The Invisible
Work Force

The Invisible
Work Force

~

*Transforming American
Business with Outside
and Home-Based Workers*

BEVERLY LOZANO

THE FREE PRESS
A Division of Macmillan, Inc.
NEW YORK

Collier Macmillan Publishers
LONDON

The Free Press
A Division of Macmillan, Inc.
866 Third Avenue, New York, N.Y. 10022

Collier Macmillan Canada, Inc.

Printed in the United States of America

printing number
1 2 3 4 5 6 7 8 9 10

Library of Congress Cataloging-in-Publication Data

Lozano, Beverly.
    The invisible work force.

    Bibliography: p.
    Includes index.
    1. Home labor—California—San Francisco Bay Area.
2. Home labor—United States. I. Title.
HD2336.U5L69 1989   331.25   89–11696
ISBN 0-02-919442-3

To Richard,
who inspires me to just keep pedaling,
when the ride is long and the hill is steep

Contents

~
Acknowledgments

A book is a deceptive thing. Something in its form conveys the impression that it came about as the result of a solitary intellectual process on the part of its author, and that what lies between its covers is the product of that singular mental effort. But nothing could be further from the truth. A book is an outcome of the collective labor of many. It embodies their mental and material contributions, their belief in the importance of the work, and the emotional labor they perform in encouraging the author. This book is the embodiment of contributions made by the following persons.

John Walton introduced me to the topic of informal work. He made extensive comments on earlier drafts of the manuscript, and in sharing with me for the last ten years his critical sociological perspective, is responsible for many of the insights that now appear as my own. I could not hope for a better mentor and friend than John.

I am likewise fortunate in having the opportunity to work with Gary Hamilton. To the extent that I have managed to avoid the temptations of economism, it is because Gary has generously shared with me his own complex view of the social world. It is a view that dignifies that world's inhabitants, and in reflecting it with such constancy, he sustains in me the belief that social actors can change social structures.

Obviously, there would be no book without the analytical contributions of my respondents. I am grateful for the hours of valuable time they spent answering my questions, and for their patience in explaining the logic that underlies their working arrangements. Kevin McCurdy provided substantial material support in the form of lodging. Had he not consented to let me stay at his house in Berkeley (along with three other housemates, eight cats, and

Wilma the Dog), I would never have finished collecting the interviews. Kenneth ("Dr. Umlaut") Umbach was the one who insisted that others might be interested in reading what I learned in these interviews, and that I should seek a publisher for the manuscript.

Once I decided to do this, my family was there to give cheerful encouragement throughout the long process of writing and revision. Among its members, I thank Andy and Breck Cushman. They created golden silences so that like my respondents, I too could work productively at home. My children, Evelyn and Frank Freitas, made their own unique contributions to these efforts, for without their irreverent humor, my work would become endlessly grim (and quite possibly self-important)! I am profoundly grateful to my parents, Rose and Manuel Lozano. They were the first workers whose labor I observed at close range, and they awakened my understanding of what it means to make a living by selling one's labor power to others.

Finally, I thank Richard Cushman for bringing me to live in the People's Republic of Poverty Flats, where work is made meaningful, sexism has been declared illegal, and all the good things in life are equitably distributed. Were it not for the hope I find there, I would not have written this book.

The Invisible
Work Force

1

~

What Is Informal Work?

In her central Italian home, Gina sits down at a sewing machine, prepared to spend the day stitching pockets to the dresses she makes for a garment manufacturer in a nearby town. She resolves to work rapidly, for one of her children has been sick and her output has fallen. On piece rates as low as the ones she is paid, Gina feels the need to make up for lost time.

Grocery shoppers in Santiago, Chile, stop at the house of the Vasquez family. The front window is open for business, and Manuel stands there wrapping a bit of flour, a small bag of sugar, and a can of soup, while in the background his daughter assembles the next order. The Vasquez home is one of several in this part of the city that serve as retail outlets for a wholesale operation. The families who live in them earn commissions on what they sell. But even when prices are high, Manuel rarely has the money to build up an inventory large enough to enable the family to get ahead. Nevertheless, the shop in the window must provide an income until someone in the house finds a job.

In Silicon Valley, U.S.A., Paula steps into the bedroom and presses the "transmit" key on a microcomputer. She has just delivered a computer program she wrote to her contractor in a San Francisco investment firm fifty miles away. The project took longer than she anticipated, so the fee to which she agreed when she started the job does not seem as generous now as it did then. But on the other hand, the firm loans her a terminal that is compatible with their computer system and so, on the whole, Paula is not too dissatisfied with the agreement.

~

At first glance, individuals like these may appear to have little in common, and in many ways their lives are profoundly different. They come from regions that occupy distinct positions in a global economy. They enjoy varying levels of formal education, and are confronted with different degrees of choice in deciding how they will go about making a living. Even within their own regional contexts, some are considered to live comfortably, while others are counted among the poor. Yet there is something that brings them together here. They are all "informal workers."

Like all workers, they are people whose labor produces an important part, if not all, of their household income. But not one of them is actually employed in the sense in which we usually apply that term. Their names do not appear on a payroll, nor are they paid a regular wage. If they are enumerated in an official census, and happen to be working when the census is taken, we are likely to include them with the self-employed. Yet, a close examination of their activities will reveal that this label is also misleading. The self-employed experience a degree of real autonomy in their work, while informal workers can be so thoroughly dependent on the enterprises to which they are connected that they call to mind the wage worker's dependence on an employer. At the same time, these enterprises depend heavily on their informal workers, for through them they gain access to a unique supply of flexible labor that supplements the efforts of their regular employees at particular points in the production process.

What makes informal workers unique? Aside from the fact that the relations of their work set them apart from both wage workers and the self-employed, they place a curious mixture of productive and personal inputs in service to the firms for which they ultimately work. Like cottage industry in an earlier time, informal work is predominantly based on social, familial, and household resources we do not usually consider to be involved in the production and circulation of goods and services. But in fact, its contribution to household income arises from the very conversion of what we thought were intimate relationships and places into productive labor and capital.

The complex set of connections binding firms, workers, and households together can be discovered in settings as far-flung as those illustrated above. These connections display similar patterns from region to region, and have important consequences for their participants and for the economy as a whole. They can be subtle— so subtle even those who are involved may fail to see them, for often they consist of nothing more substantial than friendly agreements between mutual acquaintances. And yet, subtle or not, these informal ties form the foundation on which an ongoing structural relationship between workers and firms is established and maintained. Precisely because the underlying foundation of this structural relationship is so casual, those whose labor it mobilizes may be called "informal workers," and their labor, "informal work."

Informal work, fitting neither of the two categories into which labor is usually classified, raises a number of challenging theoretical and empirical questions. First, given the historic tendency under capitalism for an increasing proportion of the labor force to depend on wage work for its subsistence, and until recently, for self-employment to decline, how has this previously unnoticed form of work, combining aspects of each of these, endured? What purpose does informal work serve, and how might the consequences for its participants differ from the reward structures associated with wage work and self-employment?

Second, given what seemed to be a clear separation of production from the household, how is it that today there is still a discernible relationship between the two? Authors of bestsellers like *Megatrends* suggest that "we are reinventing . . . the workplace,"[1] and predict that "in the future, thousands of workers in jobs involving the management of information will spend all or much of their work time at home."[2] It is a scenario, they claim, that even holds the promise of "economic independence."[3]

What is the nature of this relationship between home and work? Why does it gain currency now? Finally, in what ways does its existence condition relations between household members, between the friends, relatives, and acquaintances that make up the social matrix out of which informal work emerges?

Initial approaches to these questions were limited by the fact that they rested on dualistic sectoral models of what are more properly conceived as dynamic social processes. Such approaches were also limited by their treatment of informal work as if the informal "sector" to which it was assigned represented something entirely new. In fact, this is not the case (see Appendix A. Informal Work: Historical Antecedents and Contemporary Households). Nevertheless, these approaches provided valuable insights into the phenomenon of informal work, and when they are aligned with recent examinations of the household as an arena in which subsistence strategies are still developed, an alternative model of employment relations emerges. It is a model in which informal work is systematically contrasted with wage work and self-employment, and it provides the starting point for this empirical study of informal work.

The study is based on interviews with informal workers and firms located in the San Francisco Bay Area, a region that includes the high-tech economy of Silicon Valley. Like the Boston Triangle and Austin's Silicon Gulch, the San Francisco Bay Area is applauded as the prototype of the new urban economy to which planning commissions and chambers of commerce in other cities aspire. It is composed of what seems to be the ideal mix of light manufacturing and white-collar opportunity. Service sector employment has expanded rapidly, particularly in the case of business services. As in the United States as a whole, production employees have decreased as a share of all employees, but manufacturing employment in the office and computing equipment industries has increased. And while large firms in these industries continue to dominate the market, their share has declined as small companies and sole proprietorships proliferate. The San Francisco Bay Area therefore serves as a dynamic microcosm of life and work in the restructured economy of the urban United States.

Here, as in peripheral and semiperipheral regions, we find people laboring within the informal work relationship. Some may appear in census statistics as part of the recently augmented number of self-employed. Others remain uncounted, yet apply this label to themselves for lack of a better term. There are, no doubt, people in North America whose poverty is as stark that of informal workers in Latin America, Africa, or Asia, and who, like them labor informally because no other employment is available.

But the Bay Area is no underdeveloped region, and the focus of this study is on the surface, more mundane than that in previous studies of informal work. The people featured here do not belong to a separate "sector" of the work force made up of the poor and unemployed. They perform tasks as ordinary as any we find in an office or factory. They are technical workers, clerical workers, mental and manual laborers with skills similar to those required if they were to work at jobs in these fields. And their informal employment is not an outgrowth of underdevelopment, for we find them in a highly developed urban region, working informally when regular employment is available.

The motives of the firms that provide them with work turn out to be similar to those of firms in Third World countries. Informal workers cheapen the cost of doing business and enable firms to adjust to market fluctuations more flexibly than if they had to rely solely on wage labor. But workers' motives in the United States can differ substantially from those typically inferred from studies of peripheral and semiperipheral regions. These individuals are not driven by poverty and unemployment, but rather by tensions on the shop and office floor, where frustration with managerial authority and bureaucratic control lead some to seek escape through informal employment. And yet, informal work provides just a partial resolution of their dissatisfaction, for when firms allow work to take place away from the direct supervision exercised within their walls, other mechanisms of control are brought to bear on workers.

These motives and the decisions they prompt appear to be located at the level of isolated individuals. But taken in the aggregate, they result in the creation of a pool of a unique kind of labor, available alongside the self-employed and the wage earner. It is a pool on which firms come to rely as a permanent supplement to the efforts of their regular employees, in the normal conduct of business.

Informal Work, Wage Labor, and Self-Employment

The prevailing model of the employment relations that characterize the contemporary labor force is a dichotomous one. In it, wage workers are assigned to one category and self-employed persons to another. Employment and earnings policies are based on company payroll data in the case of wage labor, and on census information about the self-employed. Because informal workers do not appear on official payrolls, they are usually considered under the rubric of self-employment. This is a category of worker in which the number of persons has recently increased.

For instance, between 1970 and 1980, the number of nonagricultural wage and salary workers in the United States grew by 27 percent. But the number of people who claimed to be self-employed multiplied at a faster rate: 34 percent. By 1983, there were 7.6 million persons claiming self-employment, an increase of more than 45 percent over the 1970 figure.[4] Table 1–1 shows that this most recent growth in self-employment exceeds any change that has taken place in the last fifty years.

This change coincides, of course, with a period of dramatic escalation in unemployment, and we might argue that the increase in self-employment has been fed by jobless workers seeking ways to make an informal living on their own. There may be some truth to this—although the findings of some investigators suggest that those who have jobs are best placed to find informal work as well.[5] And in fact, high rates of unemployment are not the driving force behind the rapid growth in self-employment in the Bay Area.

Counties there sustained above average employment rates during the hard times of the 1980s: While 11 percent of the California labor force was unemployed in December of 1982, "only" 8.7 percent of the workers in San Francisco and Santa Clara counties could not find jobs. In San Mateo County, the jobless rate did not exceed 6.7 percent.[6] Furthermore, Bay Area employment grew somewhat more rapidly than it did for the United States in general. Between 1970 and 1980, total national employment increased 24 percent. Employment in the San Francisco–Oakland SMSA (Standard Metropolitan Statistical Area) did more than keep pace with this rate, expanding 26 percent, and the number of jobholders in the San Jose SMSA grew by 61 percent during the same period.

Table 1–1. Percentage Change in the Numbers of Nonagricultural Self-employed Persons in the United States Labor Force: 1930–1980

Years	Percentage Change
1930–1940	+5
1940–1950	+13
1950–1960	+5
1960–1970	−18
1970–1980	+34

SOURCE: Figures for the years 1930 to 1960 are derived from Table 5, page 19, in J. D. Phillips, *The Self-Employed in the United States* (Urbana: University of Illinois Press, 1962). Figures for the years 1970 to 1980 are derived from the United States Bureau of the Census, *Census of Population,* Characteristics of the Population, Volume 1, Part 6. Washington, D.C.: Government Printing Office, 1970 and 1980.

And yet, precisely where unemployment is lower-than-average and gains in regular employment are higher-than-average there is a similar trend in self-employment. There was a 34 percent increase in the San Francisco–Oakland SMSA. And in the San Jose SMSA, where Silicon Valley firms hired over a quarter of a million more people in 1980 than they had ten years before, there was a simultaneous increase of 44 percent in the numbers of self-employed.[7]

What is the significance of this trend in an investigation of informal work? Does it mean that informal work has undergone a corresponding increase? Some would argue that indeed, self-employment statistics are indicative of unenumerated trends in informal work. Portes and Sassen-Koob mention the essentially constant level of Latin American self-employment over the last thirty years in partial rebuttal of recent assertions that informal work is in fact declining.[8] Fernandez-Kelly and Garcia include subcontracting the services of "self-employed individuals" as a mechanism through which the underground economy expands.[9] Along with unpaid family laborers and wage workers without social security, Portes, Blitzer, and Curtis admit the self-employed to their definition of informal workers.[10] And percentage increases in the number of self-employed are cited as proxies underscoring hypotheses that informal work itself is increasing, or that the "underground economy" is growing. But there are several reasons for viewing these inferences with greater caution than has been customary in treatments of informal work, however tempting it is to take them as direct evidence of trends in informal work.

First, an elementary knowledge of arithmetic is sufficient to warn that the magnitude of a "percentage increase" is in part a function of the size of the original number. Thus, when the number of self-employed persons increases from five to ten individuals, self-employment has doubled, having increased 100 percent. However, should an additional five persons go to work for themselves, the percentage increase in the ranks of the self-employed has changed a more modest 50 percent. The next five entrepreneurs—or informal workers, depending on how you will have it—produce but a 33.3 percent growth rate, and so forth. Given the fact that the number of self-employed is relatively small compared to the overall size of the labor force, conclusions based on "percentage change" statistics must be viewed with circumspection.

Second, if we start with 7.4 million individuals reporting self-employment income in one time period, and note that seventeen years later, 10.8 million persons have earned income by working for themselves, the number of persons with self-employment income will have increased 46 percent. But the significance of this statistic is substantially less dramatic if at the same time the number of income earners has increased from 111 million to 170 million—that is, at a rate of 53 percent. In this case, those with self-employment income *lost ground* as a proportion of all income earners, declining from 6.6 percent to 6.3 percent of persons with income. In fact, this is precisely what happened in the United States between 1968 and 1985, roughly the period to which commentators on the informal sector refer when they use self-employment statistics to argue the case for an increase in informal work.[11] Do equivocal statistics like these mean that informal work is insignificant in its impact on the economy? Not at all!

In fact, the very importance of informal work lies in its distinction from self-employment. The self-employed person is autonomous in ways the informal worker is not, a distinction drawn so clearly elsewhere, the latter is at times referred to as a "dependent wage worker."[12] Census respondents must choose between the categories of wage or salary work and self-employment, making it difficult to tell just how much informal work there is, but this in no way detracts from the importance of investigating informal work.

Naturally, it is reasonable to assume that a careful examination of the actual working relations experienced by those officially counted as self-employed would make it necessary to reclassify some proportion of them into a third category of the informal worker. Simon and Witte point out in their work on the underground economy that many of the self-employed (according to some studies, non-filers of tax returns) work at "small operations, often out of their own homes with clients coming by "word of mouth,"[13] just as the respondents in this study do. But we remain in the statistical darkness as to the nature and the reliability of the relationship between informal work and self-employment. This makes it impossible at this time to authenticate from the sudden growth in Bay Area self-employment a corresponding expansion of informal work.

However, the Bay Area does provide a unique setting in which to examine the role and the dynamics of informal work in an advanced economy. Unemployment, a problem present everywhere, is not as severe a feature of the scene as it might be in other places. The underdevelopment typical of regions where a "backward" economy fails to adequately employ the labor force can hardly be argued here, as it is so persuasively in Third World studies of informal work (see Appendix A, Informal Work: Historical Antecedents and Contemporary Households). The Bay Area economy is a modern one, where business services grow in number and revenues, and assembly workers turn out increasing quantities of the world's most valuable goods. Here, some of the giants of high-tech industry have sunk their roots, while beside them, enterprises made up of a handful of individuals proliferate. The demand for workers increases. And although some insist that self-employment is a proxy for informal work, there is evidence that the self-employed do indeed find growing outlets for their labor in the Bay Area. But what is really needed for a better understanding of informal work is a model of employment relations highlighting the features that set it apart from both wage labor and self-employment. If informal work is neither one nor the other, what is it?

An Alternative Model of Employment Relations

Table 1–2 displays seven critical dimensions of employment that are typically used to distinguish wage work from self-employment. Four dimensions concern the material relations through which goods and services are produced—use of household resources, regularity of earnings, ownership of productive property, and control of profits. Three have to do with the social relations into which capital and labor are brought—control over the pace of work, control over the design process, and autonomous participation in an open market where work is allocated.

A comparison of self-employment, informal work, and wage labor along these seven dimensions shows that with respect to each of them, wage labor and self-employment differ from each other. However informal work combines features of both wage work and self-employment in such a way that it emerges as a third employment category, distinct as a whole from the two others that it resembles in part. At the same time, although informal workers have some things in common with the self-employed, they are in fact more similar to wage workers. This is especially true with regard to the social relations of production.

For instance, informal work depends on significant inputs from resources represented by the household, and by connections be-

Table 1–2. Dimensions of the Employment Relationship

		Type of Employment		
	Dimensions	*Self-employment*	*Informal Work*	*Wage Work*
Material Relations of Production	Productive resources and personal/household resources kept strictly separate	no →	no	yes
	Average social wage constant over comparable time periods	no →	no	yes
	Producer owns and controls essential means of production	yes	no →	no
	Profits distributed by the producer	yes	no →	no
Social Relations of Production	External controls over pace of work	no	yes →	yes
	External controls over creative process	no	yes →	yes
	Work tasks located on an open market	yes	no →	no

→ = Shared dimension

tween friends and acquaintances. Although the self-employed may maintain home life apart from their work activities, this can also be true for them. It is not uncommon for a self-employed person to use the home as a base of operations in place of a separate shop or office. Here, family members may take business calls, help with record keeping, or assist in other ways during especially busy periods. Wage workers, on the other hand, leave the employer's equipment behind at the end of the working day, and when the rush is on at the plant they do not normally bring in their relatives and friends to lend a helping hand.

Like the self-employed, informal workers tend to be paid by the piece or the project—that is, they are remunerated by results. This will mean that when work is plentiful, income will increase. But during slow periods, income will drop to a point where neither the self-employed person nor the informal worker is able to maintain health insurance, make regular contributions to social security or retirement funds, or take regular vacations. The total package of material rewards can fluctuate wildly for both informal and self-employed workers, leading to an income instability wage earners do not normally experience during the actual tenure of their employment.

But in other critical respects, informal workers differ from the self-employed, and resemble wage workers. They do not own their own means of production, for the equipment at which they work may be encumbered, if not owned outright, by those for whom they work. In addition, they do not distribute the profits their labor produces for a firm any more than do the firm's regular employees.

They will also appear more similar to the wage worker than to the self-employed with regard to the social relations that exist between them and the enterprises that engage them. Because informal workers may labor in their homes or at a distance from the firm with which they contract to work, they do avoid daily direct supervision. It is for this very reason that self-employment and informal work are discussed interchangeably, for the latter takes on the surface appearance of the former's freedom and autonomy. But this appearance is deceptive. Informal work is in fact characterized by mechanisms of external control that, however subtle they might be, result in external pressures that determine the pace of the work and the design of the product as effectively as does the direct supervision to which wage workers are subject.

Finally, if self-employment alludes to an individual's capacity to generate his or her own employment, informal workers clearly belong in a different category. Encountering limitations we will explore later, they find it difficult to expand beyond their relationships with one or a few principal enterprises. They consequently experience a dependence on them reminiscent of the employee's dependence on the employer. The manner in which these key dimensions of two employment relationships—self-employment and wage labor—are confounded with each other to result in a third type leads some to aptly designate informal workers as "disguised wage labor,"[14] or as "self-employed proletarians."[15] Indeed, this is what they are, and if informal workers seem to be uniquely exploited, it is because, regardless of their income, training, or occupation, the relationship within which they work subjects them to the worst features of both worlds: They face the risks of self-employment and simultaneously confront the wage worker's dependence on capital.

2

~

The Industrial-Information Economy
Visible Foundations of Invisible Work

This quintessential community of entrepreneurs and venture financiers espouses a gospel of pioneer capitalism that resounds far beyond the rolling hills of canyon oaks and chaparral. As role models, these people have shaped the psyches of fellow believers and in the process created a culture that promises to propagate their brand of entrepreneurial lust for generations to come. They have begun to work their ways on the political and social underpinnings of an increasingly entrepreneurial national economy.

"Beyond Silicon: Shooting for the Moon in Los Altos Hills," *San Francisco Examiner* (April 10, 1983)

Informal work was first seen through the eyes of anthropologists in Third World countries like Ghana and Peru, where cities were overwhelmed by high rates of migration from the countryside. How migrants were managing to make a living was not immediately clear, for official statistics indicated astronomical levels of urban unemployment. Informal work seemed to provide an answer to this question, and by reverse logic, many reasoned that poverty and underdevelopment *caused* informal work to appear. Such logic in turn implied that where levels of development were sufficient to sustain regular employment, or where workers possessed skills in high demand, we should not expect to find people working informally.

During the same period in which informal work was noticed in Third World regions, the United States underwent a process of economic transition. It did not always proceed smoothly, and workers in this country also suffered extended unemployment. But by the mid-1980s, a restructured economy had reemployed many of them in a rapidly expanding service sector in which data processing establishments, secretarial services, and temporary help agencies proliferated and prospered. Large firms grew larger, while at the same time, unincorporated individuals found more room in these markets than ever before. And though the share contributed to total employment by the manufacturing sector declined overall, high-tech production expanded.

The San Francisco Bay Area is a convenient microcosm in which to observe these developments, for it is a region in which national economic trends are exaggerated and manifest themselves with an intensified clarity. It is therefore possible to identify the origins and dynamics of informal work unconfounded by issues of underdevelopment. What is happening there?

In this setting, production supervisors in circuit board assembly plants are distributing "extra" work to their most reliable employees—who take it home and quietly redistribute it around the suburban neighborhood. Bank managers whose technical documentation requires constant maintenance arrange for manuals to be updated by former employees, now "freelancing" as technical writers in their living rooms. The job that proves too demanding to complete without hiring extra employees is cheerfully accepted by the owner of the secretarial agency, and then sent out to one of her friends who has a word processor at home. Even companies that provide sophisticated services such as computer programming and software development keep at hand in the Rolodex a listing of "consultants," clever hackers who can be depended upon to get the program written, even if it means staying up for days at their home terminal. Thus, it is precisely in these most dynamic and profitable sectors of the economy that an invisible work force of informal labor makes its appearance.

Closely Knitted Interests and Interwoven Transactions:
Historical Roots of the Contemporary Economy

San Francisco Bay serves as the glittering hub of an area that includes two major ports, a dynamic financial district, and Silicon Valley—all in a continuous urban space that thirty years ago was dotted by dairy farms and fruit orchards. Like many urban areas, this space has become so densely populated that a ten-mile car trip can take over half an hour, and many who commute to Silicon Valley jobs spend two to three hours daily on the freeways connecting the region's industries with its living rooms. Obviously, for some workers this alone is ample reason for working at home.

Contemporary accounts of the developments that resulted in one town spilling over into another until regional consolidation was virtually complete usually begin with the growth of the electronics, or "high-tech," industry. Silicon Valley fever, the story goes, was first contracted in the 1930s by Frederick Terman, Jr., a Stanford University professor of engineering. By infecting his students with the contagious idea of establishing their own firms locally rather than migrating east (and many, like Hewlett and Packard, did so in their garages and at their kitchen tables), Terman inspired sufficient enterprise by the end of World War II to attract federal defense funds to the area.

This trend was enhanced in 1946 when Stanford officials invited Bay Area financial and industrial leaders to join with them in establishing the Stanford Research Institute (SRI). The original purpose of this collaboration was to undertake applied research on behalf of California industry in general. The actual result was for the United States Department of Defense to become SRI's steadiest client, and for local Lockheed Corporation to become one of the region's largest employers through its successful capture of military contracts.[1]

At about the same time, the "San Francisco milieu," consisting of a "large pool of wealthy individuals and families with discretionary incomes," was integrated with the newly developing industry to the south.[2]

As the early firms spun off competitors, the complex developed its own financing system. The major San Francisco banks established offices in Santa Clara County, where bankers versed in the new technologies still weigh the proposals of venturesome scientists. While the banks provide loans, investment groups that specialize in venture capitalism buy stocks.[3]

And of course, as Lockheed official David Moffat points out, the proximity of the region's firms to Stanford University and the University of California at Berkeley provided "the right intellectual atmosphere" from which growth could be fueled.[4]

As in many rapidly growing areas, development of a high-tech economy appears to take place overnight. But it is interesting to note that the relationships that today bring together brains and money, military spending and economic development, have a history that extends back more than one hundred years. However strongly we are tempted to explain the modern boom town in terms of the 1947 discovery of the semiconductor, it is not Terman's technological vision that explains the current distribution of financial, scientific, and productive inputs to the local economy. A backward glance reveals instead that the relationships and institutions underlying this recent phase of development were in place long ago, and that these are what made possible the transformation of technology into one more profitable commodity among many that have contributed historically to regional expansion in the past.

In the Gold Rush year of 1848, San Francisco was a small settlement of 820 residents. A year later, $2 million in bullion was exported through the Golden Gate, and by 1850, the population had grown by 20,000 new inhabitants. A Chamber of Commerce commentator in 1915 described these ambitious arrivals in entrepreneurial terms similar to those we now apply to the high-tech prospectors seeking their fortunes in the region today. They were "men of all sorts and classes—except the timid and poor in spirit."[5]

In those times, as more recently, military strategy and government spending provided a powerful impetus to the economy. As the Civil War highlighted the West's isolation from the rest of the nation, Congress agreed to subsidize the railroad building projects of five men, Collis Huntington, Charles and E. B. Crocker, Mark Hopkins, and Leland Stanford. These names still identify some of the major institutions organizing contemporary development. Later, the Spanish-American War emphasized the desirability of a canal at the Isthmus of Panama. Its opening in 1914 carried with it "instant advantages to the port of San Francisco,"[6] when a two-thirds drop in shipping rates forced rail carriers to follow a competitive suit.

By the turn of the century, the population of San Francisco had grown to 343,000, and ten years later, despite the fact that the city fell in flames during the Great Earthquake of 1906, it had increased another 21 percent. The institutions that provide financial services today were already in place—three stock exchanges, an insurance industry with a 1914 annual income of $35.5 million, and a thriving banking sector.[7]

"Few people realize," mused one observer of this era, "how closely knitted are the interests of the various companies, how immeasurably interwoven are the infinite variety of transactions, hence, a sort of homogeneity of interest."[8] As this comment suggests, the current pattern of development in which a "San Francisco milieu" steps forward to provide capital and services to productive enterprise in the surrounding areas, in which public agencies and private investors jointly seek the national interest, does not emerge with the discovery of the silicon chip. Rather, the silicon chip finds fertile ground for the growth of new industry in the thick web of preexisting social relationships that have been established in the previous dynamics of economic development. The results of this long and continuous process have left their marks in the form of a particular composition of enterprise that now constitutes the urban economy and defines its labor force. We will turn briefly to a description of the main components that make up the region's industrial composition, and then begin our examination of the manner in which informal work is related to it.

The Industrial-Information Economy: Business Services and High-Tech Manufacture

Services[9]

The Stanford Research Institute proposes that the California economy is best described as an "emerging industrial-information economy." If the northeastern United States can be characterized as the nation's foundry, and the midwest its breadbasket, then California might be called its R&D center.[10] The concentration of research and development activities in the state means that technical and business services will account for a large proportion of all its economic activities. Fewer than 8 percent of California business establishments engaged in manufacture in 1984, whereas a third provided services of some kind. In fact, these figures are typical of the United States as a whole.

Business services such as computer and data processing, programming, and software development occupied 17 percent of the nation's service establishments, and between 1977 and 1982, the number of establishments providing business services increased 39 percent. Within the computer and data processing category alone, the number of firms doubled to increase their share of all business service establishments from one out of fifteen to one out of every ten. Receipts underwent correspondingly dramatic gains, nearly tripling from $7.5 billion in 1977 to $21.8 billion five years later. This 192 percent increase was achieved with just a 73 percent growth in the industry's formal labor force. Moreover, as these developments took place, payroll growth was held to considerably more modest levels (see Table 2–1). As we will see below, this is an outcome due in part to the ease with which such work can be subcontracted to informal workers off the payroll.

Table 2–1. Percentage Change in Payrolls and Receipts for Selected United States and California Service Sector Firms: 1977–1982

Percentage Change in:	*California*		*United States*	
	Payroll	*Receipts*	*Payroll*	*Receipts*
Total services	103.1	100.0	183.0	160.0
Business services	112.1	110.2	103.4	113.7
Computer and data processing	187.9	199.6	176.8	191.7
Computer programming and software	258.0	301.6	248.5	310.9
Data processing	126.4	139.7	139.4	148.9
Stenographic and reproduction	109.5	117.2	179.8	202.6
Help supply agencies	123.5	136.1	111.1	121.3

SOURCE: Figures derived from United States Bureau of the Census, *Census of Service Industries*, Geographic Area Series. (Washington, D.C.: Government Printing Office, 1982), Table 2a.

A large proportion of these developments in California can be attributed to firms and transactions taking place in the Bay Area. One quarter of the state's business service establishments had located there by 1982, bringing with them nearly 30 percent of the total receipts. The San Jose SMSA alone has over one out of every twelve of the state's computer and data processing firms, and these collect more than 17 percent of the industry's statewide receipts. The amount spent on business services in regions like Silicon Valley represents a higher-than-average proportion of the total service bill, compared to national figures: The United States business service sector collects 32 cents of every dollar spent on services, whereas in the southern part of the Bay Area, its share amounts to 41 cents of each service dollar.

As more firms enter the industrial-information economy, employment in the business service sector has also increased. Between the 1977 and 1982 censuses, the numbers of people employed in this category grew by 37 percent, and in 1982, more than 3.2 million people were listed as employees of United States business service establishments. It is erroneous, however, to imagine that all these workers are involved in the glamorous, well-paid occupations that purportedly make California the nation's R&D center.

Activities listed as "services" to business include cleaning and maintenance, window washing companies, and copy shops, and the excitement that accompanies the "high-tech revolution" obscures the fact that one of the fastest growing and most lucrative services to business is the temporary help industry. During the 1970s, receipts to firms that function essentially as labor contractors increased nearly 200 percent. This high rate of growth has continued: 1982 receipts by temporary help agencies had expanded more than 136 percent over their 1977 level. Stimulated by the demand for such labor, the number of such firms in the San Jose SMSA grew over 80 percent during that five-year period, and 18 percent of the state's temporary help establishments were located in the San Francisco/Oakland region.

Even a glance at the computer and data processing category reveals a mixed picture of what the "industrial-information economy" means. Of the 462,000 persons counted as being on the 1984 payrolls of computer and data processing establishments, only 36 percent were actually employed in firms that specialize in programming. The remainder were employed at lower-paid activities such as data entry and processing.

What are firms in the service sector like? Although we are accustomed these days to thinking in terms of large-scale organization—and in the Bay Area, firms tend to be somewhat larger than throughout the rest of the state—fewer than one out of seven establishments providing business services in the United States have over twenty employees. As Table 2–2 shows, small operations made up of three or four individuals proliferate, and the majority of enterprises employ fewer than ten people. The service sector remains an arena in which sole proprietorships, operations owned and run by a single unincorporated individual, constitute three-quarters of all establishments. Even where investment in electronic equipment such as that used in computer and data processing is required, nearly half of all service establishments in the United States were operated as unincorporated individual proprietorships in 1982. This represents a substantial increase in opportunity for small enterprise over the previous five-year period, when only a third were organized on this scale (see Table 2–3).

These figures suggest that even in the face of historical trends toward industrial concentration, large numbers of small units manage to set up shop, for as Aldrich *et al.* remind us, the functional elimination of petty capital has been far from total.[11] But we will also see that even the smallest units in the economy described by the census do not completely satisfy the needs for these services. There remains a demand that is met outside the sphere of these enumerated enterprises by individuals with no more capital than a home computer or a business card. What the prevalence of small enterprise in the business service sector emphasizes is that there is indeed room in the market for the type of activity we will examine at one remove from the census.

Manufacturing[12]

The expansion of the industrial-information economy naturally implies an employment shift away from blue-collar work in the factory to white-collar work in the high-tech office. It no longer surprises us to learn that following the 1970s layoffs in the "nation's foundry," the number of production workers declined 9.4 percent between 1977 and 1982, reducing their share of all employees by 5 percent.[13] But the industrial-information age brings with it a paradox: Insofar as information processing is embodied in a material product (the computer, the word processor, the electronic cash register), and these products result from manufacturing opera-

Table 2–2. Percentage Distribution of Selected Service Sector Firms by Number of Employees: 1984

Number of Employees:	United States				San Francisco County				Santa Clara County			
	1–4	*1–9*	*1–19*	*20+*	*1–4*	*1–9*	*1–19*	*20+*	*1–4*	*1–9*	*1–19*	*20+*
All services	61.6	81.0	90.9	9.1	59.2	76.7	87.5	12.5	60.0	79.4	89.5	10.5
Business services	57.1	74.4	85.9	14.1	53.5	70.5	82.6	17.4	52.7	69.6	81.1	18.9
Computer and data processing	54.8	70.7	83.2	16.8	57.6	69.5	82.2	17.8	50.7	67.9	79.7	20.3
Computer programming and software	55.8	72.2	84.6	15.4	58.7	66.7	80.2	19.8	48.7	64.0	75.3	24.7
Data processing	41.9	59.6	74.9	25.1	33.3	56.5	73.9	26.1	37.2	62.8	78.7	21.3
Stenographic and reproduction	72.6	88.3	95.2	4.8	70.8	87.7	93.8	6.2	66.7	84.2	96.5	3.5

SOURCE: Figures derived from United States Bureau of the Census, *County Business Patterns* (Washington, D.C.: Government Printing Office, 1984), Table 1B, "Employees, Payroll and Establishments, by Industry, 1984."

Table 2-3. Percentage of Selected Service Sector
Establishments Operated as Sole
Proprietorships: 1977

	All Services	Business Services [S.I.C. 73]	Computer/Data Processing [S.I.C. 737]
United States	75.1	71.2	33.5
California	77.5	77.3	46.3
San Francisco/ Oakland SMSA	76.6	75.8	46.9
San Jose SMSA	78.7	78.9	41.9

SOURCE: The figures in this table were derived from United States Bureau of
the Census, *Census of Service Industries, Geographic Area Statistics. U. S. Summary.* (Washington, D.C.: Government Printing Office, 1977), Tables 1 and 4.
These statistics were omitted from the 1982 *Census of Service Industries* because, according to the U.S. Bureau of the Census, many businesses were miscoded by the IRS into miscellaneous categories rather than being classified in
the specific kind of business.

tions, particular industries in the manufacturing sector grow rapidly by comparison. Thus, United States employment in the production of scientific instruments registered gains of nearly 5
percent, and in the manufacture of electronic computing equipment, and office and computing machines, the number of production workers increased more than 50 percent.

An interesting regional division of labor reveals itself in a comparison of the relative importance of Bay Area manufacturing and
service industries. In the North Bay, manufacturing activities occupied 10 percent of the 1984 work force, while a third were employed in services. On the other hand, in Silicon Valley to the
south, less than a quarter of the work force was counted in the
service sector, and 42 percent worked in manufacture.[14] It is well
known that the electronics industry has found suitable labor in
other parts of the globe. Production workers in this industry, as
in others, have also suffered dramatic layoffs such as those at
Atari and Intel. And yet, with respect to Santa Clara County, a
1983 Bank of America report agrees that:

The county's growing manufacturing center defies national
trends. U.S. employment patterns have been changing since
1950 as the nation has moved into a post-industrial era in which

manufacturing employment has a declining role in the economy. This post-industrial society—of which California is a leading example—is characterized by rapidly expanding service employment. The proportion of employees in service jobs exceeds that of manufacturing. In Santa Clara County, however, manufacturing employment still dominates the economy.[15]

In fact, 48 percent of California's new manufacturing jobs created since 1977 were in Santa Clara County, and this region's share of the state's electronic manufacturing employment rose from 25 percent of the 1973 total to 53 percent ten years later.[16] A Santa Clara County Manufacturing Group survey of future trends likewise indicates that "despite predictions that the Valley will become another Manhattan," production work will continue to grow through the 1980s.[17] What this suggests is that trends in the direction of a service economy do not preclude the expansion of particular kinds of manufacture. On the contrary, they promote it, and this in turn leads to the growth of informal work in garage-based assembly operations.

High-tech production lines are among the most productive in the country. Value added by manufacture for all goods produced in the United States between 1977 and 1982 increased 41 percent. But value added by manufacture to electric and electronic equipment grew 68 percent, and registered a gain of 136 percent in the office and computing machine industries. These rates of increase were greater in California, and greater still in the Bay Area, where manufacturing operations are highly concentrated in electronic products (see Table 2–4). The global demand for these goods is expected to quadruple to $400 billion by 1990,[18] and the proportion of value added to the final value of shipments is also higher for these products than for manufactured goods in general.[19] As Table 2–5 illustrates, the production process in Silicon Valley contributes more to the actual value of shipments than is the case for the industry nationally, or even in the neighboring San Francisco region.

Naturally, there is less room for small firms in the manufacturing sector than there is in services, for setting up a production line requires more capital than opening a secretarial service. The continuing importance of production to this region is therefore reflected in another critical fact: Bay Area firms accounted for a third of all the state's new capital expenditure in 1982, an increase over their 25 percent share five years before. Moreover, of the

Table 2-4. Percentage Increase in Value Added by Manufacture for Selected Industries: 1977–1982

	United States	California	San Francisco/ Oakland SMSA	San Jose SMSA
All manufacturing	40.8	72.0	39.7	138.6
Machinery, including computers	52.1	116.1	68.6	146.5
Office and computing machines	135.7	159.2	167.6	160.6
Electronic computing equipment	157.1	161.6	199.0	159.3
Electric and electronic equipment	68.0	131.5	80.2	185.2
Scientific instruments	79.5	123.9	192.4	106.6

SOURCE: Figures derived from United States Bureau of the Census, *Census of Manufactures, Geographic Area Statistics*, Vol. III, Part I (Washington, D.C.: Government Printing Office, 1977), Tables 4, 5, and 6; and *Census of Manufactures, Subject and Geographic Area Series* (Washington, D.C.: Government Printing Office, 1982), Tables 2a, 3, and 6.

Table 2-5. Value Added by Manufacture as a Percentage of the Value of Shipments for Selected Industries, 1982

	United States	California	San Francisco/ Oakland SMSA	San Jose SMSA
All manufacturing	42.0	47.3	38.3	59.6
Machinery, including computers	54.4	58.5	57.5	55.4
Office and computing machines	54.4	56.6	55.3	55.0
Electronic computing equipment	53.3	56.6	55.3	54.7
Electric and electronic equipment	57.2	62.2	60.3	66.3
Scientific instruments	65.0	66.7	65.8	63.5

SOURCE: Figures derived from United States Bureau of the Census, *Census of Manufactures, Subject and Geographic Area Statistics*. (Washington, D.C.: Government Printing Office, 1982), Tables 3, 5, and 6.

Table 2-6. Percentage Distribution of Selected Manufacturing Firms by Number of Employees: 1984

Number of Employees:	United States				San Francisco County				Santa Clara County			
	1-4	1-9	1-19	20+	1-4	1-9	1-19	20+	1-4	1-9	1-19	20+
All manufacturing	30.7	47.8	64.3	35.7	34.4	51.7	71.4	28.6	29.3	46.0	62.1	37.9
Machinery, including computers [S.I.C. 35]	32.7	53.2	72.1	27.9	31.0	51.2	75.0	25.0	30.3	49.5	66.5	33.5
Office and computing machines [S.I.C. 357]	25.6	37.5	48.9	51.1	29.4	35.3	52.9	47.1	17.4	25.2	35.5	65.5
Electronic computing equipment [S.I.C. 3573]	25.9	38.0	48.9	51.1	29.4	35.3	52.9	47.1	17.6	25.4	34.4	65.6
Electric and electronic equipment [S.I.C. 36]	23.7	36.9	50.2	49.8	30.9	51.5	64.7	35.3	21.4	33.7	48.0	52.0
Scientific instruments [S.I.C. 38]	28.8	44.6	59.8	40.2	37.1	60.0	68.6	31.4	21.0	32.5	48.1	51.9

SOURCE: Figures derived from United States Bureau of the Census, *County Business Patterns*, (Washington, D.C.: Government Printing Office, 1984), Table 1B, "Employees, Payroll and Establishments by Industry, 1984."

$2,799 million they invested that year, 62 percent was spent in the southern part of the region. Over a third of these new capital expenditures went into the office and electronic computing equipment industry alone.

Nevertheless, a surprising number of firms conduct high-tech manufacture with fewer than ten employees, and over one-fifth in 1984 operated with fewer than five (see Table 2–6). Santa Clara County tends to have a greater concentration of large firms. But small operations employing one to four individuals still manage to survive in market niches created by the presence of giants like Hewlett-Packard and IBM. Due to the manner in which small differences in product design, workmanship, tolerances, texture, and the like frequently translate into significant contrasts in the overall structure of production, we can observe a wide assortment of technologies and plant sizes in effect at any given time.[20]

Large companies such as the ones just mentioned do produce the lion's share of shipment value—the four largest in the electronic computing equipment industry accounted for 42 percent of the value shipped in 1982, and the fifty largest shipped 82 percent of the dollar value. However, these shares represent a 3 percent decline over the shares of the market they enjoyed five years earlier, and fifteen years earlier the fifty largest firms were producing 98 percent of the value shipped.

In part, this decline in market share is due to the fact that high-tech industry continues to accommodate rapid innovation, an arena in which small firms are able to find points of entry. It is estimated that small firms produce twenty-four times the number of innovations that large firms produce per dollar of R&D expenditure, and the ratio of innovations to sales is one-third greater in small firms than in medium or large ones.[21] According to Saxenian, "there is still no better place for a small high-technology firm to locate than in Silicon Valley."[22] This is also a type of firm that is highly likely to contract work out to informal workers, especially during the start-up phase of its development.

3

~

The Structure
of Informal Enterprise,
the Uses of Informal Labor

*S*ometimes, these outside people do a job so much
more efficiently than we typically find can be
done in a factory. In a factory, people don't have
quite the same sense of urgency as when they have
their own business. And isn't that a neat mode to
operate in?

—President of a scientific
instrumentation firm

They're taking more of a risk than we are. An in-
house programmer can sit and say how wonderful
they are, and if they don't deliver, we're paying for
them. On the outside, they can do all the talking they
want, as long as they deliver their product. And all
we pay for is the product.

—Personnel manager for major
producer of video games

Making the Invisible Work Force Visible

A Sample of Informal Workers

The thirty-five workers studied here live and work in the San Francisco Bay Area. It is a densely populated urban setting, and in this respect, they are similar to informal workers studied in other regions of the world. As in other settings, informal work plays an important role in their strategy for generating household income, and in the dynamics of the regional economy. But this group of informal workers differs from others studied in a number of important respects.

The Bay Area has its share of poor people. But this is not a cross-section of the urban poor, nor of those who have little education and few occupational skills. This group includes people whose household income is high and who have a great deal of formal training. Moreover, their occupations reflect skills valued in the most dynamic industries of the region. They are computer programmers, word processors, and electronics assemblers. In fact, the majority are white-collar workers whose occupations place them in the professional-technical category of the labor force. Eighty-nine percent of the group claim to prefer their informal employment status over having a regular job, and more than half actually left a job in order to make informal work their exclusive pursuit.

Age, Gender, Marital and Family Status

Twenty-one women and fourteen men participated in the study. They average thirty-seven years of age, with the women slightly older than their male counterparts—thirty-eight as compared to thirty-five. However, it is misleading to consider only the average, for in fact adults of all ages are represented here.

The youngest respondent is twenty-three, a young man who writes software on contract. The oldest is a sixty-two-year-old engineer who produces custom-designed scientific devices in his garage. Twelve people are forty years old or more, and six are under thirty.

Because informal work is often most feasible for those whose households include other workers as well, it is important to know the composition of the informal worker's household unit. Fewer than a third of the respondents live in single-person households, and eight of these eleven individuals are women. The remainder of the group consists of twenty married individuals, and four more who cohabit with a partner. Well over half of these are couples with children, and in fourteen cases the children still live at home.

Housing Arrangements

The term informal work often refers to work that takes place directly in the home. In this investigation, place of residence is also the exclusive workplace for all but two respondents. What is the typical living arrangement in which their work is conducted? The majority reside in single-unit dwellings rather than apartments, and of the twenty people who live and work out of a house, eighteen either own or are buying it.

It is interesting to note at this point that the cities in which these residences are located have regulations governing the conduct of home-based occupations. These codes are similar in that they specify the following restrictions on such activities: Occupational use must be secondary and incidental to the residential use of the home. There must be no employees or assistants involved in the work, regardless of how they are compensated, and business partners and family members can be counted as assistants. Client visitation is prohibited in most places, as is the use of mechanical equipment. No more than one-quarter of the floor space may be devoted to the occupation, and finally, no sign indicating the presence of the activity may be displayed.

Most interviews took place in respondents' homes, and people were often eager to point out the physical arrangements required when home life and work life are combined under one roof. Hardly any of those interviewed are aware of municipal restrictions on working out of one's residence, and it seems that most are unwittingly in technical violation of the letter of these laws. In some instances where the dwelling is small or the activity extensive, work can take over the entire home. And almost everyone engages the help of someone else—friends, partners, family members—as occasionally paid assistants (see below). The use of mechanical equipment is required by some, and two front doors of two respondents had discreet signs displaying the name of the enterprise.

Yet, insofar as the overall spirit of municipal regulation is intended to preserve the neighborhood's "residential character," residents' failure to comply is scarcely detectable. There is nothing to suggest from the street that these homes are in any way different from the ones next door, and the work going on within them remains virtually invisible to the passerby. Nevertheless, the quiet labor inside is a significant part of the household survival strategies practiced by these informal workers.

Household Survival Strategy

Respondents are about evenly divided between household survival strategies that depend completely on informal work, and those in which it is part of a mixed stategy. In fourteen cases, the informal work of the respondent accounts for all household income. In four more, respondents' earnings are combined with those derived from the informal work of a partner or spouse.

On the other hand, seventeen people combine their income from informal work with wages or salaries earned through regular employment. That is, twelve have partners with full-time jobs, three work informally in addition to holding a job themselves, and in two more households, the respondent is both informally and regularly employed, and has a partner with a job.

Household Income

In how adequate an income do these strategies result? Half of the eighteen respondents in the professional-technical category, and four of the nine who do clerical work agreed to divulge their household incomes for 1982, the year prior to the interview. There are wide disparities in the figures reported: The lowest household income was claimed by an unmarried typist who subsisted on $10,000. A more affluent couple in which the wife works informally while her husband is employed by a public relations firm enjoyed the highest household income reported in this study— $75,000 the year for which figures were requested. Average household income among those responding in the professional-technical category amounted to $45,000 in 1982. The four clerical respondents who provided data earned $17,000 in household income during the same period.

Some of these figures are above and some below the regional median household income of $21,000 reported for the entire region in the United States Census of Population and Housing.[1] Furthermore, respondents' positions with respect to the regional median seem to be related to occupation. Only one household in the ten reporting from the professional-technical category falls below that figure. On the other hand, only one of the four responding in the clerical group appears above the regional median household income.

Informally Earned Income as a Share of Household Income

What portion of total household income is contributed by respondents' informal work? In one case, an individual actually lost $1,500 the previous year by virtue of having undertaken informal work! The largest contribution, however, was more substantial—$36,000 in a household where informal earnings represent the only source of income.

Informal work alone contributed an average of $16,200 to the household incomes of reporting professional-technical workers. For clerical workers, the average contribution in 1982 totaled $13,250. It is important to note the following, given the size of these figures. If informal work had been the only source of household income, then six of the ten reporting professional-technical workers and all of the clerical respondents would have fallen below the regional median for household income.

What these patterns suggest is that informal work is best practiced as part of a mixed household survival strategy, where it can make significant contributions to the unit's income at times. Yet, informal work can be subject to a cycle of feast or famine, and the income it generates may fluctuate from year to year. This is subsequently reflected in informal workers' lesser access to benefits such as health insurance and pension plans normally associated with regular employment (see Chapter 4).

Tenure and Training

All but one of the individuals have worked informally for at least a year, and most have been at it much longer. The average length of time for the group as a whole is four years, and thirteen have five or more years of experience as informal workers. In fact, two of the people I interviewed had worked out of their garages for over twenty years.

As mentioned above, this is a group that has invested heavily in formal education. Over a third have completed college. Another third have finished some course of graduate training, including three people who have doctoral degrees. The disciplines represented are diverse and in some cases esoteric, ranging from philosophy, art, and sociology to chemistry and siliconate device physics.

Those with higher degrees are not necessarily found in the professional-technical category. Four college graduates work as typists or word processors, and one of these women holds two masters degrees. Among the eight respondents who have worked at electronics assembly, half have some college training. We might therefore consider that nearly a quarter of this group is underemployed, given the level of educational attainment represented within it.

Nevertheless, when taken as a whole, this group of informal workers presents a rather different appearance from those featured in previous studies. For the majority, informal work is a preferred choice over regular employment. They are not poor, nor are they unskilled. They design software, write computer programs, type, and manufacture high-tech equipment—tasks that are central to the business of local firms. Yet, as is the case in other parts of the world, their work makes important contributions to household income and survival, even as it depends on the household of family and friends for its existence. Moreover in this region, as elsewhere, firms rely on informal workers to perform labor in place of regular employees.

A Sample of Firms

The twelve firms that make up the other side of the story these workers have to tell represent two of the most dynamic sectors of the Bay Area economy—business services and electronics manufacture. Firms included in the study had to satisfy one of two criteria: In five cases, individual respondents specifically mentioned them as their typical clients.[2] The remaining seven companies were chosen because they are similar in size and products to firms named as typical clients.

Personnel at the higher levels of management and decision making were interviewed in seven of these companies. They include five company presidents and two vice-presidents. Because six of these are in small or medium-sized firms, they are closely involved with the day-to-day functioning of overall operations, and hence are responsible for decisions about when to subcontract work outside the firm. One of the vice-presidents spoke for a multinational corporation. But in the course of his career there he had been involved in such decisions within his own division. Also numbered among the corporate respondents are four personnel managers and a purchasing agent in charge of managing outside contracts.

Our conversations covered three basic topics. First, I asked for a brief introduction to the firm. How and when did it come into existence? How is it currently organized, and what are its principal products or services? How many people does the firm regularly employ? Second, I requested that respondents explain if, and on what occasions, the firm found it expedient to contract work outside its walls versus hiring someone to perform the job inside. At this point in the interview, I expressed special interest in hearing about people who might work for the company out of their homes. How are these contacts established and maintained? Finally, I inquired about the relative benefits and disadvantages of having work done away from the firm's direct supervision as compared to in-house production.

All the respondents in these Bay Area firms found it easy to address the issues posed in my questions, for they turn out to be issues faced in the routine conduct of company business. In fact, not only do they rely on other firms that specialize in providing subcontract services, but with one exception, they all claim to informally engage individual workers at times. The exception was a firm that had the matter under consideration at the time of my visit.

Large Firms

Six of the twelve companies must be considered large operations by almost any measure of corporate size. One of them, for example, is counted among the Fortune 500, and two more are subsidiaries of firms included on that list. These large organizations range in size from one that employs 1,350 people in its nationally dispersed plants and offices to a diversified conglomerate with over 300,000 workers on its global payroll. Four firms in this group are multinational corporations, while the remaining two have sales and production facilities outside the state.

A majority—that is, four of the six—are in the manufacturing sector, and specialize as producers of electronic equipment. Their products include video game hardware and software, laser technology, electronic business systems, and consumer appliances. In

1982, the sales leader in this group sold $26 billion worth of goods. The firm with the smallest volume of sales took in $70 million that same year, a figure that increased 28 percent by 1984.

Two large firms into which I was granted entry are providers of business services. One of them controls an internationally integrated computer network that is used to maintain payroll and equipment tracking operations for clients that come primarily from the oil industry. The other is a major accounting firm whose primary client base is made up of other corporations. Sales in 1982 totaled $90 million for the former, and well over $150 million for the latter.

Medium-Sized Firms

Three of the companies are considerably smaller in scale than the six large firms studied. Their operations are all limited to the Bay Area, and they are primarily involved in manufacturing. Two of them are similar in that they produce specialized lines of scientific instrumentation. Their work forces number twenty-five employees in one case, and sixty in the other. The third respondent in this group is a subcontract assembly house whose eighty-eight workers do circuit board assembly for local electronics companies. In fact, one of its clients is counted among the large corporations already discussed.

The smaller scale of the group's operations is reflected in their sales volumes, as well. One company found a $3 million market for its scientific instruments; the second manufacturer of such equipment sold $1 million worth of its products in 1982. Orders for the subassembly firm totaled $1.5 million during the same time period. It is interesting to note that all three of these organizations have recently experienced layoffs, whereas only one of their large counterparts in this study has suffered such cutbacks.

Small Firms

The three enterprises in this last group are all subcontractors to larger firms in the Bay Area. Again, the principal client of one is represented in the first group of six large companies. As with the medium-sized firms, these all limit their operations to the local area, and insofar as they work strictly on subcontracts, their fortunes depend heavily on trends in the regional economy. Two manufacture components for electronic equipment that is finished by its primary producer several miles away. The third company provides business services to a multinational bank that routinely engages this small firm to write technical manuals and systems documentation, and to do the word processing of these texts.

These small firms have few, if any, employees. The two manufacturers hire only eleven people between them, each calling on informal workers when things get busy in the shop. The company that contracts with the bank employs no one, relying completely on three "independents" to whom the work is subsequently contracted a second time. Only one of these respondents agreed to reveal the previous year's sales figures. In 1982, one of the subassembly firms filled $1.5 million worth of orders for sheet metal housings for computers and video games hardware.

The three groups of firms in this study differ in a number of ways. In terms of products, sales, number of employees, and scale of operations, they fall into diverse industrial categories. Yet at some point in the normal operations of each company, the issue of subcontracting some of the work arises, and according to their representatives, often the choice is to have it done by an informal worker.

How many such workers do these firms have at their disposal? It is difficult for them to say, because the arrangements that lead to such working relationships may be verbal and remain unrecorded in the company's ledgers. Nevertheless, in the course of this research, explicitly acknowledged connections could be traced between nine of these firms and at least thirty-two informal workers, five of whom were interviewed here. Fourteen of the thirty-two are accounted for in the routine operations of three of the large enterprises; nine are regularly engaged by the three medium-size firms; and nine more are mentioned by the three small subcontractors.

What does this mean in terms of the possible incidence of informal work in these sectors of the United States economy? This study uses neither a large nor a random sample from which to generalize. In fact, the firms were selected in several cases precisely because of prior knowledge of their use of informal workers. But let us speculate for a moment. There are, according to the United States Bureau of the Census, over 592,000 manufacturing and business service establishments in the United States.[3] If the patterns implied in the present study correspond to actual patterns around the country—that is, if nine out of every twelve firms find it possible to call on an average of 3.5 informal workers each— this represents an informal labor pool of over 2 million workers in these two industrial sectors alone!

Beyond such speculation, answers to the question of the prevalence of informal work must be sought in large random samples of households and firms that represent the industrial and demographic composition of the region. But clearly, this is an endeavor worth undertaking, for throughout the course of my research, I was repeatedly impressed by the ease with which I was able to locate respondents informed about a topic that until recently seemed hidden and unknown. Everyone knows someone who is doing it. Representatives from the firms discuss the practice of informal work in terms that suggest it is a normal way of doing good business. Perhaps the reason informal work has remained unnoticed until now is that, like Poe's purloined letter, it is hidden away where everyone can see it.

What sets the informal worker apart from the wage earner and the self-employed entrepreneur? What role do informal workers play in the day-to-day life of the firms that use their labor? The following section examines the structure of informal work along three of the dimensions in our model of employment relations.

On one hand, informal work resembles self-employment in that these workers depend heavily on the cooperation embodied in friendly and familial social ties. But at the same time, they are often dependent on others for the essential tools of their trade. They differ from the self-employed on this dimension. Whereas the latter own their own means of production, the former work at equipment that may be encumbered in the ways shown below. Finally, unlike the self-employed, informal workers do not seek work on an open market. They depend instead on a few regular enterprises to provide them with work.

The result of the relations thus established is that informal workers, their families, and friends come to constitute a flexible labor supply in service to firms at particular moments of the productive process. They are available to step quietly into the life of the firm and perform work for which the company would otherwise find it necessary to hire employees. And when the moment has passed, they just as quietly step back until the next time the need for their service arises.

The Structure of Informal Enterprise

The dominant labor force trend for the last two hundred years was in the direction of labor proletarianization, and workers who did not fit neatly into the "employee" category could only be lumped homogeneously together under the self-employment rubric. And yet, what does the term self-employed mean? Do we assume they own their own means of production, control the hours and conditions of their own work? Is the opportunity for profit and loss a necessary condition of wearing this label? Traditionally, these have been the guidelines applied when the question comes to a legal test.[4] Perhaps people should have five or more clients before we place them clearly outside that "gray area as to their classification as employees, or independent contractors." The Internal Revenue Service sees this as the definitive criterion.[5] Insofar as these are some of the commonly accepted features that define self-employment, respondents in this study do not fit in that category.

Freelancers and Friends

Respondents were asked how they would describe their employment status. Do they see themselves as self-employed or do they consider themselves to be employees? A number of them are unable to answer the question definitively, and it is interesting to note that their confusion centers on the issue of their enduring ties to one or a very few clients.

None of the respondents claims to be someone else's employee. But unsure of what to call themselves, their most spontaneous response is likely to be "I'm a freelancer." If they must select between "employee" and "self-employed," they invariably choose the latter—but often with qualifications suggesting their independence is not as complete as they would like it to be. For example, a woman who provides daily information on the high-tech industry to one major European publication (she does so via satellite communications from her home) responds to the question, "are you the newspapers's employee," in the following way:

No—well . . . no. See, that's a bit difficult. I'm essentially freelancing. But I'm not typically freelance in that I have a very close association with just one publication, and that takes up most of my work.

A contract programmer who is provided custom programming jobs by a single business service firm explains that, yes, she is self-employed. "But in some ways," she says, "I don't *really* consider myself self-employed, because I don't have to go out and get clients." And one of an increasing number of "independent" contractors doing word processing for large San Francisco banks expresses confusion over the ties that bind him, his intermediary, and the bank together:

*S*he hires us as . . . I guess we're considered as consultants, or subconsultants. So we're considered self-employed, and I'm more or less independent. But she gives me the work to do.

These are not employees. But they are reluctant to say they are clearly self-employed, for they recognize the degree to which the flow of their work depends on some other party's ongoing assignment of it. Such inability to describe employment status unambiguously resembles the confusion found among home-based workers in Great Britain, where a national survey showed that one in six had doubts about his or her correct employment status.[6]

Naturally, those who have a product or service for which a range of clients place occasional orders are not as dependent on clients' signals to begin working. An engineer who has made a living out of his garage for twenty-five years produces scientific instruments for at least ten government agencies from which he enjoys fairly stable demand. Despite federal budget reductions resulting in demand fluctuations so severe that he has twice had to seek short-term employment, he does not hesitate to call himself self-employed. Like others, he depends on his clients. Yet his dependence is hardly as stark or as literal as that of the programmer, word processor, or assembler who stands at the ready to provide ongoing support to the daily functioning of a single operation. The former is captive to the client's market situation; the latter is the client's captive.

The issue of employment status also has ramifications beyond these "freelancers" themselves. They rarely work alone, and surrounding my respondents we find the less obvious ranks of those who "help out," who "cover" for them when there is suddenly too much work or they must be away. Some analysts have suggested that informal work represents new business in the making, and insofar as these activities will have a multiplier effect on the level of employment, they should be encouraged. In Table 3–1, we see that indeed my respondents' activities do generate enough work to require additional help. But freelancers are as sensitive about the status of these casual assistants as they are ambivalent about their own. They are quick to point out that these are not employees in any legal sense. They are friends and family members who participate in the work by virtue of its taking place in the home or neighborhood. A couple who manufacture electrical transformer cores explain how

The whole family does it. We get the kids—they're in third and sixth grade—in on it. Even Grandpa works on it. He's ninety-two and half-blind, but he has this great big magnifying glass with a neon light. It's like a family event.

There are advantages to relying on personal social networks like these. The activity is more easily supervised than it could be if strangers were involved. Thus, the workers providing the link between firm and garage can deliver on their promise that quality will be reliably maintained. The importance of assuring quality standards equal to those expected within the firm is underscored by one woman who for three years produced electrical coils for an engineer whose own garage operation was eventually acquired by a well-known producer of office equipment:

I had helpers—usually women I had already met in electronics. I would call them up and tell them I had some extra work, and if they were interested, I would pay them by the piece. I didn't go next door to any housewives who never had any experience. I like to work with women who have some general knowledge of how to handle the tools and soldering equipment, and who know all the components.

These stories are reminiscent of the cottage industries that grew up around the factories of an earlier industrial revolution, and though the sparkle associated with Silicon Valley may seem tarnished by what appear to be antiquated methods, they remain suitable for some tasks. It is important to realize, however, that these working relationships are not peculiar to the manufacturing process. Similar arrangements bring firm and friends together for the purpose of performing mental labor. Contract programmers often share work when they are too busy to handle a sudden influx of work, or when they are consulting with the client and their own equipment is not in use. One such respondent uses his neighbor as "kind of a contract programmer." The neighbor submits an esti-

Table 3-1. Number and Status of Respondents' Helpers

Occupation	Helpers	Helpers' Status
Professional/Technical		
1. Engineer	0	N/A*
2. Engineer	10	Independent contractors
3. Market researcher	0	N/A
4. Technical writer	0	N/A
5. Programmer	0	N/A
6. Technical writer	0	N/A
7. Programmer	8	2 Partners; 6 independent contractors
8. Technical writer	1	Partner
9. Programmer/tutor	0	N/A
10. Journalist	2	Independent contractors
11. Programmer	3	1 partner; 2 independent contractors
12. Software author	21	4 partners; 17 independent contractors
13. Technical writer	0	N/A
14. Programmer	0	N/A
15. Programmer/consultant	0	N/A
16. Software author	1	N/A
17. Software author	2	1 partner; 1 independent contractor
18. Technical writer	3	Independent contractors
	TOTAL = 51	

Clerical

1. Word processor	2	1 partner; 1 independent contractor
2. Typesetter	2	Independent contractors
3. Typist	0	N/A
4. Typist	0	N/A
5. Typist	6	Independent contractors
6. Word processor	0	N/A
7. Word processor	0	N/A
8. Word processor	0	N/A
9. Word processor	0	N/A

TOTAL = 10

Production

1. Assembler	0	N/A
2. Assembler	2	Independent contractors
3. Assembler	0	N/A
4. Assembler	0	N/A
5. Assembler	5	Independent contractors
6. Assembler	0	N/A
7. Assembler	3	Independent contractors
8. Assembler	6	Independent contractors

TOTAL = 16

Total number of helpers used by 35 respondents = 77
Average number of helpers/respondent = 2.2

*N/A = Not Applicable

41

mate for each job, reports "approximately how many hours" are worked, and those are multiplied by his "wage."

There is no written contract. Though there is something called a wage, there is no employee in the accepted sense of the word. Family and friends become fellow freelancers, and employment status is rarely raised as an issue as long as the operation remains small and local. Personal networks like these can also form the basis of rather elaborate operations. A typist explains how her home-based service generates enough work to keep herself and two other women working full-time. In addition, she has four or five other people on call who are less experienced and are given the less complicated work. Finally, she has numerous friends who "work better by the hour than by the page." Her extensive contacts with the local office community enable her to refer these for temporary work inside her client-firms. There are even a couple of people she occasionally uses as messengers! Yet, she too stresses that she has no employees.

I don't want employees, per se. I make no money on this— it's all just on friendship. Of course, the benefit is that the calls always come to me. I can take what I want, and then delegate the rest.

It is not always possible to keep things on a "friendship" basis, however. When times are good, more hands may be needed in order to take advantage of all income opportunities, and at this point, it becomes necessary to rely not just on friends, but on friends of friends. The first links forged between firm and informal worker multiply until a network less easily monitored develops. The employment status of those thus involved begins to call for clarification, lest legal complications arise between what are now strangers at either end of the chain. The criteria that leave informal workers dubious about their actual degree of self-employment—dependence on a single client, control over the work process—are precisely the criteria they attempt to apply and enforce on those who now look to them for work.

This situation is a difficult one, for even the laws and agencies that govern the proper use of labor sometimes fail to agree on its exact definition. An example of the contradictory turns the issue can take is provided by a subcontractor of assembly work. Following a California Department of Industrial Relations investigation of the use of industrial homeworkers in the area, she agreed to bring her operations into compliance with the law. This simply required that she register her enterprise with the proper authorities, and that the three women who work for her obtain valid home-worker licenses. Her compliance with this set of regulations resulted in her name being added to the official list of those registered with the state to use such labor, that is, industrial homeworkers who function as independent contractors.

At this point, another agency responsible for monitoring the proper withholding of payroll benefits for wage and salary workers, the California Employment Development Department (EDD), noted her name on this list, investigated her operations, and filed a complaint against her. These authorities seized on the fact that the three women work exclusively for her, and interpreted this to signify that they should more correctly be considered her employees. This, of course, would make her subject to the regulations governing the use of wage labor. In her words:

The problem is this—when the day comes that I don't have any work to send them for a while, and I tell them to go down to EDD to file for unemployment, what do you think they're going to tell them?! They're going to say, you're not eligible— you're independent contractors, and that means you're self-employed!

This subcontractor's response to the dilemma has been to appeal her case, a costly legal process that has dragged on for three years. Dilemmas like these suggest that, contrary to definitions of informal work as unregulated labor, it is rather an instance of potentially *overregulated* labor, by virtue of the fact that it is subject to two competing definitions of employment status. Because informal work shares aspects of both wage work and self-employment, both sets of regulations may be brought to bear on the same relationship. Fernandez-Kelly and Garcia point out in their work on home-based assembly that government officials are well aware that this dilemma exists.[7] But there exists no agency with a clear mandate to resolve it.

It is important to note that situations like these are not limited to industrial homeworkers. In 1984, the Internal Revenue Service ruled against a shorthand service that claimed its homeworkers were self-employed, even though these workers provided their own computers or typewriters.[8] Section 1706 of the Tax Reform Act of 1986 now requires many professional contractors, or "consultants," as they are called, to become employees of the brokers that place them in jobs.[9] And in 1987, the Internal Revenue Service ruled that a contract technical service worker who had been placed at a utility company by a broker should be classified as an employee of the utility rather than as an independent contractor, or as an employee of the broker.[10] Apparently, President Reagan's 1984 inaugural promise to bring the underground economy "into the sunlight of honest tax compliance" extends to programmers and other technical personnel who work on contract.[11]

Respondents are understandably concerned about issues like these as they describe their relations with their own helpers. For example, an engineer who designs highly specialized scientific devices in his home overlooking Palo Alto has them manufactured by a group of informal workers in a neighboring state. Designs and components are shipped in one direction via United Parcel Service, to be similarly returned as finished products in the time agreed upon. Originally, this was an agreement between friends. But as usual, friends have "more people available as needed," in this case, six more of their own acquaintances in the neighboring state. The respondent emphasizes that:

This group is independent. We are separate entities—I hope! We planned it that way, and as far as I know, they can take on other work. They do work under my direction. But they are independent in every other way.

The process whereby the exigencies of business and the pleasures of friendships are reconstructed into "separate entities" can be an intricate one. Although the legal meaning of self-employment is violated in informal work, various paper arrangements can be imposed on these relationships to give them a new semblance of legality. Friends that might be mistaken for employees can be transformed into "partners" in an operation that contracts to provide labor only. Thus, with a somewhat abashed laugh, a man explains how he involves a friend in his word processing operation:

Well, he's a partner. He comes over three weekends a month and does a little bit of typing at so much per page. This partnership I have with my friend contracts with the partnership I have with my father-in-law—he owns the computer—to do the labor involved. So theoretically, there are two businesses operating here: one that does the labor, and one that owns the capital.

To some, the "partner" who provides the labor might seem to fit the classical definition of a thoroughly proletarianized employee. He has nothing to sell but his labor, and for a piece rate, at that! Yet their simple declaration of equal partnership protects both, for the time being, against charges of labor code violation. Moreover, the "partner" who owns the computer is able to reduce his own personal income tax liability by claiming investment tax credits.

This arrangement is not uncommon, and several respondents resolve the ambiguity surrounding their own employment status and that of their helpers in just this way. We must recognize that informal work is not so much an illegal proposition as it is a quasi-legal product resulting from participants' agreements to selectively apply one set of criteria over another to an ambiguous situation. Certainly, the choice is first prompted by the desire to avoid possible prosecution for violation of laws regulating the employment of labor. But the alternative criteria correspond to another legal category permitting, even promoting, the investment of capital through the official recognition of business partnerships. Where it may be costly or complicated to obey laws defining the employment of labor, informal workers may invoke laws that define them as different kinds of working associates. Thus, friends and family become partners, pieceworkers become capitalists, and those who send them work are called consultants when they bear a closer resemblance to the labor contractor.

A few respondents admit this troubled them, and the woman who shares her work on a purely friendly basis refers to more unscrupulous contractors as "pimps." But others see nothing unprincipled about bending rules in order to spread work that may come available. The most common explanation of one's informal working status is that "it's very, very flexible."

Equipment: Borrowed, Bartered, Liberated

Finding work on an open market is a test of true self-employment that many of my respondents appear to fail. Another criterion is access to the means of production: How do people acquire the necessary tools of their trades and how adequate do they find them? Again, variations in the degree of their ownership of the equipment at which they work offer additional reasons to consider them as dependent workers rather than independent entrepreneurs.

Respondents listed the various types of equipment they use, its value, and the means by which they acquired it. The total value and the sources of capital investment for each respondent are shown in Table 3–2.

It is not surprising to learn that computer programmers and word processors who work on home computer systems require more expensive equipment than home assemblers. What is interesting to note, however, is that within each occupational category there is considerable variation in the amount invested. For instance, one programmer values her system at less than $1,000; four others work at an assortment of terminals, printers, and peripherals worth well over $10,000. The same is true for those who provide typing and word processing services. In fact, several claim equipment outlays as costly as those used by the technical workers. And though the investment required of home assemblers is not as elaborate as that required in the clerical and technical categories, the amounts that can be committed to the enterprise cover a wide range.

Table 3–2 also shows a figure indicating dollars of gross annual income per dollar of capital investment. In some cases, the flow of work is irregular (see Chapter 4) and annual income can only be estimated, so we should view these figures with the caution appropriate to estimates and nonrandom samples. Nevertheless, it appears that for the informal activities considered here, the amount of income yielded by each dollar invested varies widely. If we assume that for any productive task there is an optimum combination of capital and labor that most efficiently yields a given combination of goods or services and income, then we must question the efficiency of some of these enterprises.

It is important to note here that the value of the equipment at which these individuals work is not necessarily the amount of money they themselves have spent out of their own pockets. Nearly all own some part of the equipment—a computer terminal, software, a soldering iron, or wire crimpers—and personal savings are a common source of such purchases. But they also rely heavily on other arrangements to acquire these items. Loans from family members, trade, barter, and rental, as well as imaginative forms of "liberation" of the electronic property of others all figure prominently into putting together the complete investment package. On one hand, these arrangements diminish strain on personal finances. But at the same time, they create additional lines of dependence and obligation that diminish autonomy and share of the profits.

The willingness of some affluent family members to loan money can be prompted by nothing more generous than the motivation to create within the family a tax shelter for their own income. This requires two things of the borrower. First, he or she must maintain records adequate enough to allow the lending kin to claim a legitimate investment with a legitimate depreciation allowance. Second, the loan must be repaid, and often the agreement is that the borrower will repay "in kind" by performing services for the lender (typing, programming, bookkeeping, etc.). Hours will be spent at work that produces no direct income to the borrower, but that yields savings on services that lenders would normally have to buy (since they often run regular businesses of their own), and savings on their tax bills.

Relying in this way on family and friends does spare informal workers the need to turn to more costly third-party leasing companies. Yet we should understand it as analogous to a highly profitable investment strategy that has sprung up around the computer industry itself.[12] A respondent in a firm that produces minicomputers describes the company strategy of setting up subsidiaries through which to lease their products. As lessors, they derive income from their lessees. As owners of the equipment, they can claim depreciation allowances. "This," he explains, "has had a lot of impact on our ability to generate revenues, hold on to those revenues, and not give them to Uncle Sam!"

A similar principle underlies the partnership between a computer consultant and his friend "who has money she doesn't know what to do with." Her investment in his equipment, as well as in that of several similar enterprises, reduces what she must give Uncle Sam. In other words, informal employment activities may represent lost public revenues not simply in terms of the actual income earner's dishonesty, but in terms of providing convenient, legal investment opportunities within personal social networks.

Others trade and barter for their equipment. A typesetter, for instance, describes her freelancing as "working on other people's equipment and getting paid under the table—or just working out trades where I do work for them, and they let me use the equipment for customers I pull in independently." For her, the arrangement works well. But for others, the bargain leaves much to be desired. Informal trades involving work for the equipment retailer in return for a future discount on a purchase may end with the work done but the discount falling short of what was verbally promised. Even in the professional-technical category, it is not un-

Table 3-2. Value and Source of Equipment, Gross Income and Gross Income Returned per Dollar of Capital Investment: 1982

Occupation	$ Value	Source	1982 Income	$ Income: Capital
Professional/Technical				
1. Engineer	MD*	MD	MD	MD
2. Engineer	15,470	Savings	44,000	2.85
3. Market researcher	1,000	Savings	0	0.00
4. Technical writer	0	N/A‡	10,000	N/A
5. Programmer	940	MD	MD	MD
6. Technical writer	3,000	Savings	MD	MD
7. Programmer	53,000	Bank loan, savings	30,000	0.57
8. Technical writer	8,300	Barter, savings	12,000	1.45
9. Programmer/Tutor	4,150	Savings	1,000	0.24
10. Journalist	6,550	Savings	32,000	4.89
11. Programmer	3,000	Barter, savings	MD	MD
12. Software author	11,300	Savings	40,000	3.54
13. Technical writer	1,200	Savings	24,500	20.42
14. Programmer	4,160	Savings	3,670	0.88
15. Programmer/ consultant	4,000	Barter	10,000	2.50
16. Software author	20,000	Barter, savings	20,000	1.00
17. Software author	22,500	Bank loan, savings	3,000	0.13
18. Technical writer	MD	Barter	MD	MD
Range	$0–53,000		$0–44,000	$0–20.42

Clerical

1. Word processor	5,000	Family loan	MD	MD
2. Typesetter	11,000	Savings	21,000	1.91
3. Typist	3,000	Savings	MD	MD
4. Typist	3,850	Bank loan	5,000	1.30
5. Typist	1,800	Savings	18,000	10.00
6. Word processor	300	Savings	11,000‡	36.67
7. Word processor	8,100	Family loan	18,000	2.22
8. Word processor	10,000	Savings	30,000	3.00
9. Word processor	MD	Barter	3,840	MD
Range	$0–11,000		$5,000–30,000	$1.30–36.67

Production

1. Assembler	100	Savings	1,250‡	12.50
2. Assembler	2,000	Savings	10,000‡	5.00
3. Assembler	0	Client	1,250‡	N/A
4. Assembler	20	Savings	MD	MD
5. Assembler	0	Client	15,000‡	N/A
6. Assembler	100	Savings	10,000‡	N/A
7. Assembler	0	Client	MD	MD
8. Assembler	3,000	Loan from friend	Md	Md
Range	$0–3,000		$1,250–15,000	$5.00–100.00

*MD = Missing Data †N/A = Not applicable

‡Estimates based on the conversion of respondents' stated piece rates and average output into hourly rates spread over 20-hour work weeks, 50 weeks per year.

49

common to hear that of the two gleaming computer systems in the living room, one is on loan and the other is being "sort of worked off from the client."

Individuals who are dependent on a firm that engages employees in work similar to that they put out may be sold surplus equipment or materials the firm has on hand for their work at home. A woman whose weekends and evenings are spent wrapping transformer coils at 50 cents apiece for the firm at which she is employed during the week showed me her home workspace in the spare bedroom. "I even have my own table from the company that I bought to do my work on," she says. "They sold it to me at a reasonable price."

Examples of high-tech benevolence like these are reminiscent of earlier periods in capitalist development. In the nineteenth century, manufacturers often speculated in the sale or rental of hand-weaving looms at the same time that they set their employees, who worked on power-driven equipment, in competition with the outworkers. Each had a place in the chain of production, and at each link of that chain large-scale enterprise benefited, while both wage earner and cottager remained subjugated workers. Today, however, there is an added benefit in selling or renting equipment to the persons with whom the firm contracts. Insofar as these people can subsequently be argued to possess their own equipment, the client can demonstrate that they are independent entrepreneurs with businesses of their own. This means the firm reduces further the risk of being defined as an employer, while the worker remains dependent on it other ways.

Even so, there are still firms willing to face that risk by engaging as "self-employed" those whose only capital investments are the business cards and stationery the firm requests them to have printed. For instance, some corporations currently practice a variant of the internal subcontracting system detailed by Clawson for the late 1800s.[13] Each day at five, when regular employees go home and leave the computer system idle, "self-employed subconsultants" take their places at the word processing stations. Here, they turn out the technical manuals and updates for company billing systems, program documentation, and other internal publications, the labor-intensive volumes generated by industrial-information economies. They receive no benefits, own nothing but their calling cards. And one young man is understandably worried over the financial stability of the firm with which he "consults." He is trained to work only at their computer system, and should last years's losses be repeated, he may be forced to look for contracts with firms whose computer systems differ.

Access to a large computer system can, however, represent informal income opportunities to regular employees. Intimate knowledge about how to enter and make one's way through the system transforms the company's capital equipment into means of production where one's own equipment is lacking. Thus, the bookkeeping needs of one company are met by their informally employed bookkeeper on the computer system of another firm where she is an employee. Concealed in the electronic maze by a password known only to her, the affairs of one business are conducted quietly alongside those of another.

Others, who work at small home terminals, meet their software needs by joining organizations like "Pirate's Cove." A modest membership fee ensures that a wide variety of programs can be "liberated," as one respondent puts it—transferred electronically onto a floppy disk at the user's end of a telephone line. All that is required is a terminal, a modem, and, of course, the pirate's telephone number!

The structure of these informal work activities is small-scale, an intimate network of people established through friendly and familial ties. It rests on flexible arrangements in which the employment status of those who participate remains uncertain, ambiguous—sometimes purposefully so. Both workers and equipment, labor and capital, come and go, to be replenished when needed from sources outside the formal labor and capital markets. Yet despite shifting boundaries (or perhaps because of them), many of these endeavors endure for years. Some of the respondents have just started out, or only engage in informal work occasionally. But for thirty, it is their only source of paid employment. Two of these have been in operation over twenty years, and thirteen more have survived in their current form between five and ten years.

Why do they not go on to rent offices, advertise for "help wanted," and expand into more visible and autonomous forms? Why do they not aspire to true self-employment or entrepreneurial status? Some do. Six of the firms in this study began in Bay Area garages and are now counted among the legendary ranks of the Hewlett-Packards and Apple Computers that were likewise born in such humble beginnings. But most respondents do not anticipate future expansion, nor do they claim to desire it (see Chapter 4). They list several limitations to growth of this sort. These limitations have to do with a shortage of capital, or with an unwillingness to take on the commitment to increased volume an expanded scope of operations would entail, even if capital were available to invest.

For example, an assembler who annually delivers to her client over $30,000 worth of transformers relies on nothing more in the way of equipment than an old converted sewing machine to wrap the coils. It is worth about $100. At one time, she engaged six other homeworkers, and remembers people "driving around to pick up the machine, and always, the arguments about how 'I want to get my work done and Mary's dragging her feet!' " She did not have the funds to provide each worker with her own machine. But a few simple modifications to the existing equipment enabled her to wind faster and more reliably. Now she completes a greater volume of work with *fewer* people at the same equipment. When times are good, she can just meet her client's demand. And when times are bad, she has no need for additional equipment. Hence, her enterprise is kept in a steady state over long periods of time, and now, she points out, "I don't have to split it with anybody."

Others explain that they can't expand because the spare room is too small, or the family car used for business is getting too old. Working out of the house is good, they say, because in a recession, "you can survive—you don't have to retrench." When a home typist considers replacing her electric typewriter with the more versatile word processor, she realizes she will have to increase business volume by $300 per month just to make the payments. This is a risk she prefers not to take, for like others, she is "in a holding pattern, happy with it staying exactly as it is."

There are other limitations as well. Some prefer not to include additional participants in the network, even where no more equipment is required. When the scale of operations increases, yet the structure of the enterprise remains dispersed throughout people's homes, it becomes increasingly difficult to maintain control over quality, inventory, and deadlines.

Finally, scientific workers who have established themselves successfully in a technological niche may find enough steady buyers for their specialized product to stay busily at work for years. But success at meeting the limited demand for one type of scientific instrument can lead to technological isolation within one's own garage. An engineer muses that, while he could try to expand by developing a device that is more widely used, "maybe I'm getting technologically outmoded." And in the Bay Area, where so many dream of starting up their own high-tech company, it is a safe bet that the device is already being designed on someone else's kitchen table!

The Uses of Informal Labor

Informal work is organized on a small and loosely structured basis, but its clients most certainly are not. The list of "typical clients" served by respondents in this study includes some of the nation's largest nuclear labs, a Big Eight accounting firm, a multinational bank, prestigious universities, well-known computer manufacturers, and members of the Fortune 500. They also name a multitude of companies in various stages of growth, from the small start-up with but a few employees to the medium-sized firm that has maintained a stable work force over a period of years.

At first glance, it seems that these respondents engage in work no different from that for which their clients also hire employees. They type. They write software, technical manuals. They assemble electronic components and design scientific equipment. Informal workers engage in manufacture and provide services; they perform both mental and manual labor, as do regular employees. Why is some work put out to the informal worker, and some of an apparently similar nature kept in-house? Where there is a demand for additional clerical, production, or scientific work to be done, why does not the firm simply hire one more employee?

The answer that comes immediately to mind is that informal labor must be significantly cheaper. Yet, a number of those interviewed claim to make more per hour than they could as someone else's employee. This is certainly true for the typist who charges $10 an hour; and four of the six women who do clerical work by the page earn over $15 per hour. The average salary for local clerical employees is only $1,000 per month; new engineers, computer scientists, and other professionals average $22,572 annually.[14] Six of the twelve in the professional-technical category who agreed to reveal their informally earned incomes earned more than this figure. Even cottage assemblers relate that they average as much as $10 per hour at times, a rate well over the $5 to $7 paid experienced assemblers on the Silicon Valley shop floor.[15]

Naturally, these earnings do not include fringe benefits, which must be foregone or purchased privately by informal workers. This key issue will be taken up in the next chapter. However, the popular assumption that informal work is defined in terms of sub-minimum wage payments needs to be questioned. Subminimum wages *directly* cheapen the cost of labor. But Beneria and Roldan demonstrate in their Mexico City study of industrial homework that there are a number of ways in which contracting work out of the firm provides an *indirect* saving.[16] Firms may be willing to pay higher rates for subcontracted work in the short run than they pay in-house employees, and why this is so this remains to be ex-plained. When is work sent out of the firm, how is its seemingly higher cost translated into a lowering of labor costs? There are four occasions on which companies rely on outside personnel, even when they have in-house workers technically capable of doing the job.

Labor-Intensive Work and Variable Demand

First, where work is labor intensive, but the demand for the prod-uct or service is variable, an outside pool of labor releases the firm from commitments to a large internal work force that must be laid off or called back as demand fluctuates. Many have the impression that high-tech industry, with its potential for automating every-thing from the office to the factory, has escaped the need to rely on domestic labor. At times this is true. But we must not overlook specific new requirements for labor-intensive work that are created in the very process of automation. And not all these de-mands can be readily met through offshoring production to Third World countries.

For example, the computer industry requires a reliable supply of basic components that can be delivered quickly. Many small and medium-sized firms compete effectively as subcontract vendors with operations overseas. One of my respondents works for such a subcontractor out of her garage, putting together the most labor-intensive portion of an assembly subsequently completed within the subcontracting firm. The firm employs its small internal crew to put only the finishing touches on a printer ultimately purchased from a subcontractor by Apple Computer. What is needed to as-semble a product that eventually will do the work of countless typ-ists in half that time?

Basically, you need accuracy. You need the pieces, a screwdriver, a pair of pliers, some glue, and some string. You can put one together with nothing more than that, and frankly, the hardest part is tying the string so it won't slip! Some hi-tech, huh?!

Although such a component could be completely assembled in the company, both floor space and supervision costs are saved. In fact, another cottage assembler produces parts that at one time he manufactured within the client company.

They used to do it, but this way, it's just one less thing to oversee. All they know is, they put in an order, and every thirty days, they get a big box of components. Just send the check, and no space problems, no employee problems—that's someone else's headache. For them, it's that simple.

The efficiency of this division of labor between primary manufacturer and "sub" is confirmed by a manager in a company that produced and sold over \$100 million worth of minicomputers in 1983 with an in-house work force of ten assemblers. According to him:

We're not doing the whole vertical production type of thing—not a lot of little tiny soldering and stuffing PC boards. Basically, we take these things that come in quantity and assemble big components into a system. That way, someone else is having all the overhead.

In addition, the fact that much research and development of new products remains concentrated in the United States means that firms are continually generating a substantial amount of "prototype" work, the production of twenty to fifty units of a product not yet placed on the market. It is obviously not efficient to send such work overseas, nor to interrupt the ongoing production carried on domestically. Rather than bring in extra employees, this work is put out to someone else. A woman who keeps herself and three cottage workers busy year-round relies solely on prototype work for her living. "Of course, when they go into large-scale production," she says, "I don't see it again."

The use of cottage workers has long been associated with labor-intensive manufacture. What is less often noted is that the transition to an industrial-information economy requires massive inputs of intensive mental labor to transform electronic devices into saleable commodities. Labor-intensive mental work can also be organized around analogous production schemes.

According to Hall *et al.*, software, rather than hardware, is

the principal constraint in the development or progressive im-
provement of computer systems. And while hardware has
changed dramatically, software development remains "a labor-
intensive and therefore extremely costly process." This means
that companies that formerly produced computer programs themselves are actively encouraging "outside independent producers"
to develop them instead. These same analysts estimate that in the
Bay Area alone there are over 10,000 "mom-and-pop" programmers; others suggest that as much as 80 percent of all software
goods and services comes from small independents.[17]

The transformation of science into sales does not stop with the
development of the software system. Someone must think through
the "friendliest" way to lead uninitiated users through the often
frustating steps of the program, or users may decide they don't
need a computer after all. Therefore, several respondents find
work writing technical manuals as independent contractors to
software producers. "There's a fine line," one explains, "between
writing a very technical manual that assumes you know what a
baud-rate is, and writing a cutesy manual that talks down to the
user." It is this fine line that often spells the difference between
a program that sells and one that does not.

The balance is difficult to strike. It results from a process requiring long hours of thought, of writing and rewriting before a manual is complete. Often, the firm for which the work is done desires
changes or modifications difficult to articulate to the person being
paid to express them. A technical writer thus describes her work
as a process of "helping others, who don't always know what they
want, clarify their thinking." It is a process that involves a risk:
If the terms of payment are based on a project rate, the individual
paid to do the firm's thinking may not be able to complete the
work within the deadline promised. Each additional unit of time
she must spend then lowers the average rate at which she works
(see Chapter 4). Hodson suggests that the creativity and risk involved in high-tech work may lead to the active reproduction of
an entrepreneurial sector.[18] However, while we can indeed see
tendencies on the part of firms to export risk by subcontracting
technical work, the result need not be the creation of a truly entrepreneurial enterprise.

Once the concepts and operations involved in a task can be routinized, the firm places in-house personnel to work on them in a
manner similar to prototype assembly that becomes ready for volume manufacture. If this is not possible, normal operations have

continued uninterrupted, the idea is shelved, and the relationship between firm and independent terminated until the next brainstorming session produces food for an outsider's thought.

Rush Jobs

Work may also be subcontracted when a firm receives a sudden influx of product orders, and someone must be found quickly to do a "rush job" and get the company "out of a bind." In good times, this "bind" is the welcome result of customer orders exceeding the firm's projections. The firm is faced with a choice between hiring additional employees or putting the work out. Because the increased demand is only temporary, subcontracting the work lowers overhead costs associated both with the hiring and with the layoffs sure to follow when the orders have been filled. Such costs include bookkeeping, additional floor space, unemployment contributions, and training. Even where average hourly labor costs for outside workers may be higher than in-house wages, the savings on administrative costs are sufficient to make up the difference.

But bad times for the high-tech industry also result in the need to complete "rush jobs." Normally, firms hire for what they consider a normal work load with a fairly constant lead time for production. However, when the firms that make up a company's market face recession, they delay placing orders until they actually need the product. Then, they need it immediately. As firms compete to survive in markets characterized by heightened instability and last-minute decisions, the local availability of outside workers—people willing, as one puts it, "to respond with blinding speed to changes in demand"—takes on new importance.

Confidential Work

A third occasion on which the outside worker is the perfect substitute for in-house personnel is when the firm must process confidential information. In an industrial-information economy, information becomes a commodity only insofar as one controls access to it. Therefore, several respondents are engaged to process salary surveys, investment plans based on confidential access to market data, market research reports, and reports on company profit-sharing plans.

The secrecy ensured by the informal worker's isolation from the daily discourse going on within the firm is useful in two ways.

First, in the case of salary surveys and profit-sharing information, it prevents employees from making invidious comparisons between their rewards and those enjoyed by others. Workers are often warned against revealing to others how much they make, and an indiscreet or disloyal secretary can provide information that becomes the basis of worker-management conflict. Second, where firms are competing to attract highly skilled labor without bidding its price too high, subscribing to confidential salary surveys enables firms to hold the line on wages and salaries without losing employees to a competitor down the street. Market research also requires discreet inquiry. A woman who contracts to make such inquiries on behalf of others describes her services in these terms:

They don't want to do the research themselves, because they don't want the competition to know they are interested. So they hire me to keep it confidential, and I find a way of sneaking around for them.

Custom Work

Finally, when firms require highly specialized skills to solve the occasional esoteric problem that goes beyond the capabilities of their regular staff, they turn to the outside consultant. Specialists with infinite knowledge of infinitesimal matters, they piece together an ongoing enterprise out of the occasional demand of a limited number of firms. There is both security and insecurity connected with what several respondents refer to as a "niche." Insofar as they win a reputation as someone who solves apparently insoluble riddles, their services command a satisfactory price. However, during recessionary periods clients may retrench, stick to production of basic products, and leave the more adventuresome project for better days. These highly specialized consultants thus become a luxury clients can no longer afford, and they must wait out bad times in the lonely niche they have carved out for themselves in the high-tech marketplace.

Summary

Informal work emerges as a paradox growing out of the very processes that create and shape the formally organized corporate sector. Just where we find the largest, most modern firms in the global economy, at the same time we discover the smallest possible enterprise existing with them, side by side. The regular economy provides jobs for a growing labor force, and simultaneously a category of worker appears whose status is so ambiguous, its members can scarcely define it themselves.

If they say they are self-employed, an examination of the most basic components of this label leads us to doubt that they are. More often than not, in one way or in several, they are as dependent on their "clients" as wage earners on their employers for access to work and the means of production. Yet no one considers them employees.

On the surface, they appear to do the same work carried out by employees of local companies. On closer inspection, it becomes clear that only at certain points in regular production is work made available to informal workers, their families, and friends. And yet, informal work can hardly be considered a marginal phenomenon in the economy. It is central to the normal conduct of regular business, for some work always remains labor-intensive relative to other work. Perhaps manual labor declines in importance. But now mental labor comes to the fore, to drive up the costs of production.

Rush jobs, custom work, confidential projects—managers describe them as rare events in the day-to-day life of the company. But when all these rare events, occurring in so many firms in the region are aggregated, we find that every day another "entrepreneur" rises to the occasion and joins the so-called self-employed. And if things go well—who knows? There is likely room in the garage, or around the kitchen table, for friends and relatives, neighbors and children as well. Informal workers are a convenient and necessary adjunct to the regular force on which firms rely. In the next chapter we will examine how the working relationships that bind workers so firmly to these companies originate, and what consequences these relationships have for their participants.

4

~

Individual Motives and Structural Requirements
The Origins and Dynamics of Informal Work

I don't like authority—that's real clear. I don't like it! I like to control my own life, and so, I got fired from my last job for keeping my own hours. Now, I didn't charge them for the hours I wasn't there, and I'd stay late, if necessary, to finish the work. And the problem was, I seemed to be having this nice life! The boss said, "Other people are noticing you, and they want it that way too. You are disrupting the pattern of the office." So now, I work at home. There are no benefits here, and you're at high risk. But I never cared about benefits. I much prefer the freedom.

—Home typist

Informal workers play a key role in corporate production. Their willingness to stretch personal, social, and material assets to the limit transforms those assets into productive capital. This capital is then placed in service to firms that would otherwise have to look elsewhere for a reliable source of the goods and services produced by these workers. Rush jobs would have to be paid at overtime rates to regular employees. Labor-intensive work, both mental and manual, would raise operating costs further if it all had to remain within the walls of the firm. Without this pool of informal workers, start-up firms would find it necessary to divert marketing and development dollars into steady wage payments, and many bright ideas would fail to make their profitable appearance in the market. In other words, the ready availability of a reservoir of *workers* (as opposed to *employees*) with skills ranging from simple manufacture to complex scientific design extends the capabilities of firms to fine-tune their operations without adding personnel.

We can see that informal workers perform important functions in day-to-day corporate operations. But to discover that something is functional does not explain how it comes into being, nor how, once established, it differs from other functional arrangements. What prompts some people to work informally, rather than as employees? What processes lead to the development of these relations between local firms and informal workers—that is, what makes them possible? Finally, what are the outcomes for informal workers, compared to the outcomes associated with regular employment? These are the issues that will be explored in this chapter.

A brief review of previous interpretations of the origins of informal work begins the discussion. These explanations may well be valid for some workers at certain times and places. But they do not correspond to the processes that lead to the activities discussed here, and an alternative explanation must be sought. In the present case, informal work arises out of a complex interaction between individual workers' motives to escape bureaucratic control, and firms' structural requirements for a flexible supply of labor.

An examination of the dynamics that govern informal working arrangements, and the outcomes to which these dynamics lead will recall the model of employment relations proposed in Chapter 1, and shows that informal work differs significantly from self-employment with respect to the dimensions of creativity and control over the labor process. Yet, it is equally unlike wage work in terms of the systems of remuneration that accompany it. These dynamics will account for the fact that informal work is uniquely characterized by the risks of self-employment, and the dependence and subjugation of wage work.

Previous Explanations of the Origins of Informal Work

A number of explanations have been given for the origins of informal, or "underground," economic activity. The one most often proposed for the United States concerns the marginal tax rate. Rational people, the argument goes, will try to maximize their income not by working more, but by keeping more of what they earn when they work. Thus, Tanzi explains his indirect evidence for growth in the United States underground economy after 1978 by pointing out how inflation resulted in sharply rising marginal tax rates.[1] Since the self-employed are consistently identified as having the highest noncompliance rate for the reporting of income, it is a short step to the position that self-employment is primarily motivated by the desire to avoid paying taxes.

But if this argument is true, we should expect noncompliance to increase with income, and this is not the case. Where tax liability is highest, we see in Table 4–1 that compliance rates are high as well. Perhaps we can safely attribute this to nothing more altruistic than the high income earners' awareness that their affluence might attract official attention. Nevertheless, these figures fail to support the existence of a straightforward causal connection between marginal tax rates and self-employment as the means to avoid them.

It is certainly easier to conceal income that does not appear on a company payroll, and two respondents are candid in admitting that they do so. But no one gives this benefit as a reason for working informally. In fact, several who file joint tax returns with a spouse find at least partial honesty the best policy, for it qualifies them to take home-based business deductions on their total household income.

A second explanation of the origins of informal work discusses it as a response to unemployment and underdevelopment. Where the level of investment in modern infrastructure is insufficient to employ the entire labor force, those forced to eke out a living in the absence of a job turn to informal income opportunities.[2] The same argument is offered when unemployment rates escalate in developed countries: The informal sector expands with the ranks of the jobless.[3] Naturally, it is reasonable to assume that some workers do survive periods of layoff through barter and cash payment for odd jobs. But one does not develop informal income op-

Table 4–1. Employee/Independent Contractor Compliance Study:
Income Tax Compliance Rates by Adjusted Gross
Income

| | Income Tax Compliance Rates (%) | | | |
| | | Percentage of Payees With: | | |
Adjusted Gross Income	Percentage of Earnings Reported	Full Compliance	Partial Compliance	Zero Compliance
Less than $5,000	51.0	30.6	2.2	67.2
$5,000–$9,999	62.8	42.2	6.4	51.4
$10,000–$14,999	72.8	50.0	5.0	45.0
$15,000–$19,999	83.2	60.5	5.1	34.4
$20,000–$29,999	86.0	64.1	7.1	28.8
$30,000–$49,999	89.0	78.1	4.7	17.2
$50,000–$99,999	94.6	77.9	7.8	14.3
$100,000 and over	99.9	88.9	0.0	11.1
ALL	76.2	48.2	4.9	46.9

SOURCE: Figures derived from Table 2, "Employee/Independent Contractor Compliance Study: Compliance Rates by Adjusted Gross Income," in United States Congress, *Description of Proposals Relating to Independent Contractors Scheduled for a Hearing Before the Subcommittee on Select Revenue Measures of the Committee on Ways and Means,* (Washington, D.C.: Government Printing Office, 1979b).

portunities out of nothing, nor overnight. Access to equipment, skill, trusted helpers, and an interested client are essential components of informal work that were discussed in the preceding chapter. The unemployed steelworker may find odd jobs around the neighborhood when word of his misfortune is circulated, but these are not likely to turn into the more enduring operations of the kind respondents in this study have undertaken. Only three respondents say they began their work due to a lack of other employment alternatives. *The rest claim informal work as a preference*

for which they have either abandoned or failed to seek regular em-
ployment. And though the existence of urban ghettos and poor
barrios provides examples of uneven development within the Bay
Area, the region as a whole can hardly be called underdeveloped
in terms of its industries, nor its level of income, education, and
employment.

A third explanation of the origins of informal work highlights
the fact that it cheapens the cost of labor. Rational employers put
work out to people who receive none of the fringe benefits received by regular employees, and for whom they have no responsibility.[4] Even where short-run labor costs appear higher, the long-
run effects do benefit the firm. But the fact that these fortuitous
outcomes are the *result* of such working relationships still does
not explain how and where they are established. Why do people
enter informal work when the "client" seems to receive a dispro-
portionate advantage? For the unemployed, financial necessity
may require them to sell their labor more cheaply than what it is
socially worth. But why do some people *choose* such an arrangement?

There are at least two possible answers: (1) They are economically irrational; or (2) the dynamics of the arrangement are such
that the disadvantage is either obscured from them, or offset by
other advantages we have not considered. For thirty of my respondents, informal work is perceived as a voluntary choice. Thirty-
two claim to prefer it over regular employment, and our conversations lead me to believe that this is not because they are irrational,
but because in fact, it seems to them that they are better off in a
number of ways.

The informal working arrangements of people like these are not
the outgrowths of high marginal tax rates, nor of high rates of
unemployment. Instead they are often generated on the shop and
office floor inside the firm, where the managerial impulse to control labor results in the desire to escape that control. It is also
within the firm that means are often created through which some
workers may succeed in escaping control, or at least in appearing
to do so. The mechanisms through which this takes place can be
impersonal ones, such as the solicitation of bids on a contract, or
the invitation to submit products or designs for review by the firm.
But very often the mechanisms are much more direct and personal, and involve face-to-face arrangements between employer
and employee, who agree to redefine the nature of their working

relationship. The employee will be "independent," and the employer becomes the independent worker's "client."

But subsequently, we also see how the dynamics governing this new relationship, a relationship rooted in the worker's desire to escape control, are determined in new ways by the firm's need to reinstitute control. Direct supervision over the pace and quality of work is given up. But corporate control reappears in deadlines and in the forms of remuneration peculiar to informal work—payment by results. These attempts to retain some control over work taking place outside the firm's walls result in increased competition, longer working hours, and greater insecurity for informal workers than we have typically associated with regular employment, at least in the past.

Informal workers will therefore seem to sacrifice material rewards for nonmaterial satisfactions. In other words, they must buy freedom and control over their own work by accepting a certain amount of payment in "psychic income." This seems economically irrational, perhaps. But two factors weigh against our judging them to be completely misguided.

First, their long-run economic disadvantage is obscured from them by the immediate experience of working without direct supervision. This represents a real departure from the authority relations they experience as employees. Second, to the extent that the disagreeable conditions of informal work—competition, long hours, insecurity, and payment by results—come increasingly to characterize today's regular workplace, informal work becomes relatively more agreeable by comparison. Considerations such as these enter into the final cost accounting respondents make in evaluating the outcomes of informal work. They are a reminder that both inside and outside the firm, employers' commitment to labor is weaker, and labor's disadvantage is growing. Informal work is not a unique instance of this. It is rather one feature of an increasingly unstable employment picture that now confronts all categories of workers in developed countries as well as in the periphery.

Authority Relations in the Firm

Popular images of the industrial-information workplace convey the impression that the spread of high-tech industry will make work challenging, creative, and fulfilling at last. Enthusiastic paeans to Silicon Valley imply that here, the division between work and toil is about to disappear. On "starkly modern, crisply manicured 'campuses,'" it is said, executives create a "brave new corporate world," a "heightened industrial consciousness," even an "egalitarian meritocracy where competence is king." Saunas and tennis courts are installed on company premises. Invitations to Friday night beer blasts around the company pool are offered as signs that "Silicon Valley managers believe in spreading the wealth."[5] Through "management by mystique," employees and profits grow simultaneously, for the "convergence of capitalism and humanism" does away with hierarchies. Instead, "there's potential power and opportunity for all."[6]

Why do people choose to leave such an Eden and face what one respondent calls "the ogre of insecurity outside the company window"? For many, it is because such images of the high-tech workplace do not correspond to their experiences as employees of these firms. Thirty-one of the thirty-five respondents have had regular full-time jobs in the industry, 75 percent of them with local companies. Their most common reaction to questions about motivations for informal work is to spontaneously offer angry, frustrated accounts of the jobs they left in order to work on their own, or of jobs they have had while working informally. Many of those jobs were held in firms featured in the popular press as being run by the "new wave manager." But there is a wide discrepancy between the tales told in the pages of *Fortune* and *Forbes* and the accounts provided by my respondents.

They claim that to them, informal work represents an escape from rigid hierarchies and managerial control in precisely those places we are told control and hierarchy are disappearing. It is an escape from the competition and conflict of shop floor politics that transform these "starkly modern campuses" into battlefields where even physical violence is known to erupt. It seems to promise freedom from all of that.

We may not be surprised to learn that for production workers decisions are still made at the top, and as one woman puts it, "the shit rolls downhill." Her description of life on the assembly line belies popular accounts of attempts to democratize operatives' work lives, and reads more like factory scenes from a smokestack industry:

*T*he people from the top would come walking through, looking around, checking up, seeing that everybody's in their position. Next thing you know, your boss is coming out in a

*bad mood and telling the supervisor we need this stuff. And
then, like pushing over dominoes, she'd come over and tell the
lead, the lead would come back and tell us—pressure, all the
way down to us, to get the job done.*

When pressure to produce reaches the line, tensions rise to levels that can result in physical violence and mental illness. Fights
break out between workers, or between workers and their supervisors. "It was always power—somebody had to be on top of somebody else," says an operative of his previous job. He describes the
day when his immediate supervisor pushed him to the limits of his
tolerance:

*I grabbed the sonofabitch by the shirt and bashed him up
against the wall. I told him—you fuck with me, that's it! I can
burn you and get both of us fired! So he laid off and found
someone else to screw with.*

Managers confirm the existence of frequent friction and occasional violence on the job. Race, wage, and status differentials
split production workers who must spend the day in close proximity to each other. When a production manager was called on to
settle a dispute between two women quarreling over the appropriate pace of work to maintain, she resolved the problem by firing
the slower employee. "Unfortunately," she admits, "there's some
pretty rough things that go on."

Therefore, compared to a setting in which monotonous physical
labor is combined with emotional strain and close supervision,
home assembly provides a pleasant contrast. The work is still repetitive. But out in the garage, where perhaps music or a ballgame
plays in the background, at least the atmosphere is tranquil.

What of white-collar workers, whose skills, status, and education presumably entitle them more clearly than blue-collar workers to the liberal privileges offered on the high-tech campus? They
too have their list of complaints. Their human capital investments
have not yielded the dividends they expected in terms of creative
opportunity and professional autonomy on the job. Programmers
and skilled office workers join the labor market expecting that the
limits to advancement will be determined strictly by their technical competence. These expectations are thwarted by a bureaucratic management that requires them to perform duties they consider extraneous to their jobs. Ideas they consider technically
superior to current company practice are routinely overlooked, or

subverted as they go through "appropriate channels" scrutinized by wary superiors eager not to be outdone. The comments of this technical writer are typical of others explaining their preference for informal work.

When I've worked in companies and large organizations, I've felt swallowed up in the bureaucracy. A lot of effort and time went into doing things that weren't productive—a memo on this, a manual on that. . . . Companies just do things to screw up people like me who would get things done if we had the chance. And I don't like that! Working for myself, much of the time I now spend devoted to work is spent actually producing.

Furthermore, "success" in the firm often means that the technically competent are themselves moved into managerial or administrative roles. The pleasure of performing one's technical or scientific work dissipates as bureaucratic duties are added onto the normal workload. An independent software author explains, "I would rather write software and get it working than argue about smoking policy, or tell people why they're not going to get as big a raise as the guy next door."

Many believe today that a degree in computer science or engineering is the ticket to a career in which alienation is at a minimum and initiative is maximally valued. Highly trained individuals accept jobs in the expectation that employers seek nothing more from them than the most innovative ideas they can produce. They are soon disillusioned when they realize that in the firm, "you've got to ask three people before it's approved." "At NASA," says an engineer, "it got to the point where I was not allowed to work— to do the things *I* wanted to do. So I came home and did them here."

Managers' refusal to yield control over the work process seems irrational and arbitrary to people who have a good opinion of what their talents are worth, and perhaps at times it is. But in fact, the process of transforming scientific technology into marketable commodities is not a simple one. Firms in the computer and software industries are confronted with highly competitive markets in which survival depends in part on innovation. However, it is innovation in product marketing, as much as product development, that gives a firm its competitive edge. This means that technically superior products may not do as well as those that are "simply more gaudily packaged and advertised."[7] "We're in the business of publishing hits," says one company executive. And so, to the dismay of people like these respondents, corporate strategy does not begin with a rank ordering of available ideas according to their scientific merit.

Managers' first consideration is likely to be the targeting of profitable markets, and only subsequently the implementation of product lines devised around specific needs perceived to exist there. All that is desired from technical personnel is that they produce the most efficient materialization of product ideas determined by someone at a higher level in the hierarchy. The creative process can be rationalized by dividing the task into components that are delegated to work groups within the firm.

The meetings, memos, and manuals that prove such an annoyance to my respondents are in fact necessary to the smooth management of large-scale projects, for without a constant level of "interfacing" between work teams and management, the product may not come in on schedule. At the same time, managers find themselves trying to control a process in which they remain dependent on personnel whose specialized technical contributions they find difficult to understand and evaluate. Antagonism develops between managers communicating in the crass language of the marketplace and workers who feel they need only answer in the nobler tongues of science! Both sides agree this leads to insoluble conflict over the issue of control, and in fact, turnover rates appear to be highest in larger firms and those with more of a factory-like environment.[8] A twenty-three-year-old designer of video games describes people with high-tech talents as a breed apart from the ordinary person:

Computer people are different from other people in their work attitudes. Your brain is dedicated to a project. You cannot establish a norm for everyone and say, this is what we're going to do, and set up a schedule for everyone, because everyone functions totally independently. The way we operate, we're almost like mavericks! You can't fragment pure thought—and that's where the control problem comes in.

Perhaps his comments sound like the mere self-congratulation of a young man whose skills are currently in demand. But a representative from a video game firm that must transform such skills into products shares the image the "maverick" presents us:

These people are unique! Horrible to manage! I've got a group of them here—our games programmers. They're the worst! Socially inept, don't know how to deal with people! They prefer dealing with things, and when it comes to meetings— how to get things done through people—they have a terrible attitude: argumentative, unrealistic, and impractical. They don't want to deal with it.

The tensions that result are handled in two ways. First, pure thought *can* be fragmented, and if it loses some of its purity in the process, this does not make it any less profitable. Firms learn to hire what one manager calls "grunt workers" to do their programming wherever possible. These are trained in-house, often use software packages so simple "a secretary can learn to use them," and are given written specifications that can later be translated into measures of their productivity. Second, the mavericks can either decide, or be encouraged, to leave. After trying to improve their situation by going from one firm to another of those reputed to "manage by mystique," they strike out on their own into informal work.[9] Often, their clients will be the same firms that found them so horrible to manage (see the section entitled "Initiating Informal Work").

The pressures to produce and the control that enforces those pressures are but one aspect of the dissatisfaction prompting a desire to escape the workplace. As often as respondents complain of being watched and clocked, they paradoxically complain of long, meaningless hours spent on the line or in the office with nothing to do. Production dictated by the vagaries of the market can be what one manager describes as "very lumpy," and when parts shortages occur, word goes out to assemblers that it is time to slow down in order to avoid layoffs. Even when idleness is caused by nothing more than awaiting return of one's work from the quality inspector, time drags, and "you've got to pretend you're working so they'll think you're busy." Secretaries who pride themselves on typing speeds of 140 words per minute find their work completed by mid-morning, and one claims she "sat around eating candy bars, just to stay awake." Professional workers find themselves subject to "the norm of working late." "They all stay after five," says a programmer, "and you end up hanging around just bullshitting with them until eight, because nobody *really* has anything to do after five. But it's used as an index to see who's working."

Much of the dead time on the job is filled with gossip and socializing that some come to find dull, for the work group begins as a collection of strangers thrown together day after day. The tedium of confinement is alleviated by inflating issues of status into full-blown office politics, by the "secretary to this vice-president out-dressing the secretary whose boss is only the something-or-other." By contrast with the time they spent inside the company, informal workers work if there's work to do, and if not, they rest or play. If they work hard, they get tired. But this is different from feeling drained, sapped, or sucked dry, as they report having felt on the job.

These individuals are not motivated to work informally by unemployment, or because they can find no place in the wage labor market. They do so precisely because they have had jobs, have been employees, and reject what regular employment has come to represent to them. The expectations they brought to the high-tech workplace, the industrial-information firm, soon dissipated in the face of realities that revealed it to be a workplace like any other.

These structural realities are determined by the need to rationalize and control the labor process, and result in the enforcement of managerial authority over workers of all kinds. This enforcement of authority leads to confrontation between workers and managers, confrontation that produces at the level of the individual a motivation to escape. Such motivation in turn ensures that there exists a group of workers ready to work outside the firm on behalf of other structural requirements, those the firm has for a flexible labor supply.

Initiating Informal Work:
Personal Agreements and Market Mechanisms

A desire to escape one situation does not automatically open the door to a better one. Many employees share the frustrations outlined above, yet not all leave their jobs to become their own bosses. In order for that to happen, an opportunity must be created, one that promises an immediate flow of work and income. The best place to create this opportunity turns out to be the same place the motivations for informal work originated—right on the job.

Informal work is initiated and conducted most effectively where previous working relations have established trust between individuals agreeing to contract outside the firm work that was once performed in-house. Former employees are more likely than strangers to understand standards of quality, formats for written materials, and the firm's way of doing things in general. They have already been observed on the job. They are known and tested quantities whose only shortcomings, after all, are a bit of indiscipline in the face of authority and resistance to company routine. But provided they have proven their technical competence, self-control can be substituted for direct managerial control in getting a job done.

Nearly a third of the respondents began informal work as a result of face-to-face agreements with immediate supervisors, purchasing agents, or production managers inside the firm while they were still engaged as employees. An important feature of such agreements, of course, is that the changed status of each party be clear in order to avoid future legal complications. But where people are already acquainted with each other, the process of clarifying the change is not really too mysterious. The president of an instrumentation firm explains how his cottage assembly program works:

We do have several people who you might say "spun off" from this company to do their own thing at home. Somebody has to say, look—I've got a problem. I want to be home more, but I need to work. And we say, well, here's what the law says about that—you think about it. And we kind of review that with them . . . sometimes give them some ideas to perfect their thinking. . . . We may say, well, did you think about this test they often apply, and that test? And if they say, yes, I know what it takes to be a private businessperson, so we each know the responsibility we have if we're ever attacked by the IRS—then we're both set to explain our positions!

When people don't know what it takes to be a "private business-person," the issues about which their thinking may need to be perfected include local registration as a fictitious business, the purchase of business cards or stationery, and the occasional demonstration of attempts to solicit other clients. Satisfaction of these conditions, particularly the latter one, amounts to adequate legal proof of autonomy from an employer, and true self-employment. But there is a catch, in practice. A successful contract relationship that endures for years may occupy the former employee so thoroughly that there is no time left to expand the client base. As the same executive admits in the next breath, "We give them so much work, they can't look for other clients!"

Impersonal hierarchies and bureaucratic systems of control that lead to worker frustration may be the most prevalent impetus to work informally. Yet it is important to keep in mind that simultaneously, companies are daily constituted out of the social networks, friendly alliances, and personal relations forming themselves out of the production process. These in turn are transformed into opportunities of mutual benefit. For example, a manager faced with a rush job may seek workers willing to put in extra hours at home. The owner of a subcontract assembly company reveals how the selection is made: "When you work as close as I do with the people on the line, you know who's got problems out there. So if there's work we want to subcontract, we usually give it to the needy, and let them do it at home." This may seem cynical to the outside observer. Yet, to the participants in these agreements it seems natural, practical, and just. One more step is sufficient to make this the normal pattern of operations. "When the guys get a little independent," as this man puts it, and decide to "go out on their own," a call and a quote are all that are required to keep both parties engaged in a working agreement.

The personal ties that provide the ground out of which informal work grows need not involve the firm's upper-level decision makers. Just as often, they exist between former co-workers who remain friends after one leaves the firm. The friend inside serves as a conduit of information about available work, and is right on the spot to make personal referrals when internal discussions of needs for outside workers arise.

It is convenient to have former employees ready to do rush jobs and labor-intensive work outside the regular payroll. It is even more to the company's advantage when several employees leave at the same time to work as a unit. These "partnerships" may bring together peers who did similar work in the firm's internal division of labor. But they can also represent cross-sections of company structure. For example, when a technical writer and a word processor, or a production engineer and an assembler, leave at the same time, the firm is subcontracting to an external unit that is known, and differentiated as to skill and function. In a sense, the firm has generated a new department without incurring any additional overhead.

Of course, it is not always the individual's employer that subsequently becomes the client. Every day, people from outside the firm come in to do business on behalf of companies they represent, and ambitious employees thinking of striking out on their own make it a point to get acquainted and be remembered. Salesmen who call on dozens of firms throughout the area are invaluable sources of the "word-of-mouth" referrals nearly all respondents mention as critical sources of work. A production supervisor in one plant may ask his or her counterpart in the company down the block for the name and number of someone interested in "side work," trusting that the fastest and most skilled worker will be named as the candidate. At dinner parties and local "watering holes," work passes from hand to hand through the highly permeable social networks that make up the regional economy. Even the 24 percent rate of employee turnover conspires to facilitate the establishment of informal working relations, for the vigorous circulation of workers throughout the regular labor force multiplies the contacts out of which informal work grows.

However, firms do not rely solely on the chance provided by personal encounter to meet their needs for outside workers. The fortuitous outcomes of friendly agreements are supplemented by the establishment of impersonal market mechanisms designed to encourage others to work for the company without appearing on its payroll. For instance, patent ideas that might yield $2 million in revenue hardly justify setting up production lines in a company that, as one executive explains, has "$200 million ideas floating around." Yet employees might be encouraged to go out and set up production on their own. The company provides them rights of manufacture and in return receives a "piece of the business." Government research labs also stimulate the private production of innovations that the public sector is prohibited from manufacturing on a commercial basis. Thus, two respondents make their living producing devices they designed while employed by such an agency. One locates the origins of his garage operation in the following dynamics:

> *One of the claims the government research lab I worked for makes to justify its existence is that inventions resulting from the space program are made available to private industry, and thereby enhance the industrial position of the United States. So when I decided to leave to produce my own inventions, they were more than happy to give me an exclusive license to manufacture the device.*

Often the relationships that spring up around "spinoffs" like these are purposely left in a gray area about which the parent firm can be quite sensitive. Following an interview with a broker of cottage assembly, I conducted a blind interview with his contact inside the firm in which he and his assemblers had previously been employees. The fact that an employee had been set up in this type of business was elaborately sidestepped and the issue was discussed in abstract, circuitous terms like these:

A number of companies have developed around here that act as brokers for people who work at home. Someone comes in and says, "I have the greatest bunch of assemblers you ever saw!" The thing he doesn't make a big deal of is the fact that these people aren't all working together in a factory. You see, it would be extremely difficult for us to tell at any given time where a particular board was done. I mean, we know—but we don't know. And for that matter, we don't really care.

There is nothing actually contradictory in what he says, for there are two levels at which these relationships are embodied and can be known. On one hand, there is the specific contract, either written or verbal, in which one party agrees to provide a product, and the other agrees to pay for it. On the other hand, it is general knowledge around the region that contracts can be satisfied through a variety of working arrangements—regular employment, legal or illegal homework, job shops, temporaries, and so on. Which of these is in effect in a particular situation can remain unknown without participants suffering any negative consequences. In fact, the less known at this level, the better for all concerned!

There are intermediaries in the mental labor market as well. According to Osborn *et al.*, between the software end user and its author stands a new entrant into the industry, the "software broker." These, along with publishing houses and independent software firms, "actively support the efforts of individual entrepreneurs who produce products compatible with theirs."[10] The ultimate beneficiaries of such efforts are actually the computer manufacturers, for each useful computer application embodied in a software program extends the market for the hardware on which it runs.

The importance of stimulating software development for this purpose is demonstrated by the fact that some computer firms are electing to bypass costly brokers altogether. Instead, they establish their own internal divisions to solicit independently produced programs. Software packages submitted to Hewlett-Packard Plus, or Atari-Apex are periodically reviewed and tested by company staff, much as the works of more literary authors are reviewed by book and journal editors. The exclusive rights to software deemed to have a profitable chance on the market are purchased in exchange for royalties that are either fixed or may increase with sales. Later, the author of an especially successful software package may be sought out to work for the firm on a contract basis. So successfully do these practices minimize the firm's commitment to a regular technical labor force, the personnel manager for a major computer and video game producer notes that their entire home computer division employs only four programmers.

*A*lmost all the software we sell to the outside world comes from independents, and we have hundreds of programs that were all developed on the outside. These come from independents who say "we want to do things our own way—we don't want to belong to this big bureaucracy."

And so, they do not "belong" to big bureaucracies. They merely submit their work to them, without belonging, in the hope their labor will result in the next "PacMan" or "Wordstar," and be rewarded accordingly by the market. The relationships constituted between firm and worker by these intermediate structures differ on the surface from the personal agreements that arise in the shop and the office. They are less personal. Nothing is guaranteed. Each hopeful software author seems moved by the pure, risk-taking, entrepreneurial impulse. And yet, a market organized into a system of brokers, intermediaries, and publishing houses confronts the individual authors and transforms them into a pool from which large firms can dip. The cost of replacing this pool of mental labor with in-house employees, who must be paid for producing the failures as well as the "hits," goes beyond the resources of firms already struggling to stave off the bankruptcies periodically announced in Silicon Valley. Survival depends on unpaid labor, and those whose video games are passed over provide precisely that.

The structural origins of these convenient arrangements are within the firm, where formal structures of authority and control breed resentment, monotony, competition, and disappointment. These unhappy features of the workplace culminate for some in the desire to escape. What would happen if such actively disaffected individuals had no choice but to remain on the job? Might their resentment turn into resistance to authority? This is an issue the firm need not confront with them. Their desire to escape the formal structure of authority can instead be actualized through the informal structure of social networks, also generated within the firm.

Thus, it is the corporate sector itself that provides the breeding

ground out of which informal workers emerge, to be reincorpo-
rated at a later date in forms that cheapen overhead costs and
remove any threat of face-to-face confrontation between worker
and manager. This dynamic is further stimulated by the establishment of impersonal mechanisms, again located in corporate enterprise, to facilitate the connection between firms and workers that
do not appear on their payroll.

For these reasons, the origins of the informal work discussed
here are found in the complex interaction between the individual
motives of workers and the labor requirements of capital. These
origins are not external to the productive process. They exist
within it, in terms of the structural realities that give rise to both
individual motives and corporate needs, and the social arrangements through which these new working relationships are established.

Therefore, to a certain extent, elimination of informal work, or
the so-called "underground economy," would require one of two
programs. Either the workplace must be transformed into an
arena where discontent is handled democratically, or firms must
be prevented from converting their employees into "self-employees." It is unlikely that either of these programs will be undertaken in the near future.

The Dynamics of Informal Work:
Piece Rates, Deadlines, and the Reassertion
of Company Control

The popular impressions of work life inside the modern firm do
not hold true for those who choose to leave and work informally.
Not surprisingly, they discover that managers still dictate the
tasks and projects at which they will work. They tell them how to
go about doing their work, and decide how much it is worth. The
daily facts of life here are not concealed from them behind lush
office shrubbery, nor softened by recessed fluorescent lighting.
Capitulating to what few believe can be changed, they attempt
to get out from under the boss's thumb by becoming their own
bosses.

How successfully do they elude externally imposed control over
their work? In some ways, they seem to succeed quite well. Most
respondents report great satisfaction with the freedom they enjoy
to decide the hour at which their work day begins, how the work

area will be arranged, and whom they will allow into it. They are free now to take calls from friends without suffering the supervisor's watchful gaze. If they want to take a break in the middle of the day for jogging or running errands, that is also up to them. And within the limits set by clients' technical specifications for the work, they control their own immediate labor process.[11]

But none of this means that firms relying on them have yielded all control. Maintaining control over the subcontracting process turns out to be an important issue for companies that they resolve through two principle mechanisms—insistence on adherence to short-term deadlines and payment by results. These two mechanisms are characteristic of informal work and result in important consequences we will explore below. Tasks or products that cannot be easily broken down into units of time and money are likely to be reserved for the in-house work force, and never enter the circuit of informal production.[12]

What types of work lend themselves to short-term deadlines and payment by result? They include rush jobs with a well-defined beginning and end, labor-intensive work in which the unit can be clearly priced (i.e., a piece, a page, a project for which a standard can be estimated), or custom work for which in-house costs would exceed average costs a firm attempts to maintain across its labor force. The imposition of deadlines and payment by results for such work enables firms to establish indirect control where direct supervision is lacking in two ways.

First, the deadline ensures that regardless of the hour at which outside workers choose to *begin* their working day, they will either extend it or increase its pace to the point at which the deadline can be met. Rush jobs are by definition urgent jobs that the firm's average work force cannot handle. Custom work may be awaited as an integral part of an ongoing procss, and again, delay must be avoided. Labor-intensive work is likely to comprise but one phase of some continuous production. Therefore, the work that is put out carries with it a sense of urgency in the deadline as well. This fact is reflected in the ways respondents qualify accounts of their freedom, now that they no longer have a boss. For example, a home assembler is ambivalent about the degrees of choice versus compulsion in her work.

I like it because no one requires me to do it. Oh, occasionally they do. . . . They say when they need the stuff and I'll have it done by those times. But I do tend to put it off, and finally, my

husband will say, "Humph! Mary! You know, we do have a
commitment!"

When commitments become extensive and, as a home word
processor puts it, "Mr. Financial Report comes in pressuring and
saying he's in a hurry for this," the work week can run as long as
sixty hours. The free-floating schedule in which work and play
seem to find their own natural place in one's life is more often an
ideal than a reality, for social life is still planned around the hours
deadlines dictate as necessary to complete the work. A typist explains:

*Y*ou *set your hours—to a certain extent. I mean, to another*
extent, they're set by your clients saying, "I need this by such-
and-such a time." You can kind of decide within those
parameters when you're going to get around to doing it.

Pre-stipulated deadlines allow the firm to exercise some control
over the pace of work. The manager's vigilant stare is not required
to ensure that the worker is working. Instead, the clock, the calen-
dar, and the worker's self-discipline set the length and pace of the
working day. Informal workers generally agree, in fact, that they
are working harder now than they did before. Seven-day work
weeks in which their minds, if not their hands, are continually applied to the tasks before them are not uncommon, especially as the
deadline approaches.

*W*hen *your brain is dedicated to a project, you eat, sleep,*
and breathe it—the code, how to write it more efficiently.
Sometimes, when I'm designing a video game for one of the
people I contract with, I'll work for twelve hours, sleep in front
of the computer, have food delivered in, and just work, work,
work!

A number of people admit that when they struck off on their
own, their original intention had been to work less than the forty-
hour week required by their jobs. By leaving their jobs, they hoped
to "control the terms of their own existence" and to make work
a less consuming activity in their lives. But pressures from clients
and the need to save up for future rainy days by working as hard
as they can when work is available result in many being "swept
away." There is a tendency to postpone both daily breaks and annual vacations, a tendency one woman assures us is "not motivated by greed, but by insecurity." And a good reputation for

meeting deadlines reliably often leads to more work from the same clients, who increasingly depend on this source of labor on a regular basis, and whose expectations escalate with each contract.

Obviously, the quality of work performed under pressure may suffer, and quality, like speed, is an issue over which firms also reassert control. The best way to offset tendencies for work to be performed so hastily that it won't meet minimum company standards is to apply a system of remuneration that only rewards acceptable results. The direct supervisor is here replaced with some form of a piece rate. Work that fails to meet client specifications is rejected and done over, usually at no extra cost.

Although Marx pointed out that "the piecewage is the form of wages most in harmony with the capitalist mode of production,"[13] the hourly wage became the normal form of payment, and we tend to look with surprise on the persistence of piece rates today. It may be true for a firm's employees that social insurance legislation "effectively establishes a minimum wage, . . . constraining the use of payment by result."[14] But informal workers are not legal employees. Thus according to one contemporary manager, what was true before can remain true today for informal workers: "You can't pay hourly outside, because you have no control over how their time is spent. If they want to build up speed, that's fine. But we don't pay for anything that is rejected in test. So they are building their own salary." If the deadline introduces a sense of urgency into the pace of the work, payment by results confers importance on its quality.

It is clear how such payment can be applied to the manufacturing process. Homeworkers are paid so much for each coil they wind, each circuit board they load with components, each joint to which they touch a hot iron and melt a bit of solder. The correspondence between effort and result is direct, and subcontractors find explicit ways to maximize this correspondence. A woman who provides her home assemblers with an evening of practice on new assemblies pays that same night for pieces made in training. "A little check in hand as they walk out the door," she says, "is a great impetus to do more." Another intermediary has his own "motivator" for his two home assemblers to cut production time below the estimate he has given the company. "When I go to their homes," he explains, "I have a blank check for fifty dollars in my pocket. If one has an idea *both* can use, I pay her a bonus."

Some clerical work also lends itself to payment by results, so that many home typists work by the page. Striving to maintain both speed and accuracy, they describe their outlook on work as "production oriented." Unfortunately, clients arrive expecting much more than mere production of typed pages. They are also looking for the services they are accustomed to receiving from office secretaries on an hourly wage—punctuation, spelling corrections, grammatical revision, and at times, professional editing of half-baked handwritten drafts! Some typists advertise themselves as "editor-typist" as a way of attracting business. Yet this mental work slows down the production process, lengthens the time it takes to produce a page, and lowers average hourly earnings. Therefore, several home typists and word processors assert that they "don't want to think about the material—it's too intrusive." In the interest of increasing production, they prefer that clients think for themselves.

It is unfortunate, but this means that where informal work was prompted by the desire for more creative, intellectual work, that desire is now compromised by the need to sustain high levels of volume. Clerical personnel employed in the firm are often required to do the boss's thinking, and their efforts go unrecognized much of the time. However, the hours spent editing or rewriting a report, the hours spent typing it, and perhaps the short break afterward are all paid at the same rate. The boss is credited as the source of the product's literary brilliance, to be sure. But there is still the paid opportunity for a secretary to use mental as well as manual skills. In the case of my respondents, several of whom have college degrees, skills may remain underutilized as they strive for speed and accuracy on the first draft.

Some who provide contract clerical services do charge hourly rates in order to relieve the pressure piece rates exert to turn out page after perfect page. An hourly rate would seem to ensure that time spent making corrections or modifications—that is, bringing the work up to clients' quality standards—is paid in full. But in fact, this apparent hourly rate is transformed into a piece rate when the initial agreement includes, as it always does, a close estimate of the number of hours the total job will take. The number of pages, for example, is translated into a length of time it will take to type them or to format and print them on the word processor. If it takes much longer than estimated, it may be possible to squeeze from the client some additional remuneration.

Yet many report they are not always successful, because the client's expectations have already been established. They consequently find themselves providing some additional, unpaid effort until the client is willing to accept the work as finished. The manner in which hourly rates for informal work represent little more than psychologically tolerable forms of piece rates is illustrated by this home typist:

If I charged by the page, I'd make more than my hourly rate of ten dollars. But there's something about having to get that many pages out of the machine. . . . Oh—I can get them out! But there's something in my mind that says, "you gotta produce!" And I make mistakes. It's like piecework in a factory, you know? This morning, I typed a thirty-eight page report and it took me three and a half hours. At ten dollars an hour, I made thirty-five dollars. At a dollar a page, I'd have made three dollars more. But the mental pressure is just not worth it.

In fact, clients often insist that the quoted hourly rate be explicitly translated into a quotation of the average time it takes to produce a page. Subsequent corrections taking less than an hour can then be prorated, if they are paid for at all. Needless to say, the most common understanding here, as in home assembly, is that there is no reimbursement for rejects.

The form of payment is also an issue for informal technical workers whose finished product is clearly the result of mental labor— a manual, a program, a scientific instrument. It is not possible for them to break the task down into manual operations they will provide versus mental processes they will leave to the client. The very task for which they are paid is to "think about the material," and the "piece" for which they are rewarded is the client's total project. Such work is described as "translating the client's ideas into documents," "satisfying someone else's image of the product," "helping the clients clarify their thinking," or "acting as an interface between people who know nothing about computers and people who do."

The working relationship may begin with the client's description of what seems to be a clearly defined technical need. Following the worker's estimate of how long it will take to complete the project, agreement on either an hourly rate or a project fee is reached. But more often than not, initial implementation of what clients *think* they want serves merely to clarify in their minds what they *really* want, and this is usually something quite different from the original work for which they contracted. Now, the cost of the project must be renegotiated, or the estimate of the hours necessary for its completion revised upward. For either modification to occur, the client firm must be persuaded that the problem lies with their original communication about the nature of the project, and not with the quality of the worker's efforts.

Misunderstandings between clients and contractors can be costly. For example, in the midst of 40 percent growth, Wang Computers contracted a project out to a small, independent consulting firm which failed to complete the work. With the project estimated to be costing Wang $10 million a year, the contractor was dismissed three years later. Wang's director of computer operations and technical services explains that "the biggest problem was simply that Wang executives had no idea what they wanted."[15]

Because, in the words of one programmer, "clients can be real flaky," informal technical workers are ambivalent about quoting project rates. It is difficult to estimate how much time is required before the thought process succeeds in laying a conceptual foundation on which the more routine task of implementation can be carried out. It is easy to "get burned," to charge $100 for something estimated to take four hours, when in fact it turns out to require ten. Some people offer an hour of free consultation to establish whether the project is even "do-able" as originally conceived. Others charge an advance, asking for "money up front," so that when clients claim their specifications have not been met and withhold payment, losses can be minimized.

Many of these working relationships are based on personal connections between family and friends. This means that the client may be willing to place the worker on the "honor system" and pay an hourly rate. But even here, there tends to be a clear understanding beforehand of how many hours the job should take. Spoken or unspoken, the deadline serves to enforce the honor system. And many people feel such a strong sense of honor, they are likely to err on the side of cheating themselves out of payment for time they have actually worked.

It is understood in the firm that work can be interrupted for short breaks within limits set by the law and enforced by the supervisor. Office and shop floor culture may extend these limits to include an occasional personal phone call, or a chat with co-workers by the copy machine without a loss of pay. The limits of tolerance for such respites during informal work are determined in part by the deadline, but are also narrowed by the worker's self-control. It becomes difficult for some to actually compute the hours they feel are owed them, for under the honor system, one's honor is included as part of the total package sold the client. A technical writer who has tried charging both project and hourly rates complains of the latter:

Charging by the hour is very frustrating to me. I am very conscientious about trying to keep track of the time I spend. I might be in the middle of something, the phone will ring, and I forget to look at my watch. And by the time I get rid of that person, I'll say, "Now let's see—did I talk for five minutes or was it ten?" I really feel as if they get a lot for their money!

And indeed, managers are quick to agree that they do get a lot for their money. "Quality control is easy," they say. "It either goes or it doesn't go!" "If we send it out, we don't have to worry about payroll taxes, benefits, vacations—or anything. It's *their* responsibility." "When we have deadlines, we put it out. We don't want to hire half a dozen programmers and then figure out what to do with them when the project is over." "This company's never had a layoff. We keep a small work force, use subcontractors, and deliberately orient ourselves to making them lay off their helpers so we don't have to lay off ours." These testimonials to the use of outside workers are typical of the reasons firms give for putting out work. But while the benefits of what some call "off-loading" are numerous, they can be summarized as part of a single strategy firms use to stabilize day-to-day operations in a competitive and unstable market context. It is the market dynamics faced by the firms that result in negative material consequences for informal workers.

Lumps, Glitches, and the Cycle of Feast or Famine

It is clear now that firms reinstate control over the pace and quality of informal work through the system in which it is remunerated. As a result, informal workers may work longer hours at a faster pace than they would as employees hired to do the same kind of work. There is in effect a second dynamic that places informal workers at an additional disadvantage: Instability in the market situation faced by the firms that employ them leads to instability of informally earned income, a difficulty encountered in some degree by all informal workers.

Although the Bay Area unemployment rate remains lower than

the national average, large local firms have contributed their share of massive layoffs and spectacular bankruptcies to the economic crises of this period. Like Osborne Computer Corporation, a company can make a fortune on one day, and on the next become a "victim of 'creative destruction'" wrought by an IBM's entry into the market.[16] In fact, high-tech economies like that found in the Bay Area are characterized by rapid start-ups and sudden failures: Even a giant like Warner Communications suffers serious losses when its subsidiary, Atari, fails to maintain its market lead.[17]

Employees are suddenly unemployed, and plans for retrenchment invariably include the subcontracting of both R&D functions and manufacturing.[18] According to Paul Ely, Jr., executive vice-president of Hewlett-Packard, such instability means that "management must be prepared on almost a daily basis to make adjustments to plans and budgets."[19] An important source of such adjustments is the use of contract labor, and the personal flexibility sought by informal workers ends up redounding to the benefit of firms seeking market flexibility.

This does not mean, of course, that each individual firm is constantly confronted by the spectre of failure, or that management does not attempt to make long-range decisions. Firms project sales and, based on such projections, forecast production schedules. But when orders are cancelled, or when unexpected orders come in, what some managers call "lumps" appear in the production plan, making it "lopsided" in terms of the amount of work to be done versus the size of the work force to which the firm has committed itself. Rather than making short-run adjustments in its average work force, the firm smooths the "lumps" that appear in its production cycle by subcontracting work to its outside labor pool.

The high-tech industry can also be subject as a whole to cyclical variations in product demand, availability of essential components, or technological innovation. Industry-wide variations in supply and demand are referred to as "glitches," and though they are regular features of the market at the aggregate level, individual firms experience them as atypical events for which subcontracting is a temporary solution. Needless to say, however, the cumulative effects of these periodic disturbances result in the creation of a constant demand for informal workers. Thus, informal work itself becomes a permanent feature of the economy alongside the firms that generate it.

The fact that informal workers are in general demand at all

times does not imply that all of them are at all times working. Demand on the part of individual firms fluctuates, and at most, informal workers have but a few firms as clients at any given time. This is why most respondents describe the rhythm of their work as "feast or famine." For months at a time, they work day and night. Then, mysteriously, the phone does not ring. For no apparent reason, a "dry period" sets in. Newcomers to informal work experience panic, advertise their services in local newspapers and laundromats. Perhaps, in desperation, they go so far as to look for a job. But the more seasoned hold out in the knowledge that the lull is temporary. The phone will ring again, as inexplicably as it fell silent, and they view the abrupt slowdown in their work as their annual vacation.

The convenient availability of a work force characterized by instability, a work force to which the corporate sector has none of the commitments required by law and custom when employees are hired, means that firms present a stronger appearance of internal stability than they would otherwise. This stable image allows a firm to enjoy what one manager values as "first crack at the regular work force—especially the high-caliber people," for workers know who is prone to layoffs and who is not. Company reputations for being able to maintain job stability for employees depend in a real sense on their ability to fine-tune operations through the judicious use of "self-employees."

Thus a national study of flexible staffing patterns reveals that 13 percent of the firms surveyed use subcontracted labor as a means of protecting their employees from downturns in demand.[20] And at a California Department of Employment Development seminar on "contingent workers" (i.e., part-time workers, leased employees, at-home workers, and self-employed contractors), a representative of the California Chamber of Commerce confirmed that it is these workers "that keep the rest of us working full-time."[21] To use the idiom of the day, the use of informal workers is a normal business practice which enables firms to stay "lean and mean."

The use of informal labor also lowers the cost of doing business. This is not necessarily because informal workers accept subminimum wages. Many report they make more than the legal minimum, and in fact, those who work on hourly rates charge more than they earned at their previous jobs. Even pieceworkers claim their piece rates result in higher hourly earnings than the local office or factory wage.

What informal labor reduces is what some firms call the "burden factor," that is, the costs associated with hiring employees, providing them with space, equipment, and benefits. Depending on the industry, private firms employing between 50 and 250 people provide 65 percent of them with paid sick leave, 75 percent with paid rest periods, and 99 percent with paid holidays and vacations.[22] By 1982, social security, workers' compensation, and other legally required payments added 8 per cent to total labor costs in the manufacturing sector, and employer contributions for other programs increased these costs another 13 percent.[23] In the high-tech industry, where workers remain largely unorganized, these costs are still within 1 percent of the average for all industries. It is therefore possible to pay informal workers at a somewhat higher rate than wage and salary employees while saving some portion of what normally must go toward employee benefits.

In addition to these contributions, firms also compute as part of the burden factor the costs of stocking and handling inventories, providing floor space and equipment, and maintaining administrative services. According to one respondent, he is able to provide for $153 an assembly unit that cost the firm $179 when he managed its production as an inside supervisor. And yet, the two women who left the company with him to assemble the unit at home now average $10 per hour, in contrast to their previous hourly wage of $6.15. He attributes the saving to the firm and the apparent increase for his assemblers to the fact that his burden factor is much lower. Where the firm faced 3.6 percent in overhead costs, he adds only 1.8 percent to the cost of each unit because assembly is done at home, and he and his workers receive no benefits.

The higher short-term rewards are experienced as positive by informal workers. They feel as if they are making more money than before. But as already noted, the "lumps" and "glitches" in which informal work is rooted are ultimately translated into cycles of feast or famine. The long run, in which the job is completed and the labor no longer needed, brings no disadvantage to the firm. The income of its outside workers, however, can suddenly drop from double what they earned as employees to nothing. If short-run earnings are higher for informal work than for regular employment, this is because firms are willing to pay a little extra for labor to which they have no enduring commitment, and which can be broken up into discrete hourly units or pieces. Employees are paid for the entire day they spend on the employer's premises, regardless of whether they are fully occupied all eight of those hours. In contrast, informal workers are paid only for the time they actually spend working, as demonstrated by the results of their labor.

Company representatives are quick to point out that their "self-employees" are free to plan for the future by providing themselves with privately purchased health and retirement plans out of their earnings. But the cyclical variations in work flow, once translated into income variations, discourage informal workers from making these investments. Only twenty-six out of thirty-five respondents have health insurance. Eleven of them are covered under an employed spouse's plan,[24] and for five of them informal work is a part-time activity and health coverage is provided through regular employment. In other words, fewer than 30 percent of the informal workers in the sample provide *themselves* with health insurance.

Those who are not included on a spouse's policy report putting off decisions about health and retirement plans, and realize they are leading a precarious, "high-risk existence." One woman's solution to the financial consequences of catastrophic illness, should it come, will be to "sell" her clerical business to a friend for $1, declare herself destitute, and apply for MediCal as an indigent. Others push worry to the back of their minds and express the hope they will never fall seriously ill. "I've never had health insurance in my life, except for the brief time I was married," says one home typist. "That's a drag. But then, I don't plan to get sick."[25]

Informal work may serve best as part of a mixed income strategy in which some member of the household is regularly employed. Recall that nine of the ten professional-technical workers who divulged information about their incomes enjoyed household incomes that were above the Bay Area median. This was also the case for one of the four persons who reported from the group of clerical workers. But had these households relied on their informally earned income alone, none of the clerical, and only four of the professional-technical workers would have attained the regional figure for median household income. When forms of payment such as health insurance are included in an assessment of material rewards, the picture becomes even more clear: Those who rely strictly on informal work (and half of the people in this sample do) find themselves at a disadvantage.

In addition to allowing firms to maintain a smaller average in-house work force and reduce their overhead costs, informal workers provide them with another, more subtle advantage. Their accounts of why they left their jobs include tales of resentment at being told what to do, frustration with bureaucratic procedure, and refusal to play the game of company politics. They describe themselves as mavericks, and the firms agree. They seem to disrupt the pattern of the office. They cause problems on the shop floor. Thinking they have a better idea, they fail to see why they shouldn't have their way.

People like these pose potential problems for management. Not only is it difficult to gain their quiet acquiescence to authority, but they threaten to infect other workers who may be equally unhappy. When a secretary argues a reasonable case for being placed on a flexible work schedule, the good sense in her argument is apparent to her co-workers as well. An engineer's designs prove more sophisticated than those proposed by the vice-president of R&D, who suffers a case of "Not-Invented-Here Fear" when his competence is called into question. And when a production worker suggests that organizing may be the only way to keep the pace of work within tolerable limits, some workers raise anxious objections that the plant will close down.

When managers explain their strategies for maintaining an "average" internal work force by using outside help as a supplement, they do not simply refer to a *numerical* average. They also have in mind what they perceive to be a *different type of worker* for their in-house needs. These workers may not be the fastest, nor the most brilliant, but they can be relied upon to keep regular hours and do as they are told. These are the "grunt workers," who one manager says "come back from lunch on time and have a good attitude."

Regular employees of these companies were not interviewed for this study, and so it is not known if their attitudes toward authority differ substantially from those of their informal counterparts. It would not be surprising to learn that they share the resentments that drive some from the firm, and that what actually differs for many of them is the degree of opportunity to go out on their own. But what is clear is that managers *believe* there are two kinds of worker, each with a proper place in the chain of production. A representative of a home computer firm contrasts them in these terms:

There is an average assembler, and they're easier to manage, because you don't have to deal with someone who is really good. We prefer to have everyone doing the same amount of work. Otherwise, the really good one gets to be a bit of a prima donna, the others start fighting, and it becomes a management problem.

Another executive describes the preferred "average" workers as possessing a "certain psychological profile" that enables them to carry out routine work on a daily basis "without trying to excel at what they do."

The voluntary exodus of the "prima donnas," whose "psychological profiles" mark them as threats to managerial authority, also allows firms to maintain internal control *and* access to their labor. And as already suggested, informal workers' escape from company control is far from complete. Even as they labor, now at a distance from the direct supervisor, the pace and quality of their work is still dictated by management in the form of remuneration by results and the terms of its completion. In fact, it is the corporate sector that solicits this work from them.

There is a final point at which the dynamics of dependence between firm and informal worker result in the latter being drawn back under the total control of the former. Some of the more efficient, enduring, and innovative informal operations are acquired by companies. Thus, several respondents in this sample report pressures from venture capitalists (also known as "vulture capitalists") to expand beyond their living room walls. There is, of course, the promise of profit, once access to capital greater than that available through friends and family is offered.

But with this promise comes the condition that investors will have a voice in the management of daily affairs, for according to one corporate representative, the founders do not always have a "good handle on where the money is going." The original satisfactions sought in being one's own boss begin to disappear as the informal enterprise is formalized. A software author confronted with this dilemma at the time of our interview discusses his ambivalence:

I'm not sure it's a good idea, but there are a lot of pressures to sell out. We're going to be forced to do it, actually, and it's just going to get us into a classical mode of work, with offices and secretaries—the whole infrastructure. Now, I don't have a tremendous desire to run a huge company, because I've been through that bit and there are a lot of problems with it. But I've got this other problem—that for some strange reason, I

don't like to miss the opportunity to make a lot of money. So I
do some outrageous things to myself. If I were smarter, I'd
probably pass it up . . . but I guess I'm just dumb. . . .

The pressures he feels are located in corporate rivalry to acquire the best and most proven talent, thereby making it inaccessible to competitors. Several corporate respondents describe the strategy of buying small operators that have demonstrated their capabilities as the fastest, most economical way of entering a market without "going through the growth pains." As one of them puts it, "Acquiring skills is much more attractive than trying to grow them internally."

The most widely publicized examples of reasserting control through acquisition occur in the software industry. But included in this sample alone are an engineer and an assembler whose three-year association in their respective garages culminated in the acquisition of their product by the company to which they had supplied it. For a time, they were reconverted into employees before leaving to undertake a new project. There is also a technical writer who, at the time of the interview, had turned down her client's offer to "buy her" and transform her back into a salaried worker. Finally, one respondent, a home-based word processor, stubbornly refused an invitation to take her clientele into a larger operation where she would receive a steady income but sacrifice her freedom.

A gross accounting of the distribution of benefits between informal worker and firm reveals that in both the material and nonmaterial sense, the firm seems to come out ahead. The greater instability that characterizes informal employment relations is a necessary element in maximizing the stability of wage employment relations. Informal income, seemingly higher in the short run, is subject to the cycle of feast or famine, and becomes variable or lower than wage earnings in the long run. Yet throughout this process, careful firms manage to reduce costs without sacrificing speed or quality. And in the end, the control workers seek to escape in exchange for accepting the insecurity is reasserted in different forms when firms agree to put work out to them. In fact, some groups who occupy positions of low status within the workplace—clerical workers, for instance—can experience *decreased* autonomy when they leave to work informally.[26]

Why do some continue informal work when it appears to place them on the losing end of a bad bargain? Why do they consider regular employment "a fate worse than death?" There are two possible reasons: either they are economically irrational, or there are costs and rewards associated with each choice for which we have not accounted. If the latter is the case, then perhaps the net outcomes must be assessed differently.

The Realities of Employment and Illusions of Freedom

During their interviews, respondents were often challenged to explain just how they justified their preference for informal work in light of the dynamics detailed above. Their answers indicated that they are not irrational or poorly informed individuals. Instead, they suggest that the sharp contrasts we make between regular and informal employment are in the process of being blurred, with much of the change coming from the side of regular employment. It seems that increasingly, the promises that came with having a job—a permanent career with one firm, raises, benefits, and a little social security at the end of it all—no longer inspire belief among these respondents.

If informal workers buy what they call freedom at a cost to their long-term security, they do so in a context in which regular employment ties are currently perceived as weak. Their preference for being homeworkers, cottage workers, freelancers, and consultants, and their withdrawal from the workplace must also be read as their withdrawal of belief in the capability of our current production system to provide regular employment sufficient to supply life's necessities. Faith in the corporate sector diminishes, and it seems that for these informal workers insecurity becomes a more legitimate feature of life in the industrial-information age.

This more general cost accounting is made when workers' expectations that education and experience will pay off in higher income and greater autonomy prove mistaken. What they observe all around them are wage givebacks, business failures, and periodic rates of inflation that erode income in both relative and absolute terms. Their realization that employers are more interested in having a "warm body that will sit in the office for eight hours" than they are in the human capital embodied in a hard-earned college degree is further disheartening. These respondents are not making their choices in a vacuum, for they all have friends with jobs. One man explains:

Many of the people I went to school with are in really bad straits right now. They are living as poorly as they did in the sixties—many even worse. And most of them haven't made the great professional achievements they hoped they would. I don't think there's any reason to believe I would have ended up any better.

The actual monetary costs of merely holding a job are perceived as excessive. The effect of the mid-1970s escalation in gasoline prices on commuting to work, the corporate image even poorly paid secretaries are expected to project by adhering to exorbitant "dress-for-success" codes, the lunches out, and all the other costs of labor force participation have risen faster than wages and salaries. Informal workers see all these as savings they make by virtue of *not* having a job. And though the future may be uncertain, our contemporary dilemma over the long-term viability of the social security system leads many to dismiss the program now as "a joke."

Given the disparities between regular employment and informal work, we are tempted to draw sharp contrasts between the two. But as Rubery and Wilkinson point out, "the lower the unit costs and the lower the fixed labour costs (for instance, guaranteed wages, holiday pay, sick pay, tax and social security payments), the more similar direct employment will be to outwork."[27] This was highlighted for me during an interview with a word processor whose single "client" was a multinational bank, and whose sole proof of "self-employment" was the business card they suggested he have printed. I found myself frustrated with his apparent satisfaction with the arrangement, and blurting out that I thought the bank was exploiting him, I asked, "Don't you really think they're just using you?" He readily agreed. Yet, having worked in the same capacity as the bank's employee, he added, "But then, they're using us all." And of course, he has a point.

Other respondents had similar reactions. When reminded that their income extends only as far as the life of each contract, they countered that today they see their parents' generation facing layoffs after giving their lives to a single firm. They see their friends riding high one day on the sparkling waves created by flashy start-up firms, and unemployed the next as those firms go under. "You suddenly realize there's a fallacy on the other side, that there was security where you were. The idea that the corporate job is secure? That's ludicrous!"

But what of the "freedom" that was supposed to make it all worthwhile? Doesn't it prove somewhat illusory too? One man admits as much when he agrees that in fact, he now works longer and harder than he did as a salaried engineer. Nevertheless, he insists:

*J*ust *the* idea *that you* could *have more freedom gives you a sense of well-being. You have a feeling of freedom, even though it may not be a reality. In this business, at least you feel like you have the possibility.*

Informal work as a subjectively experienced phenomenon is not so much a matter of exchanging secure, well-paid, fulfilling work inside a firm for the misguided dream of having one's own business. It is rather a choice between two illusions: the illusion that the corporate sector is as capable of providing us with a secure livelihood as we once thought it was, and the illusion that we can escape from it. Both illusions have their origins in the corporate sector. It is here that firms continue making promises about what sunrise industries can offer workers in the industrial-information age if only they will acquire the necessary skills. It is here, too, that the same enterprises generate the discontent that moves some to walk out the door. And just outside, in the world of informal work, we find the corporate sector again—ready now to do business, still on its own terms, with its "self-employees." The origins and dynamics of these informal working relations are not located in underdevelopment of the economy, nor in the underdevelopment of personal morality. They are integral features of a single system of competitive production in which firm and informal worker are complementary parts growing out of the antagonisms fostered by capitalist competition.

5

~

Bringing Work Home

*Typing via word processor. Former top secretary
going into business at home. 17 years
experience. Excellent work. I can spell and handle
commas, too. Margaret.*

—Classified ad in Bay Area
community newspaper   (mid-1980s)

*The home environment is very good for business—
particularly in this area. There's lots of people who
think that it's very neat that you start out in your
house.*

—Palo Alto software author

*Picture this: one of our Irish cottage knitters puts
aside the sweater she's just finished. Sighs with
satisfaction. And turns to her morning chores. She
could well have just finished her two or three
hundredth handknit Aran Crew. Each of the
sweaters she knits is her own family pattern. (To
knit any other so unconsciously, between chores, she
would first have to forget the ones she knows now.)
But, because we employ hundreds of cottage knitters,
all of our patterns are different.*

—Advertisement for $128 sweater
Lands' End mail order catalog
©Lands' End Inc.

A key dimension of informal work is that its conduct depends heavily on the use of personal and household resources. Family and friends provide an important supply of auxiliary labor for the informal worker. The family car and the home phone become essential means of production, and for all but two of the people interviewed, the home is the primary base of operations. These intimate inputs are subsequently channeled through the connections that develop between informal workers and firms, where they are transformed into productive ones that ultimately add to the corporate output of goods and services. This unique combination of home life and work life raises a number of theoretical and empirical issues that are addressed in this chapter.

It may seem ironic that at a time when we thought home-based production a thing of the past, we should find it necessary to consider it anew. But as the industrial-information economy gets underway in the 1980s, there is growing interest in the home as workplace. This interest is manifested under several headings, depending on whether the work involves the use of electronic equipment. Where it does, the activity is referred to as "telecommuting" from the "electronic cottage." Where it does not, terms include "flexiplace," or "worksteading."

The unifying factor underlying all these labels is that work normally done on an employer's premises is instead performed in the worker's home. Such homework makes its appearance on the contemporary scene as a potential solution to problems as diverse as the energy crisis and the child care problems of working mothers. Thus this aspect of informal work must be discussed in the broader social context where home-based production is claimed to be increasing, and according to some, even desirable. These claims are touched on in the following section.

Finally, a number of empirical questions are addressed, arising from the ways informal work involves household members and resources. What happens when production is incorporated into the intimate environment of personal relations and home life? How are household members affected? And perhaps most important, given the current gender division of labor, what differing implications might this feature of informal work have for men and women? Based on the empirical findings about informal work in the home, I propose an alternative perspective to the dualistic theories of production and reproduction considered below. (See "A

Second Look at Theories of Production and Reproduction" [pp. 125–129].)

Contemporary Homework: Estimates, Projections, and Politics

It is difficult to assess the accuracy of estimates regarding the prevalence of home-based production. Yet the sources of such estimates tend to agree that it is widespread. A 1977 Census Bureau survey shows that nearly half of all female-owned businesses are conducted from the home, and unofficial counts suggest that between 1.2 and 3 million women fall into this category.[1] An AT&T survey reveals that 7 percent of the United States work force now labors full-time at home, and an additional 6 percent is occupied there part-time.[2] The Current Population Survey for May 1985 produced a figure of 1.9 million individuals whose home was their exclusive place of work. About two-thirds of them were women.[3] It is interesting to note that of the 7 million telecommuters currently counted by an Electronic Services Unlimited survey, only one out of every five is actually registered as an employee of a company. The remainder are considered "self-employed."[4]

Many anticipate that more people will work at home in the future. The United States Chamber of Commerce projects that by 1990, home-based workers will number nearly 11 million.[5] An even more ambitious projection is offered by Nilles: He estimates that by 1990, the number of telecommuters alone could increase to ten million.[6]

Alongside these claims there emerges a disturbing sociopolitical agenda, one that blends patriotism and technology, home and industry, in ways that make uneasy bedfellows of feminist and conservative. For instance, Newt Gingrich's (R-Georgia) Family Opportunity Act proposes tax credits for people purchasing home computers for nonrecreational purposes. The intentions of the congressman are to

> . . . increase individual economic opportunity, expand the potential for individuals to own their own businesses, *restore the family setting by allowing families to learn and earn together at home* [emphasis added], develop opportunities for America's handicapped and disabled citizens, provide a growing pool of

computer-literate young people who can enter the jobs of the future and man the sophisticated military of tomorrow, and to decrease home-to-office commuting and national dependence on imported oil.[7]

On the surface, it seems to be the electronic magic of high technology that will unite family, state, and economy in such felicitous harmony—what Berch describes as "an explicit fantasy of futurism, with the ideology of liberation through self-employment."[8] But in fact, the interrelationship of home, state, and market in initiatives such as these is based not on the availability of the home computer, but on the escalated penetration of the home by industry that this legislation allows. The impulse to promote this penetration is clearly evident in current initiatives like the 1984 Freedom of Workplace Act sponsored by Senator Orrin Hatch (R-Utah). This proposal is not limited to high-tech homework, but would remove existing restrictions on industrial homework as well.

Using as his reference point workers whose legal right to manufacture garments at home is currently being questioned, Hatch promises that passage of his act will "allow the Betsy Rosses of this country to make their flags at home without fear of being prosecuted by the Department of Labor."[9] The conservative senator supports his patriotic alliance with the "Betsy Rosses" by citing "the feminist author, Betty Friedan . . . who offered homework as a solution to the problems of young working mothers."[10] It is ironic to recall that during the 1930s debate over whether to abolish or regulate homework, women reformers lobbied for its *abolition*—though in ways that justified their position of inequality in the regular labor market by arguing that mothers ought not to be working for wages at all.[11]

It is inevitable that homework raises issues having to do with the gender division of labor. Newspaper articles noting that "computers and babysitting have a lot more in common than most people realize"[12] make it clear in modern-day terms what those issues are. A computer in the home enables women to earn income while providing their own child care. But in fact, the computer itself is to the electronic cottage what the knitting machine was to nineteenth-century cottage workers—only a tool. In order to grasp its apparent utility in simultaneously increasing economic opportunity, restoring the family setting, and fostering national independence, it is necessary to look beyond technology to the social mechanisms now rearranging taken-for-granted patterns of production and reproduction into alternative configurations. It seems that informal work, combining as it does corporate capital with primary social ties and the resources of the household, is just such a mechanism.

When considering the contemporary political focus on home-based production as a household income strategy, keep in mind the following facts. Over 40 percent of women with children under age six participate in the labor force.[13] Working men's attitudes toward marriage grow increasingly negative.[14] And given budgetary deficits, the state is less likely than ever to subsidize child care and support of the unproductive population. Informal work at home seems to offer a cheap and convenient solution to some of the immediate needs of capital, state, and family in the 1980s.

That this should be so contradicts both popular and theoretical notions about the North American home and what ought to go on within it. Although the "pacified imagery of suburban life" in the United States has been ridiculed as commercial and conformist,[15] or as promoting a "lifestyle of relentless consumption" for women,[16] 92 percent of young Americans in the mid-1970s considered owning a private home a virtual necessity.[17] The home has been conceived of as the center of personal and emotional life, a retreat from the harsh, competitive world outside its walls.[18] Social critics diminished it to nothing more than the "means of refitting the worker to go back to work," which with defeating circularity was then reduced to nothing but a means for maintaining the home.[19] The very privacy of "tacky one- and two-family tract houses" could be blamed for promoting "a kind of trivialized, inward-looking social provincialism."[20]

Nonetheless, the stereotypical North American home has for some time been defined culturally and historically as a place reserved for rest, recreation, and family life. Home is where the heart is. Thus, to the extent that the home has been invested with particular meanings, its proposed transformation confronts its inhabitants with new dilemmas.

Who will work at home, and under what conditions will they work? If paid work in the home increases, what effects will this have on both the home life and work life of participants? And perhaps most important, how will the overlap between the space of production and the space of reproduction affect women? To say

that a man's home is his castle implies something quite different
from saying that a woman's place is in the home. When the division of labor in the work force is superimposed on the division
of household labor, the consequences will differ depending on the
gender of the worker.

The issue of a latter-day resurgence of homework also presents
a challenge to widely accepted theoretical notions about the separation of society into two distinct and mutually exclusive spheres—
the public realm of production and the private realm of reproduction. In order to understand how the current transformation of
the home as a place of rest and reproduction into a place of work
and production can be accomplished with such ease, we must first
reevaluate our theoretical assumptions about both. The existence
of informal work suggests that the lines between them are too
sharply drawn.

Theories of Production, Theories of Reproduction: Two Cases of Double Vision

In *The Division of Labor in Society,* Durkheim drew an essential
distinction between primitive and modern societies in terms of
their respective gender divisions of labor. He claimed that in the
former, "female functions are not very clearly distinguished from
the male. Rather, the two sexes lead almost the same existence."[21]
The latter he characterized by the degree to which

> . . . woman retired from warfare and public affairs and conse-
> crated her entire life to the family. Since then, her role has be-
> come even more specialized. Today, among cultivated people,
> the woman leads a completely different existence from that of
> the man.[22]

Of course, the notion of women's "retirement" from public life
was highly questionable even when Durkheim wrote this in 1893,
for working-class women were participating in the labor force in
addition to performing their roles as wives and mothers. But the
idea of distinct spheres of activity for men and women carried over
into later functionalist theories, and resulted in a dualistic model
of social organization.

Work life and home life were presented as quite separate in
function, with the family unit built on "a limited sexual-emotional
basis . . . removed from other major social spheres except for the

segmental, external ties of individual family members."[23] According to Parsons, the differentiation of labor, from the nineteenth century on, "distinguished the work-role complex from the family household," and one's occupational role was

... specifically contingent upon status in an employing organization structurally distinct from the household. Usually the employing organization has only one member in common with the household; it also has premises, disciplines, authority systems, and property distinct from those of the household.[24]

Parsons concluded that as a result, "The differentiation between employing organizations and households removes most economically productive activity from the home."[25]

It may indeed be true that from the time of the industrial revolution onward, increasing numbers of people were drawn into wage work and away from the mixed subsistence strategies common in the past. The geographical separation of industrial district and residential suburb did seem to be reflected in a greater social distance between associations at work and associations among family members and friends. But the conceptual separation of social life into well-defined public and private spheres became little more than a constraining cliché, underlying not only the work of functionalists like Parsons, but of Marxists and Marxist-feminists as well.

Historical trends associated with capitalist development were treated as if they were linear, irreversible, and by the twentieth century, virtually complete. The space in which home life and work life continued to overlap went unnoticed, and the world was divided into two mutually exclusive categories—the public sphere of production and the private sphere of reproduction. This resulted in the equally exclusive assignment of other analytic categories to one sphere or another, depending on the primary physical location in which they were then assumed to take place. For instance, according to Bernard:

Any division of labor implies that people doing different kinds of work will occupy different work sites. When the division is based on sex, men and women will necessarily have different work sites. ... When the factory took over much of the work formerly done in the house, the separation of work space became especially marked. Not only did the separation of the sexes become spatially extended, but it came to relate work and gender in a special way.[26]

Before the industrial revolution, the family was said to serve as a key institution of social life, production, and consumption. Now, claims Braverman, capitalism has left only consumption as a shared activity, and "the function of the family as a cooperative enterprise pursuing the joint production of a way of life is brought to an end."[27] With no common economic task, "work and family life are separate enterprises; families consume as a unit, but do not produce as a unit."[28]

The relegation of production to a site outside the home, with reproduction, consumption, and the family now confined within it, led to an additional set of assertions regarding gender in this spatially defined division of labor. Insofar as women remained primarily responsible for reproductive activities, and those activities were located far from production, within the private sphere of the consuming unit, women were cast in one of two roles: They were consumers, appearing to be "more of a burden than a contributor."[29] Or, as "home labor becomes uneconomic compared with wage labor by the cheapening of manufactured goods," women were driven "out of the home and into industry,"[30] or "forced" into a wage-labor sector.[31] So detached was one world assumed now to be from another that capitalism was described as an irresistible structural agency that "manipulates the household by shunting individuals, particularly women, back and forth between the two spheres."[32]

The dichotomy between public and private sphere also served as a line of demarcation between productive and unproductive labor, for activities carried on within the household were not considered to produce exchange value, whereas those conducted outside did. However, increasing numbers of women moved *into* the paid labor force and, by implication, *out* of the home. The functions of home life were diminished still further then, as reproductive activities were themselves transformed into commodities for sale in the service sector of the economy. Women who labored there as chambermaids, laundry workers, and cooks now became productive workers, until finally, "all work is carried on under the aegis of capital and is subject to its tribute of profit."[33]

The consequences of this conceptual separation of home and work into private and public aspects of social life, and the subsequent appropriation of the former by the latter led to a premature conclusion: It was wrongly assumed that all home life, all family and primary relations suitable for serving productive functions had been obliterated.

As the family members, more of them now at work away from the home, become less and less able to care for each other in time of need, and as the ties of neighborhood, community and friendship are reinterpreted on a narrower scale to exclude onerous responsibilities, the care of humans for each other becomes increasingly institutionalized. . . . In this way, the inhabitant of capitalist society is enmeshed in a web made up of commodity goods and services from which there is little possibility of escape except through partial or total abstention from social life as it now exists. This is reinforced from the other side by a development which is analogous to that which proceeds in the worker's work: the atrophy of competence. In the end, the population finds itself willy-nilly in the position of being able to do little or nothing itself as easily as it can be hired done in the marketplace by one of the multifarious new branches of social labor.[34]

The result was that social solidarity was broken down and the futility of family life increased. Finally, it was said of this family (as if it were not already unhappy enough) that "the cash nexus robs it of every vestige of affection and community."[35]

There is no doubt that the perspectives rooted in the public/private dichotomy did capture important changes that occurred historically in both work and family life at the aggregate level. But often they are guilty of sliding from useful social theory into various forms of romantic social criticism. When this happens, they no longer constitute a theoretical framework in which to anticipate and explain the current preoccupation with the electronic cottage, the new political debate over industrial homework, or activities of the sort presented in the preceding chapters. Szelenyi therefore points out that in continuing to apply these approaches, we are also "accepting the hegemonic view" of gender, home, and work.[36] In summary, these theories fail us in four ways.

In the first place, a certain amount of industrial production continues to take place in the contemporary home. This production cannot be understood as the vestigial remnant of old crafts that somehow escaped absorption into the factory system. The goods and services produced by the people in this study are peculiar to the newest sectors of the economy—electronics equipment, business services, computer programs, and software systems. They make their appearance in the home office and workshop as suddenly as they do in the high-tech industrial park. If the persistence of tradition does not explain their presence there, what does?

Second, it is through personal, social, and frequently familial relationships that these activities are channeled from the firm to the home. These working arrangements can endure for extended periods of time. Even when they do not, they provide sufficient impetus to set in place other associations maintaining the home as a place of productive work. Family structure may indeed change over time. Women may enter the labor force in ever greater numbers. Kinship networks may no longer provide the basis of a system of subsistence production, and Glatzer and Berger are right to point out that changes in household composition will have consequences for the role households play in the production process.[37] But it is wrong to conclude that family and friends do not continue to collaborate in maximizing income through whatever opportunities become available. It is in fact the very vestiges of affection and community that are constantly being recreated that form the basis for the cash nexus here!

Third, informal work literally unites under one roof the full range of activities included in the social division of labor. Certainly, production, consumption, and reproduction are conceptually distinct aspects of social life that engage women differently than they do men. But these differences do not rest on their geographical confinement to a public sphere made up of office buildings and industrial parks on one hand, and a private sphere tucked away in suburbs and apartment buildings, on the other. Informal work is a mechanism that can transform the American home from a place in which the worker is refitted to "go back to work," into a place where female workers simultaneously produce and reproduce. The reproductive division of labor remains unchanged in this setting, cheapening the costs of both production and reproduction.[38] Consequently, the implications of growth in home-based informal work will differ for men and for women, regardless of the fact that they may both work at home. Nevertheless, insofar as female homework implies a double "advantage" to society, social policies promoting homework will be framed in terms encouraging and legitimating female participation.

Finally, claims that the household's reproductive role itself has been so thoroughly commodified that "the development of market relations substitutes for individual relations,"[39] or that "the household is becoming a less effective storage unit for temporarily unused labor"[40] must be reevaluated. They overstate the degree to which the public and service sectors provide suitable alternatives to home-based child care, home-cooked meals, and the expense of daily commutes on crowded freeways. Among all employed women with children under five years of age, only 12 percent use institutional child care facilities. Seventy-eight percent of the child care on which this group relies takes place in someone's home, and in 56 percent of the cases, the care is provided by a member of the nuclear family or by another relative. In fact, as many mothers with preschool age children care for the child *while they are working* as the number who use institutional child care facilities—that is, 12 percent.[41] Families with working wives eat out no more often than families in which the wife is not employed outside the home.[42] And it is doubtful that families relying on the single wage of an unmarried woman can afford restaurant meals as a frequent substitute for dinner at home.

Moreover, assertions that under advanced capitalism, "state intervention separates the reproduction of labor power from the process of production by establishing minimal levels of welfare irrespective of work performance"[43] are indeed questionable. Eligibility for public assistance remains subject to rigorous means tests. Between the high costs of privately purchased substitutes, and the low income required for eligibility for public subsidy, the commodification of reproduction is also incomplete.[44] Coupled with the fact that women still bear primary responsibility for reproductive tasks, this implies that incentives to work at home will be greater for women than they will be for men.

The walls of the North American home turn out to be much more permeable than the theoretical barrier between public and private spheres allows. It is therefore necessary to look closely at how the actual interpenetration of home and work affects household members, depending on their age and gender. Until now, we have focused on the structure, function, origins, and dynamics of informal work in general. This work depends heavily on the conversion of what are traditionally considered personal consumption and savings items into capital goods. It is in part through this conversion that the costs of production are cheapened. Short-term commitments on the part of the firm and systems of payment by result subject workers to a cycle of feast or famine in which income fluctuations prevent long-term planning and security. Yet in spite of these material disadvantages, informal workers express a preference for their employment status because of the ways in which it appears to free them from direct managerial control.

Having established these as general characteristics of informal work, their specific interactions with gender, home, and the social ties that form the substratum of such work can now be examined. Do the shop and office floor factors motivating a preference for informal work differ for men and women? Does work performed in the home, or work done outside a clearly defined employer-employee relationship involve unique consequences, depending on gender? In what ways do employer perceptions of gender within the firm carry over into the informal employment relationship? Finally, how does the merger of production and reproduction into the same space affect each of these processes?

The Home Factory: Taking Care of Business and Baby

It is possible to find both men and women working informally at any of the occupations conducted within the firm. As Table 5–1 shows, respondents in this study include men doing assembly and clerical work as well as women engaged in professional-technical tasks. However, nearly two-thirds of the men are found in the professional-technical category, while only nine of the twenty-one women are included here. The remaining twelve women do assembly and clerical work.

The group of individuals discussed here is, of course, a small one, and was not located as the result of random sampling. It is therefore statistically questionable to generalize its quantitative characteristics to the general population of informal workers in the region. But it is important to recall that these respondents consistently report their regular employment experience as the starting point of their informal work. It is the occupational skill developed and recognized within the firm that is subsequently re-established under a contract relationship. Assuming that this is a common path to informal work outside this sample, this means that those in more desirable positions in the regular work force will encounter more desirable informal income opportunities. The greater prevalence of women in the clerical and assembly categories here may well be a reflection of their greater concentration in these poorly paid categories of the local labor market.[45] Thus, to the extent that this is so, the manner in which informal work originates may be instrumental in reproducing the gender division of labor found within the firm in the productive world outside its walls.

It is also interesting to note that in this group nearly three-quarters of the men are married, whereas only slightly more than half

Table 5–1. Gender, Occupation and Marital Status
of Respondents

	Professional/ Technical		Clerical		Production		
	Married	*Single*	*Married*	*Single*	*Married*	*Single*	TOTAL
Male	7	2	1	1	2	1	14
Female	6	3	3	4	3	2	21
TOTAL	13	5	4	5	5	3	35

of the women have a spouse. Moreover, the single women are concentrated in the clerical and manufacturing categories. With no
second income in the household, these women rely entirely on
their informal income for support, or combine it with full- or part-
time work. Of the six respondents in the group who "moonlight"—
that is, hold a regular job and work informally—four are women
and only two are men. One of the women works half-time as a
programmer for a local university; the other three are assemblers
who hold full-time jobs in addition to their "side-work" at home.
Furthermore, in the professional-technical category, five of the
nine women report working for only one client, whereas all of the
men in this group had at least two or more. The degree to which
these individuals can be considered "high-tech entrepreneurs"
varies considerably, with the women appearing more clearly in the
position of dependent wage workers of one firm.

But all these respondents, regardless of gender or occupation,
find their work at the kitchen table or out in the garage preferable
to their situations at the company desk or assembly line. This is not
surprising, for there is no reason to assume that women like being
told what to do any more than men do. In fact, they report they
do not. However, women express two additional incentives for informal work that men do not mention.

First, women seek to escape not mere authority but, in many
cases, specifically patriarchal authority, gender stereotyping, and
the occupational elitism through which it is expressed in the workplace. Second, the desire to ensure that children are being well
cared for makes the flexible rhythms of informal work appealing
to many women. This is especially true where work can be done
at home.

In what ways do women find themselves stereotyped on the job? The details of their complaints may vary according to their occupation. But their common resentment is located in a system in which male managers continue applying what we prefer to imagine are outdated assumptions about women and work.

Where the work is repetitive and tedious, as in the case of electronics assembly, company respondents would say that women are especially well-suited to the task because they "have patience." Women like to sew, they explain, and according to one manager, assembly work is very much like sewing. Such theories about women and work correspond to those encountered by Beneria and Roldan in their study of homework in Mexico City. Like employers in that region, managers in the United States explain their use of female homeworkers in terms of what those investigators term the "nimble fingers argument."[46]

In Malaysia, General Instruments Optoelectronics Division informs female employees through its company newsletter that women can endure worse pain than men. This is because they must endure the pain of childbirth, and therefore "women are also better than men at carrying on with their job while in pain."[47] And a world away, in Silicon Valley, the president of a scientific instrumentation firm described his preference for female assemblers with reference to character differences he assumes exist between the sexes:

The women seem to like the repetitive jobs in which manual dexterity is involved. They're not bothered by the repetitiveness of it. Whereas, more often, fellows seem to want to be creative and make one of something.

In Mexico's *maquiladoras*, Fernandez-Kelly describes how supervisors of assembly workers insist on having "only the prettiest workers under their command, thus developing a sort of factory 'harem.'"[48] And north of the border, a homeworker insists that some supervisors don't like to contract work out not only because quality might suffer, but because "they like to have a bunch of beautiful women on their production line. And if they put it out, they'll lose control over that, too!"

Even when gender is not made an explicit category through which female labor is interpreted and rewarded, the overlapping structures of managerial authority and occupational elitism result in unique frustrations for women. Female assemblers working at low rates of pay find themselves subject to supervision by male engineers paid high salaries to perform what seems like very little work. Some women, often in a mere attempt to alleviate boredom on the line by upgrading their skills, manage to acquire competence in the technical aspects of the job. This occasionally places them in a position to advise new and inexperienced engineers on the design or layout of a product. But the elite status enjoyed by those with formal technical training prevents these women from being recognized for their contributions, for after all, their knowledge is only based on practical experience. One such assembler explains her resentments:

If you ask me, the person that does the hardest damned job in there is the person who builds it. I mean, what does it take to sit there and test it out?! Not much! But they have that high-headedness wherever you go.

Managers justify their "high-headedness" and its correspondingly high material rewards by stressing that engineers and other white-collar professionals are valued for their creativity. Assemblers, on the other hand, "are not getting paid to create on the line—they're getting paid to do exactly what has already been set up and structured for them to do." Naturally, assemblers are "allowed to give suggestions"—where these suggestions result in cost savings to the company. But the rigid status distinctions between technical and manufacturing personnel, and hence, between men and women, are well understood by all in the firm. It is distressing to learn that even women who manage to move off the line into supervisory positions continue to enforce these divisions.[49] A woman who worked her way from home assembler to production manager of the firm that grew out of her informal work efforts, gives the following reason for her preference for female assemblers:

Men don't stay long on the line—they're a little bit too ambitious. But women don't have a lot of desire to move up. There's not too many girls that want to get ahead. They don't really want to progress—although they do fight each other when there's an opening for position of lead.

For many women, the only path out of this system is to hire themselves out through job shops for short stints at different firms, or to work out of their homes at a distance from this well-ordered hierarchy. As independents, often working for start-up companies with no labor force in place yet, they suddenly find their manual and technical expertise in demand. A few even manage to formalize these operations into full-fledged subassembly firms.

Needless to say, clerical workers encounter similar situations in which authority, status, and gender come together in ways they find unacceptable and intolerable. A home typist describes her previous employment, and the change in her self-awareness that today prevents her from working in someone else's office:

The boss would come around and throw his chewing gum wrappers on my desk—and then demand his coffee! When I was younger, I didn't notice that these things bothered me, because I didn't have such a sense of my rights. But as I got older, I started feeling condescended to a lot.

The discovery that women in low-status occupations continue to be subjugated to the control and condescension of high-status male managers is not terribly surprising. But what is just as dismaying are the reports from professional women with formal technical credentials. A technical writer working at her desk is mistaken for a secretary. More than one young female programmer admits to wearing glasses in order to appear older, serious and more experienced than her male colleagues will assume her to be. Some women say they feel they must "take on a male personality to survive."

This type of impression management is important, because according to one respondent, a woman with technical interests can easily be mistaken for nothing more than "a girl who wants to hang around with the guys." When women report their belief that in order to be considered qualified for a job they must be more competent than their male competitors, it is because their technical competence must be projected past the gender identity men see first. A woman who both has children and a Bachelor of Science degree in physics recalls with rage a job interview she once had. "The trouble with you working housewives," the firm representative complained, "is that when little Johnny gets the chicken pox—what happens?" When her second interview with the man had to be rescheduled due to *his* family's illness, he perceived the situation differently because:

He was using a double standard. He was looking at me as the housewife. And the only way I can overcome that is by working a lot harder than the rest of them.

It is important to acknowledge here that in the workplace some men are subject to the authority, often irrational and overbearing, of other men who are less technically competent, but at the same time more powerful than they are. The motivation to escape direct managerial control is common to all my respondents, irrespective of gender. But the bases of this control differ for men and women. Men resent the bureaucratic authority exercised over them as less powerful, lower-status members of a hierarchy. And yet, it is not an authority to which they are subject because they are men, but rather because they are workers. Women, on the other hand, must bow before (or resist) two forms of control: Managers tell them what to do because they are workers, and men tell them what to do because they are women.

That women seek to escape the gender discrimination that permeates the workplace through engaging in informal employment does not mean, of course, that gender does not remain an issue. Gender stereotypes are likely to maintain women in a subordinate status even when they work outside of the well-defined role of employee, particularly if they do so at home. In some ways, they can be more directly disadvantaged than before. But informal work does allow women to avoid direct, face-to-face confrontation with masculine managerial authority. A bossy client can be referred elsewhere. One's boss cannot be so easily dispatched. For this reason, many women report finding informal work less obviously oppressive than regular employment. They are similar in this respect to the female proprietors interviewed in Great Britain by Goffee and Scase: Many of them started their own businesses to escape frustrations connected to male-dominated control structures.[50]

But in addition to this pressure from within the workplace, women feel a pull from another direction that none of the men interviewed mention as a primary motivator for informal employment. Women with children find that flexibility in scheduling their own working hours and working intermittently on contracts punctuated by periods of nonwork enable them to earn income without having to entrust their children to someone else. For some, the cost of child care is the primary concern. Child care expenses are, after all, an opportunity cost of holding a full-time job outside the home and must be deducted from earnings women already find to be inadequate. Moreover, their working day is lengthened by the amount of time they must travel through congested rush hour traffic to and from the provider's home or facility.

But there is more to their concern than these material consider-ations. Most women find it virtually impossible to find child care that they consider a truly perfect substitute for their own supervi-sion and nurturance. Many actively desire to be with their pre-school age children, and even when a spouse's income is high enough to permit the purchase of full-time day care, these women do not want to sacrifice the experience of parenting their infants and toddlers. With a job comes the commitment to be available to one's employer, regardless of the needs of one's family, or of one's own need to be with them. At the same time, the choice of mother-hood often seems to involve an interruption in the pursuit of ca-reer ambitions. Working at home provides an opportunity to re-main professionally active, earn income, *and* raise children. One woman describes how telecommuting between her Silicon Valley home and her client in Europe resolves a number of dilemmas:

I worked for about five years, and had ambitions career-wise, right? So there I am, twenty-five, pregnant with my first child, and what do I do—give up? Have this big gap in the middle and then try to pick up the pieces later? I wasn't going to be happy just doing housework. It was the worst time in my life. But I really do value being around the children. So after six months, I started to freelance at home on a manual typewriter, and that got me to a certain level with my client.

Several women report that even though they enjoy being home with their children, they become bored and restless when confined to the parental role. Informal work provides the "something else" to life that their children do not.

However, when the work site is located in the home there are disadvantages as well. "Always," says a computer programmer, "the home interruptions! Kids running in and out, the 'mommy-I-want-a-drink-of-water' kind of thing!" Some women find that the only time they can actually concentrate on their work is when chil-dren are napping, or asleep for the night. Thus, the working day is prolonged into the night as these informal workers perform the double duties of production and reproduction that now constantly confront them.

Men who work at home do admit to its having both costs and benefits. They enjoy the convenience of being able to stop work and read the paper, or go jogging in the middle of the day. Men express relief at not having to make daily commutes to a job, at not having to wear a necktie. If there are any complaints at all, they tend to center on the fact that work located "in the office right next to the bedroom" can easily come to dominate life more completely than it did at the firm. These are typical evaluations made by men who work out of the home, regardless of whether they have children or not. The advantages lie chiefly in the greater flexibility with which leisure can be integrated with work. Disadvantages are described in terms of how work occasionally intrudes on social or leisure-time pursuits. The balance women must strike is a different one. It is not between work and leisure, but between two kinds of work, the productive and reproductive. Obviously, informal work cheapens the cost of both in several ways, whether it is performed by men or by women.

First, some of the worker's consumption fund is diverted from its exclusive use as a means of reproducing labor power, and is reemployed in additional production. The costs of the spare bedroom or garage now used as an office or factory are itemized under mortgage or rental payments. But in fact, they represent savings of floor space to firms that would otherwise have to seek larger quarters to accommodate production. The same is true of utilities, business calls from the home phone, and deliveries made in the family car. Furthermore, the costs of participating in the labor force are cheapened when workers can avoid the expense of having to "dress for success," of lunches out, and the obligatory drink after work. Money saved by virtue of some people not having jobs is money they need not claim as necessary to their survival, and the aggregate costs of social reproduction of the labor force itself are lowered by that amount.

However, the most substantial contribution informal work seems to offer the overall social economy is a promise based on a more literal and immediate reproductive activity: The simultaneous maintenance of the worker who is able to earn income at home *and* the reproduction of future labor, for which no child care costs need be claimed. The worker who stands ready to make this contribution is much more likely to be a woman than a man.

For this reason, every discussion of cottage industry, flexiplace, worksteading, and the electronic cottage celebrates the so-called advantages such arrangements provide for women.[51] Conservative Senator Orrin Hatch lobbies vigorously for modification of the industrial homework restrictions in the Fair Labor Standards Act claiming that "the women of this country are letting it be known that they are tired of being pushed around in this area."[52] Engineers point out that women with home responsibilities make up a large portion of the work force engaged in information-related activities, and that flexiplace is "an idea whose time has come."[53]

Perhaps the clearest picture of what that idea entails is provided in a widely cited evaluation of telecommuting by Nilles *et al.* In it, they fantasize about a future in which this example of the "ultimate organizational diffusion" becomes a reality: A home-based secretarial force is accessed via a service broker who contracts with business organizations. Fees are charged according to how rushed the job is. In their scenario, a fictional "Mr. Nehring" of "You Bet Your Life Insurance Company" calls the number provided by the broker, dictates a letter, and transfers it via modem to the "Secrepool." And in some anonymous home a woman puts her sick child, "Johnny," to bed, activates the necessary electronic equipment, and gets to work. When the letter is processed and transmitted, "Mr. Nehring" presses the MAIL key, and his nameless, faceless secretary returns to her son, who now "wail[s] for orange juice and affection."[54]

If the female respondents in this study are any indication, many women in this country are indeed "tired of being pushed around"—if not by little Johnny, then certainly by their predominantly male employers. But the current interest in these working arrangements in no way signals an end to their subordination, nor is it prompted by an agenda to equalize men and women in the labor force. It comes at a time when publicly subsidized child care is an overly progressive item for the conservative fiscal budgets of the 1980s. Allen points out in her study of British homeworkers that "dependent children are not the whole explanation of why women engage in homework." But culturally, she adds, "this explanation is very strong."[55] This cultural strength is exercised in an economic context where high-technology and information-processing firms seek to cheapen labor costs by subcontracting to every corner of the globe, be it a Third World country or the living room down the road.

Subcontracting does not always involve homework, of course, and contrary to many popular notions, homework is not always a substitute for purchased child care.[56] But where these factors can be made to work together, a significant effect is to cheapen the cost of reproducing labor. If Burawoy is right in proposing that the criterion underlying a society's determination of wages has been the minimum possible level required by a head of a household to maintain his or her family,[57] then informal work in the home lowers that level to its cheapest point by diminishing the costs of reproduction. At the same time, profits are enhanced by the lowered costs of home-based production. These aims are accomplished most efficiently by encouraging female participation in particular, for women still bear primary responsibility for reproductive work.

But how likely is it that home-based work will really resolve the dilemmas and maximize the opportunities posed by women's dual roles as workers and mothers? Early evidence suggests that although proponents may continue to employ the concept as an ideological justification for informalizing the employer/employee relationship, child care will remain an issue. Women with children often find it difficult to combine their productive and reproductive activities in one place, and this fact is not lost on employers. Thus, while some organizations are willing to subcontract work to homeworkers, or to institute telecommuting arrangements, they may also require assurance that workers will not be distracted by the needs of their children. Such assurance can be exacted from workers by obtaining their agreement to terms like those found in the draft telecommuter's agreement proposed by the Southern California Association of Governments:

> Telecommuting is not to be viewed as a substitute for child care. Telecommuters with pre-school age children are expected to have someone else care for the children during the agreed-upon work hours.[58]

There is another serious issue that arises when production penetrates the spaces and relations we have considered to be personal and private. Child labor is virtually unthinkable in the factory, where today the troublesome image of children toiling has been legislated from our memory. But when work is moved into the home, it is inevitable that children will participate in this new home activity. In the case of a software author whose children help package diskettes after school, the activity seems rather benign. But when mother works a full-time job by day, and assembles circuit boards out in the garage by night in order to make ends meet, the picture is not as innocuous. One woman explains how this worked in her family:

> *I trained my kids. They were, oh—five, seven, and nine years old. They would stuff the boards, and I would solder them, and we made $2.50 a board, or some outrageously low rate like that. Later, my two sons and a friend of theirs worked on it, so I had three boys working in one room. All I*

*was doing at that point was supervising—making sure they got
it done.*

*It was like having contract people working in my home. All
of it was in my name. I wouldn't pay them by the hour,
because kids have no tolerance for sitting long periods of time.
But if I paid them by the piece, they would work for hours,
because they'd figure, "If I do twenty-five of these at ten cents
each"—well, they would just go crazy. And any rejects, they
would not get paid for. Consequently, my children are just
fantastic workers now that they are grown.*

This activity continued for five years. It constitutes a clear violation of labor codes governing the employment of children, and perhaps tempts us to fault parents who put their children to work in
this way. But in this woman's home, as in others, this is perceived as nothing more remarkable than what one person calls a
"family event." The wintertime discomforts of a cold garage, the
rush to get work out at the end of the month—these are understood by participants as the normal hardships families must struggle collectively to overcome. People feel pride, not shame, when
they succeed in doing so against difficult odds. The more important question is, how widespread is the practice of child labor
today?

It is impossible to give accurate figures on a phenomenon that
is hidden, and that until recently seemed in little need of counting.
In 1977, the California Department of Industrial Relations issued
490 citations for child labor violations. The following year, 1,171
citations were made. By 1980, the figure had risen to 1,674. In
almost three-quarters of these cases, the violation consisted of the
minor worker simply not having a work permit, and although the
number of citations has shown a dramatic increase, it is difficult
to know how this is related to the actual incidence of illegal child
labor.[59]

However, where work takes place in the home, examples such
as the one given above are probably common. This study alone
yielded six separate instances in which children under twelve
years of age participated in the work on a regular basis. Four of
these involved direct manufacturing activity as opposed to simply
assisting with product packaging. In three cases, the product manufactured with the labor of children was actually successful
enough to enter regular production in a firm following a period
of three or more years of home production. Perhaps it is mere
coincidence, but two of these products manufactured by unrelated

respondents in the sample were ultimately acquired by the same major producer of office equipment.

If this company's officials were confronted with the role child labor played in bringing their product to market, they would probably respond with surprise and dismay. Despite recent attempts on the part of employer associations to lower the minimum wage for teenagers, I did not meet anyone who openly promoted the return of children to the factory. But then, this is not necessary, for the mechanisms through which children still come to participate in production are both subtle and effective.

They are mechanisms located first in the realities pointed out by an anonymous executive who relies on home assemblers to extend his regular work force. According to him, "The only way we in this valley can expand to be competitive with the Japanese and other countries is to either automate or cut corners. We're cutting a lot of corners."[60] It is subsequently, when work slips quietly into the home, into the familial and social relationships that organize informal workers into a viable alternative labor force, that child labor appears. But here it is constructed as a family, rather than a legal, event. The "natural" authority of parents over children is effectively transformed into the managerial authority of capital over labor.

Of course, proponents of home-based work see nothing sinister in the involvement of children, and some actually recommend seeking activities in which they can participate. For example, a contributor to *Parents' Monthly* points out that "some enterprises offer more inherent [sic] roles" in which to involve children, and suggests "posting a work schedule, just as most 'big companies' do . . ." This will "help everyone remember when they are to be at work, and just as importantly, when they are not to be." Though at times it is necessary to have "little hands busy with filing and envelope stuffing and stamping," occasions of intense concentration may require their absence.[61]

We see here the very commodification of personal relations that capital's critics claim to be a necessary feature of its development. Yet we see it in a different form from what theory leads us to believe must inevitably take place. Rather than the reproductive functions of the family being converted into commodities for purchase on the market (more meals out, greater reliance on institutional day care, etc.), the reproductive functions are left to family members, and these relationships themselves are converted into the commodity of labor power.

For instance, the president of a firm that began with the home labor of his wife and daughter now subcontracts a portion of to-day's operations to his daughter-in-law. What brought them to-gether initially, of course, was her affection for his son. But there are limits to the part primary social ties can play in doing business together. He is quick to admit that their close family relationships facilitate production, for, since "conversation is natural," his daughter-in-law is willing to produce an order before a written contract is even drawn up. On the other hand, he requires her to submit to closed bidding procedures in competition with other vendors. He says of this process:

She gets the opportunity to come in the same door the other vendors use. But it's nice that it's in the family. Sometimes there are clues I can give her about new designs coming out, or little advance warnings so that she can prepare quotations a little faster than other outside people our purchasing agent might identify.

But according to another family member, this procedure recently resulted in her accepting a bid that amounted to only 30 percent of the value the next lowest bidder placed on the work.

She submitted the bid, the minimum amount she would be willing to do it for. Then she waited. She worried. She didn't sleep for days! Now she's upset that they're getting this big take. Hell—she didn't know what this was worth!

The tendency for the interplay between normal business practices and primary social ties to end in resentment is not limited to parent-child relations. A number of women report friction between themselves and their husbands as the latter attempt to advise them about proper entrepreneurial conduct. The husband who, as one woman puts it, "sort of acts as a business manager" may push his wife to expand her work beyond its current level, pressure her to charge higher fees, or take a tougher approach with clients who seem to exploit her good-natured eagerness to please. Other men resent the fact that the working day in the home can spill over into the family evening, and insist that business be restricted to normal business hours. However, informal work does not always lend itself to a strict nine-to-five schedule, and so these conflicts will arise periodically. And when marital partners become business partners, the most loving of couples can experience tension over feeling "cooped up together."

Such reports call into question the utility of contemporary theories that nostalgically contrast the happy preindustrial pair with the beleaguered couple under capitalism. Theories like these imply that when the household was the primary unit of production and its members could see each other laboring collectively for the common good, harmony reigned between man and woman, parent and child. For example, Bernard claims that:

> When men and women work in an economy based in the home, there are frequent occasions for interaction. . . . When [they] are in close proximity, there is always the possibility of reassuring glances, the comfort of simple physical presence. But when the division of labor removes the man from the family dwelling for most of the day, intimate relationships become less feasible.[62]

Perhaps such companionship did exist in some more romantic era. This is a question for historical debate. But what is clear in the industrial-information society is that couples who work together must do so without the traditional norms and expectations that governed this arrangement when it was widely practiced. For this reason, one respondent explains the occasional tension between himself and his wife by saying, "I married my wife for better or for worse—but *not* for lunch!"

A Woman's Place

If the North American home remains hospitable to the production requirements of the corporate sector, it is still a dwelling in which long-standing images of marriage and family, parents and children, men and women, continue to reside. It is at once an arena in which personal relations can be commodified, and at the same time, preserved in their traditional appearances. Consequently, what others perceive when production is going on in the relational space designated as personal and private may conform more to appearances than reality. This is especially true with respect to gender, for when women are at home, they are seen in a special light.

Insofar as women remain responsible for reproductive work, the consequences of informal work differ for them. But even single women with no children to care for report that without the clearly defined work role associated with regular employment, others fail to perceive their activities as constituting "real work." Unlike the man whose home-based software endeavors qualify him in the eyes of his friends as a "high-tech entrepreneur," his female counterpart is more likely to be thought of as dabbling in business. An older woman complains:

Nobody (men in particular) is going to allow me to be the expert that I am. They think of me as the grey-haired librarian, the friendly family secretary. Friends will call up and ask me, "How is your little business going?" It really makes me mad!

Often, these calls are not mere expressions of encouragement from well-wishers. They are requests for a ride when the neighbor's car has broken down. They come from acquaintances seeking volunteers for some charitable activity. The telephone rings, and the caller is someone in need of a sympathetic ear. People who would not dream of calling to chat on an employer's time now have difficulty understanding that their friend is working, sometimes under greater pressure than before. Regardless of the number of women who enter the regular labor force, a woman at home tends to be perceived as a housewife. There, she appears to be available for the purpose of nurturing not only her children, but anyone else who needs her help as well. Her refusal to meet these needs on demand may leave friends feeling insulted or hurt, and many women are reluctant to test valued friendships by telling the caller they are too busy to talk. One describes her frustration with this constant dilemma:

I am the "mommy," being kind to everybody. People think that women are always free in case of crises. If I had any sense, I would barricade myself off in some area of my apartment and refuse to do anything outside of it.

Finally, a number of female respondents spontaneously raised a disturbing and unexpected issue in connection with working at home. They are not just vulnerable to friends, but to strangers as well. We have noted already that trusted friends and clients are the best sources of referrals for new business. Yet as time goes on, the social network on which the enterprise rests comes to include referrals that are not as well known to these workers. Occasionally, a stranger calls with an offer of work. This raises the stark question of how to deal face-to-face with that stranger away from the greater security some women associate with the collectively organized workplace in the firm. "What if someone came and decided to rape me?" wonders a home typist. Another raises the same question, but then answers philosophically by shrugging her shoulders and wryly pointing out that, "Of course, that can happen to you on your way to a job and back. And where would you rather be murdered—on the street, or in the comfort of your own home?!"

These are not simply speculative fears. One late night caller with a rush order for typing (and these are not uncommon) nearly succeeded in gaining the home typist's address before informing her of the condition he placed on the job: Would it be all right if he stayed "to watch her type?" Another woman describes the response to her first attempt at advertising her services. The business cards she posted around town resulted in three obscene phone calls. One came from a man claiming to have a "report" he wanted word processed. This fictitious report concerned human sexuality, and after several minutes of listening to the caller discuss its graphic contents, the woman finally realized "he was just out for fun and games," and hung up. She later discovered that several other women who worked out of their homes in her community had been harassed by the same individual.

Women who work at home employ a number of strategies to reduce their vulnerability to attacks from strangers. They keep a dog. They leave an item of men's clothing draped conspicuously on a chair. If it is late, they call the neighbor guy to come over and hang around until they can "get a feel for the client." They screen calls on the telephone, hoping that "the one psycho in a million will ask the wrong question" and unwittingly reveal himself as a threat. Hunches and intuition validated by experience are the next best thing to the safe referral provided by friends and acquaintances. But some women stop advertising their services and decide to rely solely on word-of-mouth networks for building their clientele.

This means that for women, unlike for men, the limits to expansion are set by fear. They are more clearly fixed by the limits of primary social ties, rather than the limits of the market. The situation that most completely minimizes the threat represented by the stranger in the home is one in which the informal worker deals exclusively with one or two well-known clients. This is also the situation that most closely approximates dependent wage work, and the prospects for developing the enterprise into a more formal, profitable entity are low.

Informal work at home, based on the notion that "business is where the hearth is,"[63] is today offered as a way for women to achieve independence from the confines of the job. Conservative legislators claim to be on the side of feminists in the support of home-based work for pay, and on the surface, this would seem to be the case. Even *Ms. Magazine* has featured an article on the topic. The piece is illustrated with a picture of a woman making phone calls as she lounges in bed. Surrounded by the pleasant morning clutter of her coffee cup and typewriter, a cat languishing there with her as she makes a living in peace, she tells readers:

> *I stayed in bed almost all day yesterday. Friday wasn't a "sick" day; it wasn't even a holiday. My boss just knew I needed a day off. Two years ago, the boss would have said "No." Not only that, she would have been shocked at the suggestion.*[64]

The point of the article, of course, is that now she is her own boss, free to decide things for herself. The image is a highly appealing one. Given estimates of the growth in home-based production and increases in female self-employment, it seems to be an image many women are tempted to realize. But women's decisions to break off regular employment do not automatically mean that their entrepreneurial inclinations will be richly rewarded. Fifty-eight percent of the women with home-based businesses in 1977 collected less than $5,000 in annual receipts.[65] And wherever women work, they continue to face the obstacles created by others' perceptions that what they are doing is "women's work."

Employers often classify, manage, and reward women according to gender-based stereotypes of their nature and needs. They also tend to view homework as uniquely suited to women, based on these same stereotypes. One employer who is proud that he provides women with work they can do at home acknowledges that "there's a lot of people out there who want to be their own independent self. Women's lib has a lot to do with that, and I'm all for women's lib." But just as often, the use of homeworkers is justified on the basis of the fact that "people who are tied down through the auspices of a child will always be able to make a living meeting the off-loading requirements of industry." Needless to say, the people so tied down are nearly always women. Thus, homework is established in a contradictory social space in which women can be perceived as at once tied down and liberated, depending on the needs of the observer.

In fact, the woman who works at home may still face sexual harassment, only now it can be of a more direct and threatening kind. She may be a freelance technical writer, but some will still mistake her for a home secretary. And if she is a home secretary, the local PTA will assume she is just a homemaker with a little business on the side, ever available for committee work.

When men work out of their homes, however, they are perceived as differently from women as when they worked in the firm. They are creative, risk-taking entrepreneurs, building a start-up company out of the nothingness of the garage. They need not wear eyeglasses unless their eyesight is poor, for there is no need to manipulate other's perceptions of their competence beyond providing the normal technical credentials and references.

This is not to say that women cannot succeed in establishing companies as a result of their home-based efforts. Balazs Analytical Laboratory, for example, was developed by a woman at home, and today provides semiconductor wafer testing for firms like IBM and General Electric. But its founder still complains of the initial difficulties she encountered with bankers and insurance brokers who "did not take a woman seriously enough to realize she is really starting a business."[66] Society at large still assumes women's work will be secondary to, or conducted in conjunction with, women's primary responsibility to home and family. At the same time, when work and home, production and reproduction are brought together, husbands become managers, children become workers, personal relations are commodified in unanticipated ways, and women are doubly exploited.

A Second Look at Theories of Production and Reproduction

The dualistic theories introduced at the beginning of this chapter are based on profound conceptual distinctions between work life and home life, production and reproduction, public and private spheres. To a certain extent, these distinctions describe important trends that took place in the organization of social life during a long historical period of capitalist development. The effects of such trends are likely to remain visible for some time to come. Many take these long-accepted conceptual distinctions for granted and assume they are the additive, linear, and irreversible outcome of the accumulation process. But they are not. For this reason, these theories fail to explain contemporary trends that now seem to pull us in opposite directions.

If the surburban home has become such a private and impregnable fortress of emotionally based goals, how is it that every Bay Area suburb is penetrated in some degree by high-tech capital? How can female proletarianization and the commodification of reproduction coexist so comfortably alongside these examples of home-based informal work and political attempts to "restore the family setting" through its promotion? No one should assume that the early changes wrought within the family and the lives of its members were ever completed, or that they cannot be undone at some later time. In fact, the same forces that account for those earlier transformations can be seen at work in the trends examined here. The failure to see this is the result of confusing the physical geography of factory and residence with the social geography of human relations out of which the two can be unified. It is a common mistake.

In *The Accumulation of Capital,* Luxemburg set out to unravel the problem of how the enlarged reproduction of capital can take place in a society consisting solely of workers and capitalists exchanging their corresponding portions of the social product. This problem had engaged many theorists before her, and she proposed that the way out was to realize that actually, "capitalism in its full maturity . . . depends in all respects on noncapitalist strata and social organizations existing side-by-side with it."[67] Of course, what she was referring to was the growing exploitation of peripheral countries by the core. The former provided not only raw materials, but inexpensive labor contained within "the social reservoirs outside the dominion of capital . . . [reservoirs] drawn into the wage proletariat only if the need arises."[68] This, she suggested, was the very key to the reproduction of capital itself.

Almost a century later, of course, it is difficult to name a country or region that exists outside the modern world system. Where might we locate the necessary noncapitalist "strata," the noncapitalist "social organization" of which Luxemburg spoke? Although she had in mind newly colonized countries as examples of the process to which she referred, she was careful to point out even then that we must "think in terms of social economy rather than of political geography."[69]

If few countries have escaped being touched by the trends highlighted in dualistic theories of production and reproduction, even fewer have abandoned completely the forms of family life in which the household is preserved as a distinct entity. In this household, nonwage workers continue carrying out the important tasks of

child care, or reproducing wage labor—of doing all the socially necessary work that turns out to be too unprofitable to shift into the
marketplace and too costly to fund out of public revenues, given
current national priorities. The "political geography" of these
households (suburban neighborhood as opposed to office high rise;
urban apartment as opposed to industrial park) offers no obstacle
to the exploitation of their "social economy." Benston is in part
correct to suggest that

> . . . each family, each household [is an] individual production
> unit, a preindustrial entity, in the same way that peasant farm-
> ers or cottage weavers constitute preindustrial production units.
> The main features are clear, with the reduplicative, kin-based,
> private nature of work being the most important.[70]

However, we must not think that because the household main-
tains its potential as a distinctive production unit, it is somehow
insulated from the larger context in which it is embedded. Mitchell
provides additional insight:

> The belief that the family provides an impregnable enclave of
> intimacy and security in an atomized and chaotic cosmos as-
> sumes the absurd—that the family can be isolated from the com-
> munity, and that its internal relationships will not reproduce in
> their own terms the external relationships which dominate the
> society.[71]

When the forms of social economy to which Luxemburg referred
(the natural and peasant economies, for example) are destroyed,
some form of the family or household still remains. Thus, in some
places where wages are low, rural women are induced to become
wage earners on electronics assembly lines. And in other places,
where wages and demands for increased productivity are relatively high, urban women are induced to return home and continue
their assembly work there. But the home provides no special shelter from the dynamics that characterize production outside its
walls. Someone must manage. Someone must work, and work
hard. If it is no longer necessary to drop the kids off at the baby-
sitter's house, still, someone must provide them with care.

Informal work is thus a mechanism by which the social economy
of the family is integrated into the larger system of production
and the market economy. The result is not at all a return to the
(supposedly) more bucolic relations of artisan production or domestic manufacture, with each family in possession of its own

means of production, able to produce its own subsistence. It is instead, as Mitchell says, a reproduction in its internal relationships of the external relations which dominate the society. These include the exercise of managerial authority by some people over others, discord between them over the hours and conditions of work, a gender division of both productive and reproductive labor, and violation of child and other labor laws. All this occurs now in the context of the home, the family, and personal relations that are often wrongly considered as existing "outside" the marketplace in a conceptually separate and "private" realm of their own.

In his work on informal employment, Mingione proposes a promising alternative to analyses of capitalist development based on assumptions of continuous linear trends that result in the neat separation of public and private spheres. He suggests that at any given time, reproductive units have available different combinations of resources they can utilize in order to subsist. The predominant combinations will vary culturally and historically, so that it is necesary to think in terms of "cycles of social reproduction." We can arrange the activities making up these cycles along a continuum which at the present time has regular wage and salary work at one pole, and direct, nonwage home production of use values at the other. Between the two extremes, which correspond to dichotomous analyses of the "public/private sphere" type, lie other strategies the reproductive unit might also adopt. These include barter, informal work, illegal employment, moonlighting, cottage industry, cultivation of vegetable gardens for self-consumption, and the like.

For a time, as industrialization proceeds, wage and salary work come to cover a more significant portion of the costs of social reproduction. Self-employment plays a less important role, and as women enter the wage labor force, home-based production of use-values may decline. But by the 1970s, Mingione notes, industrial nations began to experience high rates of unemployment, the relative loss of manufacturing jobs, and a growth in the low-wage, low-productivity service sector, conditions summarized as "deindustrialization." With these have come heightened pressures in the workplace to raise productivity through increased supervision and control of the work force.[72]

It is at this precise moment that declines in self-employment start to reverse themselves. Barter becomes a public issue and a personal pastime. The family and women's roles within it are "suddenly" featured at the heart of political debate and renewed religious fervor. Employers and unions struggle over proposals to institute subminimum wages for teenagers. The disabled are invited to labor at home. And as the nonproductive and reproductive members of society are fitted to new patterns of personal activity and capital accumulation, the dominant trends associated with previous patterns of development are blurred.

If industrialization provided the basis for a predominantly wage-based cycle of social reproduction, deindustrialization may well signal the emergence of a different cycle, one in which social reproduction is increasingly informalized in core countries. Here, where gender equality has been linked with women's progress toward equality in the regular labor market, this process may threaten the gains women might make. And even as preservation of the nuclear family is elevated to the status of a cherished national goal, the purpose and dynamics of that former "haven in a heartless world" are changed: The promotion of informal working relations within the home transforms the family itself into a potentially more heartless institution, suited to the changing needs for labor in the industrial-information society.

6

~

Concluding Thoughts on Informal Work

*W*e're the world's leading publisher of camera-
ready art for the graphic arts industry. And
we're looking for professional electronic illustrators
with top-notch portfolios. . . . We expect consistent,
high quality artwork delivered regularly as
assigned. . . . If the thought of on-going assignments,
comfortable deadlines, competitive rates, prompt
payment and a receptive attitude toward your
creative input sounds inviting to you, please submit
samples of your capabilities. . . . to Electronic
Review Committee.

—Full page advertisement, *Bay Area
Computer Currents*   (January 1988)

What is informal work? What role does it play in advanced economies, and how does it compare to regular employment, or to work
in peripheral settings? These are questions we are now in a better
position to answer. How prevalent is informal work? How likely
to increase in the future? One can speculate about issues like these
with greater certainty than before. But perhaps the most important point is that, based on what has already been noted about the
distinctive features of informal work, it is possible to investigate
these issues with finer discrimination than we could in the past.

Moreover, we can also reexamine with more clarity some of the
theoretical assumptions that caused informal work to appear as
such a novelty, when in fact, it is not.

What Is Informal Work?

Previous studies of informal work were organized around a sectoral division in regional or national economies. The informal sector was conceptualized as a residual category consisting of all income-producing activities that remained unenumerated or
unregulated by the state. It is true that productive activities of
the kind discussed here do not lend themselves well to the normal
census or regulatory processes. But a sectoral analysis is less a
conceptual aid to understanding informal work, and more an artifact that arises from the manner in which the processes of enumeration and regulation are themselves designed and conducted.

Census takers address the issues of employment and productivity by concentrating primarily on the firm and on those that appear on its payroll. Firms are not required to keep similar records
on work that is subcontracted to someone outside their walls.
Even for their own accounting purposes they find it sufficient to
list the product of that work under "purchases," or "material
costs," rather than as a labor item. The census of population does
enumerate the employment status of household members, of
course, and respondents can claim self-employment, if they are not
wage workers. But no attempt is made to determine the nature of
the work in the sense we have elaborated here, and so a determination of who is truly self-employed and who is more properly considered a "self-employee" of one or two firms cannot be made.

A sectoral division based on regulatory mechanisms is likewise
unsatisfactory. First, many informal working arrangements are
not, per se, illegal. They exist in the legally ambiguous space between the status of the payroll employee and the clearly self-
employed. Each of these categories is subject to a distinct set of
regulations, and informal work becomes problematic because, as
we have seen, it cannot be neatly assigned to one category or the
other. The primary principle underlying its ambiguity has to do
with the nature of the relationship between those who perform
the work and the final consumer of their labor power.

Informal work is based on the agreement, voluntary or involun-
tary, of some labor force participants to take upon themselves the

responsibility for ensuring that the returns on their labor equal the average social wage for such work. The agreement may be verbal, or it may involve a written contract. But it differs from self-employment in that informal workers, like employees, may not have access to their own means of production, to an open market for their services, nor full control over the labor process. It also differs from wage work in that its average value varies according to the terms of payment and completion, both of which are set before it is known what external contingencies might arise to affect the work and its outcome.

A firm's employees are guaranteed by law that they will be compensated the same amount for each hour they work. This compensation includes a fixed wage or salary, as well as the legally required employer contributions to social security, workers' compensation funds, or whatever the culturally and historically determined legal norms include. When the costs of materials increase, when managers' estimates of production time prove faulty, or when product markets fluctuate, employees continue to be compensated (for a time, at least) at the same rate, and adjustments must be made out of the income of the firm. Needless to say, when market fluctuations are exteme, employees may lose their jobs, or be forced to accept wage reductions. The fact that informal work is in many ways less secure in its outcome than wage work should not blind us to the fact that all workers in capitalist countries face income insecurity in some form, and that none find subsistence guaranteed.

However, the piece rate and the deadlines through which the firm attempts to maintain control over production performed away from direct supervision are peculiar to informal work. Payment is usually conceived as a strict unit price, in contrast to the employee's wage, which is determined according to the number of hours the employee is available to engage in production under the direction of the firm's managers.

At times, informal workers are successful in estimating and negotiating a rate that ensures average or above-average returns on their labor. But when work takes longer than anticipated, or when unexpected costs are incurred, the average rate of payment, as a function of time spent on the work, begins to fall. Periods of idleness, too short to effectively seek additional clients, but long enough to make a significant dent in income, may also ensue. Hence, informal workers face income fluctuations as a regular feature of their work in a way that employees do not.

The fact that the informal worker has agreed to work under these conditions is *not* registered on the company payroll, and unless census takers inappropriately assign the worker to the ranks of the self-employed, the activity remains unenumerated. It is equally true that informal workers' failure to appear on a payroll means that income fluctuations cannot be monitored by state regulatory agencies. Previous investigators of informal work were right to feature these issues in a discussion of its implications, for as they pointed out, many informal workers resemble employees more closely than they do the truly self-employed. It is therefore reasonable to argue that they are entitled to benefits they do not receive.

But to reiterate, enumeration and regulation of labor are cultural and historical phenomena that vary across time and place. Today, a more accurate count of those who work outside the normal employment relationship may result in more people being placed under the official self-employment rubric. But this does not mean that by tomorrow informal work will have diminished in importance, and that informal workers will play a smaller role in the production cycle.

Finally, informal work is distinct from wage work and self-employment in terms of the unique manner in which it places the household, its members, and its resources in service to corporate production. Friends and family provide labor in addition to that performed by the person with whom the firm contracts. Goods normally understood to belong to workers' consumption funds (i.e., home, automobile, utilities) are diverted from their reproductive use and transformed into means of production for the market. Family relations begin to incorporate aspects of commercial relations, as mothers supervise their children's labor, and spouses negotiate the hours and conditions of work in the home.

To summarize, informal work is an employment relationship within which are confounded the features distinguishing wage work from self-employment. Like the self-employed, informal workers are subject to income variation. But in regard to their ownership of the tools of their trade, access to profits, and control over the creative process and pace of their work, informal workers appear more similar to wage earners: dependent on the firm that provides them the work.

Like informal workers, the self-employed may also rely on personal and household resources. But because the latter enjoy an independence the former are denied, their personal and household resources do not enter the circuits of corporate production as directly and immediately. Confounding as it does these essential dimensions of two distinct employment relationships, informal work emerges as a third category, in which both the risks of self-employment and the dependence and subjugation of wage work are evident.

Is informal work increasing? The answer to this question demands a new way of assessing the degree of variation within the group of workers who labor away from the firm. To what extent do they enjoy independence, autonomy, access to profits—traits that characterize the self-employed? To what extent are they in fact dependent wage workers? On how many clients can these workers depend for a steady flow of work? How do they establish a relationship to their clients? How often are clients actually former employers who have persuaded (or been persuaded by) employees to perform work off the payroll, while maintaining the same social relations of production as when they were on the payroll? Who owns the equipment, sets the price, controls the pace? These are not questions the existing census apparatus can answer, for the census is currently based on the dichotomy between wage and salary workers, on one hand, and the self-employed, on the other.

However, they *are* issues that can be investigated through the use of large-scale survey techniques using the household and its members as the unit of analysis. These are essential in order to determine the prevalence of informal work through measurement of the variables proposed here. This will in turn provide a baseline against which to measure increases or decreases in the importance of informal work over time. Unfortunately, it is impossible to say with assurance how "big" the "informal economy" is, or how fast, if at all, it is growing, until such data are collected.

Certainly one can speculate. The increase in officially counted self-employment is suggestive, for its long-term decline has shown a steady numeric reversal over the last eighteen years. Furthermore, a close examination of the working relationships that make up its increase would show many workers falling into the informal work category as determined in this study through the use of non-random qualitative methods. The conditions that motivate the establishment of informal ties between firm and worker are also more obviously in effect than they were before. According to Edwards in his historical study, *Contested Terrain:*

[In the 1970s] there appeared for the first time a serious tension between the job guarantees of bureaucratic control and the firm's need to be able to adjust the size of its workforce. . . . The conflict between the need for flexibility and the need to provide job security has been put off in several ways. . . . Subcontracting to small producers provides [an] expendable labor force; the core firm can simply cancel contracts during a recession, thereby only indirectly firing workers.[1]

The tension to which Edwards refers—between bureaucratic control and the need to adjust the work force, between flexibility and job security—corresponds to the central motivations prompting a preference for informal work mentioned by the firms and individuals in this study. Recent cycles of recession and (partial) recovery create conditions favorable to subcontracting work previously maintained within the firm. One national survey of flexible staffing indicates that 13 percent of the firms surveyed increased their use of contract work since 1980, compared to 6 percent who contracted less.[2]

In addition, the question of potential increases in informal work is closely tied to the prospects for increases in electronic homework, since employees who leave the physical space of the firm are likely to leave their benefits behind as well. Because telecommuting seems to offer simple solutions to urban problems like traffic congestion and high office rents, we can now detect active attempts at different levels of the state apparatus to promote remote work. For instance, in 1987, Los Angeles Mayor Tom Bradley released an eight-point plan to relieve the city's acute transportation problems. The plan states that:

Working at home will become an important component of the Los Angeles economy in the next decade. To facilitate telecommuting and thereby reduce traffic flows, the City will make narrow changes to its zoning laws to permit telecommuting.[3]

The State of California is also implementing a pilot program that involves twenty state agencies and about 200 employees. This project will include both work-at-home and satellite-office forms of telecommuting.[4] It is likely that in cases like these, where employees are protected by a union, they will maintain their regular employment status and the benefits to which it entitles them. But where workers remain unrepresented by employee organizations, telecommuting will no doubt include the transformation of employees into informal workers. Thus, there are many good reasons to believe that informal work will indeed increase.

On the other hand, there may also be limits to the degree of insecurity workers are willing or able to tolerate. In some regions of Italy, where informal work makes up a substantial portion of total employment, recent indicators suggest that informal work has now leveled off, or perhaps even declined. As De Grazia points out:

> What is difficult to tell in this case is whether the reversal of the trend is related to the deepening economic crisis or to a change in workers' attitudes or outlook; some workers are beginning to refuse not only to be slaves to the large-scale factory but also to be subjected to the pressures of work in the black economy.[5]

An example of such refusal is provided by eight telecommuters working for Cal-Western Insurance Company. In January of 1986, they filed a suit challenging the company's practice of putting telecommuters on independent contractor status. Their grievance claimed that this amounted to company discrimination against them, when compared to office-based employees doing identical work.[6] In the words of one of these workers, "We didn't have freedom as independent contractors—they told us what to do and when to do it, or we would lose our jobs." The court ordered in this case that the company must settle with its contractors for an undisclosed amount.

Ultimately, then, the answer to the question of whether informal work will flourish at the end of the twentieth century depends on the outcome of a complex dialogue between capital, labor, and the state. But each of these players is pulled in contradictory directions. Capital is driven to cheapen the costs of production, and yet must maintain control over the labor process. Workers seek to escape the oppressive hand of managerial authority but, having nothing but their labor to sell, encounter limits to the amount of "psychic income" they can substitute for real wages. The state is confronted in some of its departments with the tasks of promoting capital accumulation and alleviating the effects of urban congestion, while in others it is charged with regulating capital's use of labor and collecting revenue to maintain its own operations.

Given the dependence of all these actors on the continued accumulation of capital, informal work will certainly not disappear, for it offers, if nothing else, an efficacious method of dealing with uncertainty and cyclical variation. To the extent that uncertainty, periodic recession, and international competition characterize the present period, it is reasonable to anticipate that informal work will be a common, if not intensively practiced, form of work, and that indeed, more people will work informally. However, one must remain leery of informal work scenarios so calamitous that they disregard the degree to which wage workers are themselves exploited by capital.

The Role of Informal Work in Regional Economies: Comparisons and Implications

If informal work of the kind discussed in this study increases, will that increase signal a "peripheralization" of the middle and working classes in core countries like the United States? Can we expect that a large proportion of the labor force in these core regions will come to depend on the tenuous subsistence strategies that characterize the lives of informal workers in Africa, Asia, and Latin America? A comparison of the role of informal work in different countries reveals many similarities. But these purely economic functions must be interpreted in light of profound contextual differences that condition the form, meaning, and feasibility of the spread of informal work on a massive scale. As Portes and Sassen-Koob caution:

> Any explanation of the resurgence of an informal economy in the advanced countries must start by recognizing that these activities, although structurally similar, have had different origins in different places and also vary in their modes of operation in different economic sectors. There is a common logic in the drive to increase flexibility of production and decrease labor costs, but the timings of the decision to informalize and the ways in which it has been implemented have varied widely.[7]

As in other regions, the existence of small-scale operations such as the ones described here makes it possible for local firms to enjoy a number of advantages not found when regular employees are hired. Informal workers reduce the costs of doing business insofar as (1) they allow the wage to be transformed into a piece rate; (2) they tend to convert items of consumption into capital goods, thus lowering overhead costs; and (3) they enable firms to adapt more rapidly to fluctuations in the economic cycle. In addition, there is evidence that informal workers can be a source of innovation and product development that local firms may be unwilling to undertake themselves.

At the more general level, informal work serves other functions as well. The costs of social reproduction of the labor force are lowered when productive and reproductive activities are carried on simultaneously by the worker. Many of the expenses associated with regular job holding can be foregone. This means that pressures to increase wages or to publicly subsidize reproduction are somewhat alleviated.

Furthermore, the status quo in the regular workplace can be legitimated in two ways. First, informal work provides a convenient arena into which some disaffected workers can be quietly and productively shunted. Their resentment toward direct supervision and bureaucratic control no longer need enter the discourse taking place on the shop and office floor. Managerial authority is challenged less often than it would be otherwise. Second, the ready availability of informal workers enables firms to maintain a regular work force at its lowest possible level, thereby avoiding the direct layoffs that would ensue if employees were hired. Instability within the firm is exported to the invisible workers beyond its walls. As a result, employers enjoy a more legitimate standing vis-à-vis their own employees.

It seems, then, that informal workers generally serve to lower the average wage, diminish pressures to publicly underwrite reproduction, and provide firms with greater market flexibility. It is true that studies in the Third World have focused primarily on the urban poor, whose motivation to work informally might look quite different from that mentioned by workers in this study. But even in this respect, important similarities exist between workers in the core and workers in peripheral regions. Birkbeck, for instance, points out that his "self-employed proletarians" picking garbage on the dumps of Cali, Colombia do not always prefer regular employment over their difficult plight, for like the workers in this study, some find their work agreeably flexible in its structure and discover they can earn more on piece rates than factory workers in the same region.[8] Payment by results is apparently a mechanism that promises individuals everywhere an opportunity to make more than the wage worker on the assembly line, and the entrepreneurial impulse is not limited to Silicon Valley.

Some observers of informal work in the Third World suggest that its increase in the core signals a process of "peripheralization" in the developed economies, for where a growing proportion of the work force labors without benefits, the overall standard of living comes to resemble conditions in the underdeveloped world. However, we must remember that the sociocultural context in which informal work is embedded differs greatly from core to periphery. This fact conditions the degree to which the practice of informal work strategies will be feasible and acceptable on a broad scale. We should therefore keep in mind the following considerations.

First, the average level of educational attainment among core workers is higher than that found in Third World countries. This means that although some U.S. workers may be willing to take their rewards in the form of psychic income, others may not. The belief that formal educational credentials entitle one to a certain level of consumption and security coexists alongside new ideologies of austerity, and many are likely to maintain higher expectations regarding the kind of stability they anticipate as a result of labor force participation. They may simply be reluctant to accept informal work as an alternative to a job.

On the other hand, educational attainment can also lead to disaffection among workers who find their need for occupational or professional gratification thwarted in the bureaucratic organization. It is this very disenchantment that can lead to the search for autonomy and creativity in the role of freelancer, consultant, or would-be entrepreneur. The acceptability of informal work as a primary source of income will in part be determined by the complex interplay between contradictory appetites for security *and* occupational satisfaction that arise out of workers' investment in educational credentials.

Second, the organization of family life in the core is not identical to that in the periphery. We have noted that the viability of informal income strategies rests in large part on participants' access to extended social and familial networks, resources, and support. Primary social ties in the United States do continue to provide this important base for informal workers. Nevertheless, the dispersal of the extended family places more restrictions on the efficacy of the networks on which participants here can rely. Direct subsistence production is also more difficult to carry on as an additional income subsidy, given patterns of land use zoning in urban areas. It is ironic, but workers in affluent countries may be poorer in some of the social resources that necessarily underpin the large-scale practice of informal income strategies.

A third consideration emerges when we look at differences in the composition of regional economies. Informal work is dependent on corporate production and is likely to reflect opportunities connected to the typical tasks generated by locally based firms. Studies in peripheral regions tend to focus on a wide range of extractive activities such as rag and garbage picking and other forms of material recycling that ultimately find their way back into the manufacturing sector. Given extremely high rates of unemployment and low wages, much attention is also given to small-scale retailing, repair, and construction which serve to subsidize working-class consumption.

Recent trends in the United States, however, underscore the relatively greater importance of the service sector, where information processing occupies a growing portion of the labor force. It is here that the most vigorous debates rage over the "electronic cottage" and the promotion or prohibition of informal working arrangements. Ambitious projections are made about the implications of what unions allege will become "electronic sweatshops," and it is already possible to find examples of abuse. However, major domestic growth in this phenomenon is certainly not a foregone conclusion, at least with respect to the activities considered here. Again, there are both incentives and constraints that will shape the future of informal work in the service sector.

Computer programming, word processing, and other forms of data entry can all be done at sites remote from the firm. Data entry in particular is an easily routinized occupation that primarily employs women, the primary targets of those encouraging a relaxation of homework restrictions. Futhermore, pressures to increase productivity are strong, and there is some evidence that conducting data processing on a piece-rate basis succeeds in achieving this end. These factors weigh in favor of an increase in informal work in the business service sector. On the other hand, the following two constraints on growth will have a mitigating effect.

The first is technological. Unless firms intend to provide large numbers of homeworkers with equipment compatible with their own computer systems (an investment that will diminish whatever savings are gained by contracting out the work), potential electronic cottagers will have to make the investment themselves. Though many may be willing to do so, there is as yet little standardization in the home computer and software markets. Some people do manage to make the match between their own systems and those of the client. But we must keep in mind the technological limits that currently constrain firms and individuals from extending electronic homework as far as they might wish.

The following scenario is the more likely one. Alongside a modest growth in home-based informal work, intermediary firms with access to capital will establish satellite offices close to residential areas. There they can find rents lower than in the financial centers and a ready supply of women willing to work on a casual basis. In addition, offshore office production will undoubtedly increase. It is clear that expanded telecommunications systems enable a housewife in South Carolina to labor in her home for a New York firm. But those same systems render workers in Barbados or Taiwan equally accessible, and these workers can be paid a cheaper rate, making domestic informal labor nearly as uncompetitive as domestic employees.[9] This trend, referred to by critics as "telescabbing," is in fact what appears to be happening.

In other words, there are undeniable incentives in the United States for employers to establish informal ties to workers outside the firm. The incentives are similar to those that drive informal work in other parts of the world. But differences in the social and economic contexts introduce constraints on potential clients and providers of informal labor in the United States. To suggest that informal work in the core will increase is not to predict, as some have, that informal work signals a "peripheralization" of life in core countries. Informal workers do not enjoy all the benefits to which regular employees are entitled—it is true. The relationship many have to their "clients" is so similar to that of the employee, it can only be viewed as an instance of labor abuse. But to imply that the objective consequences of informal work at the aggregate social level in the core amount to an emiseration on the order of that lived in Third World countries is to gravely overstate the case.

Theoretical Considerations

A belated awareness of informal work on the part of social scientists fortunately provides an opportunity to reexamine the theoretical assumptions that perhaps prevented them from including it in studies of economy and society at an earlier time. They are inclined to reify their notion of "the economy" and its effects on social life by conceptualizing it primarily in terms of those productive activities going on in the highly visible firm. Reliance on easily quantifiable categories that mesh nicely with census data has tended to support this narrow economistic outlook. Although the new labor process studies focus on the ways in which productive relations are in fact social, even these do not capture the degree to which such relations may be personal, intimate—even, at times, familial.

Given what is now known about how informal work is established and maintained in so many cases, social scientists are reminded to exercise greater caution in limiting analyses of "the economy" to variables such as wage rates, gross national product, shop floor phenomena, and the like. Corporate productive arrangements are themselves a matrix out of which primary social relations are formed. These may then constitute the ground out of which informal production emerges, only to flow back into the circuit of corporate activity.

The nineteenth-century transformation of social relations into market relations is a partial change, it seems. In the economic market, actors still seek personal advantage through their access to family and friends, home and hearth. This is not to say that the spread of capitalism did not transform social life in important ways, nor that the nature of people's reliance on each other was not changed by the intrusion of market forces. However, the emergence of informal workers reveals the need to look beyond the normal economic categories in order to understand the broader social framework out of which these very categories are structured, experienced, and modified.

The result of not doing so is that social scientists will continue with fruitless attempts to organize complex and dynamic realities within dualistic conceptual frameworks. Personal relations are assigned to a private sphere; market relations to the public arena. Production and reproduction are likewise split, and historical tendencies toward labor force proletarianization and commodification of reproduction come to be seen as linear, cumulative, and immutable. It becomes habitual to overlook the micro-processes that make up home life and the daily round of work. Then, when structural factors converge to reorganize and aggregate them in new ways, they make their appearance in our sociological awareness "suddenly," as troublesome anomalies with a poor fit in existing theory.

The existence of informal work is just such a discovery. The income and production strategies that informal work embodies have not been superceded in the modern world and can still be practiced when they are needed. The familiar and friendly social networks on which they rely, though perhaps modified, have not yet been eradicated by the bureaucratic mechanisms of the twentieth-century market. Is it necessary to reorganize our theories of economy and society around a new dualism made up of formal and informal sectors?

The answer is no. A sectoral division of production arrangements was helpful for a time, insofar as it highlighted a wider variety of working relationships than we had previously noted going on around us. It was an aid that refocused our attention on dynamic processes and social relations that could not be conveniently reduced to strictly economic phenomena. At yet, paradoxically, it opened a door on the same theoretical flaw that prevented our observing those processes and relations in the first place—the tendency to view complex realities in simple, dualistic term.

The concept of informal work is not useful as a rigid category of analysis. But by turning us away from old theoretical dichotomies it can extend our understanding of social organization and illuminate the multiplicity of arrangements that make up social life. It reminds us to consider the myriad ways in which people struggle to make a living, reproduce themselves and the social arrangements that sustain them, and at the same time, to transform those arrangements, however imperfectly they succeed.

~

Appendix A
Informal Work:
Historical Antecedents
and Contemporary
Households

I have tow kids and my husband has oly 2 days work and we can hardly live from it. You can think whats 2 day pay. my kids are to little to let home alone. Perhaps yous let me take work home from the factory so that I can earn a few dollars for my kid clothes and eats.

> —Letter from Mrs. Thomas D. Herb
> to the National Recovery
> Administration Homework
> Committee   (June 1934)[1]

At one time, a lot of husbands and wives worked here, and many of the wives worked in manufacturing. Then, they no longer worked here, but they would work at home—and that's basically how it evolved. Our ten cottage assemblers are either friends with someone who used to work here, or they're married to someone who works here now.

> —Personnel manager for producer of
> electronic business systems   (June
> 1983)

The distinction drawn today between formal and informal work did not exist in the working practices of the early nineteenth-century labor force. Wage work was on the increase, but as part of a mixed income strategy in which direct subsistence production, barter, cottage industry, and self-employment remained normal ways of making a living. In *The Wealth of Nations,* Adam Smith discusses the manner in which fluctuations in the fortunes of manufacturers are reflected in fluctuations in "extraordinary work" on the part of laborers:

A great part of the extraordinary work, besides, which is probably done in cheap years, never enters the public registers of manufacturers. The men servants leave their masters to become independent laborers. The women return to their families, and commonly spin in order to make clothes for themselves and their families. Even the independent workmen do not always work for public sale, but are employed by some of their neighbors in manufactures for family use. *The product of their labor, therefore, frequently makes no figure in those public registers of which the records are sometimes published with so much parade, and from which our merchants and manufacturers would often vainly pretend to announce the prosperity or declension of the greatest empires.*[2] [Emphasis added.]

In other words, a certain amount of economic activity went unenumerated, not because citizens sought to escape the tax collector, nor because peripheral economies were being restructured by late capitalism. It happened because in the early capitalist core, both wage work and other employment practices existed side by side as alternative strategies routinely adopted by the labor force. A longer historical glance reveals the real novelty is the emergence of wage work, with its gradually more protected nature, as the predominant working relationship on which the labor force came to depend. And even this did not occur as a straightforward linear process, but one in which wage work and other employment relations continued to be fit together in changing ways.

For example, E. P. Thompson points out that in Britain,

. . . the numbers employed in the outwork industries multiplied enormously between 1780 and 1830; and very often *steam and the factory were the multipliers.* It was the mills which spun the yarn and the foundries which made the nail-rod upon which the outworkers were employed. Ideology may wish to exalt one and decry the other, but facts must lead us to say that each was a complementary component of a single process. . . . Indeed, we may say that large-scale sweated outwork was as intrinsic to this revolution as was factory production and steam.[3]

It is essential to note, however, that although nonwage work survived the transition from a system of manufacture to a factory system of production, this does not mean that its character remained the same. The "independent laborer" to which Smith referred returned home to family, friends, and production for local needs. In the relations Thompson discusses, the activities of cottage workers depended on the factory output of wage workers and on the development of a stratum of subcontractors who coordinated the work of both for an external market. Now, the nonwage worker could be employed at equipment rented from the intermediary, and incur debts for materials which subsequently had to be worked off in kind. Outworker Carolus Charles, a filesmith, describes such entanglements with his employer in 1792:

> Yesterday week, I had not my due by near half, yesterday the same, he will pay only 10s. pound of the Clear neat Cash when all is deducted, and I can't take truck for the remainder at his price.[4]

Seven months later, he found himself heavily in debt and complained, "I wish I was well out of his clutches."[5] A hundred years later still, we may assume that Charles had found freedom from his debt bondage, if only in death. But in 1892, other outworkers continued to take his place in the production of files.[6]

At the same time that outworkers were maintained in poverty by their dependence on intermediaries for access to means of production and markets, some wage workers managed to transform their employer's means of production into profitable opportunities for themselves. In his 1867 work, *Some Habits and Customs of the Working Classes*, journeyman engineer Thomas Wright describes an interesting division of labor typical of the "inner life of workshops." Before the apprentice is even taught the names of the tools, he is trained to "keep nix." "Keeping nix," Wright tells us, "is a really important job," and consists in maintaining

> . . . a bright lookout for the approach of managers or foremen to give prompt and timely notice to men who may be skulking, or having a sly read or smoke, *or who are engaged on "corporation work"—that is, work of their own.*[7] [Emphasis added.]

This practice continues today in offices and factories in England, where it goes by the name "fiddling,"[8] and in the United States where machinists and other skilled workers put overtime and lunch hours to profitable uses.[9] It is therefore apparent that the growth of a proletarian class associated with the factory system entailed no obstacle—but provided new opportunites—for proletarian self-employment!

Nevertheless, the generalization of the employer-employee relation came to dominate society's vision of what constituted the realm of legitimate work. By the turn of the century, Helen Dendy contrasts "the industrial residuum" with the class of "true industrials" in a manner foreshadowing today's discussion of the informal sector in Third World cities. Although somewhat inclined toward what now seems an embarrassing kind of social theorizing—the members of the residuum had both a "low order of intellect" and an "impulsive recklessness"[10]—she distinguishes them from the true industrial class by their low skill level, the dependent nature of their activities on "respectable firms,"[11] and the manner in which some of their activities subsidized working- and middle-class consumption. In proposals similar to those of contemporary agencies, the reformers of Dendy's day suggested organization of the industrial residuum for the purpose of more effective self-help. But to Dendy, this would only delay the trend that seemed inevitable and indispensable to society—the trend toward a stable wage earning class of "true industrials" who supported themselves at jobs:

> After all is said and done, organization is only one amongst many means of self-help; it is impossible to organize dead matter from the outside, and the true Residuum is economically dead. It may be possible to galvanize it into a temporary appearance of life, to raise up a social monster that will be the terror of the community; but the best that can really be hoped for is that it should gradually wear itself away, or in the coming generation be absorbed into the industrial life on which it is at present a mere parasite.[12]

Yet wishful thinking was not sufficient to bring the entire labor force into the factory. At the turn of the twentieth century, handwork and domestic industry in Germany, for example, showed hardly "any sign of rapid extinction,"[13] and were subject to the forms of exploitation that Carolus Charles knew so well a century earlier. Artificial flower makers in France, Germany, and England now competed with one another to supply the changing needs of fashion a world away in Canada and Australia, and it was well known that the "darker side of flowermaking" was homework,[14] where factory regulation was circumvented.

"In these days of civilization and machinery, it seems strange that the human hand should still be employed in sifting and sorting the refuse of our houses," mused an observer of London's dust-women in 1900.[15] But as with the rag pickers and "vultures" of contemporary garbage dumps, this trade thrived as a source of profit for the chain of contractors and subcontractors who set the piece rate and divided up the spoils of the dump, and as a source of income for the women who did it. Again, the notion that such forms of employment endured alongside the "normal" wage relation and the "normal" gender division of labor in which female factory work had become common, arrived as a surprise:

> We are glad to forget the waste of the house as soon as it leaves our door, and if by chance the dust-cart in the street brings an undesired reminder, we turn quickly to escape the unsavory whiff or shower of dust. The idea that some women actually spend their lives carefully picking over and sorting such loads of nastiness is a thought too foreign to enter our heads, or too disgusting to be dwelt upon.[16]

Clearly, both capital's increased employment of wage labor—often organized into trade unions—and the increased intervention of the state in regulating that particular relationship differentiated the now predominant employment form—wage and salary work—from other employment relations such as subcontracting, cottage industry, or self-employment based on other forms of payment. These latter practices did not disappear for a time and then re-emerge in the 1970s as a new sector of the economy. Rather, they continued to play changing roles shaped both by the activities of the state and the firm in a single system of production.

In the United States, for example, the inside contracting system in which wage employees and subcontract workers on piece rates work within the same companies persisted on an occasional basis in numerous industries, until 1914.[17] Clawson points out that:

> . . . contracting was not a specialized tool, but a perfectly normal method of organizing production, which could work well for any type of work problem.[18]

The manufacturing sector phased it out in order to shift income from the contractor to the firm, which now hired foremen at lower rates of pay and lower social standing than had been acceptable to contractors.[19] Nevertheless, just such a system can be found today in white-collar occupations such as technical writing and word processing done for multinational banks. The problem is not one of determining what in the current economy "creates" an informal sector in the Third World or an underground economy in the core (see below). Rather, the task is to discover how the social relations that characterize informal work as distinct from other forms of employment are generated in different times and in different places, and how these relations fit together in a changing global economy.

Likewise, the contemporary state does not "create" informal work directly by virtue of its role in enumerating and regulating economic activity. Informal work arises out of the interaction between the complex array of possible employment relations through which people can make a living, and firms' requirements for labor that can be employed under a variety of arrangements. The role of the state thus becomes problematic, for the manner in which these relations are counted and regulated is an important determinant of state revenues, on one hand, and of the collective well-being of the work force, on the other. And this, we must recall, is a role shaped by political processes that differ by time and place.

In other words, this means contrasting the attitude of today's core states in fiscal crisis with, say, the 1930s state management of economic crisis. For instance, during the Great Depression in the United States, a "reciprocal economy" was actively subsidized among the unemployed, who were encouraged to produce and barter the necessities of life for themselves as an alternative to public relief. The state was willing at that time to adopt such a stance in opposition to merchants and Chambers of Commerce that claimed these activities hurt business.[20]

The reciprocal economy today takes on the sinister connotations of the underground economy, for this is a time when the state lays claim to a portion of barter and cash income in order to resolve the pressing fiscal crises. But simultaneously, there are vigorous attempts to reverse the New Deal regulations that banned a wide range of homework occupations in the 1930s. Homeworkers' alleged lack of precision in reporting their income and social security taxes may be more than offset by the manner in which they cheapen the cost of labor, and this represents a positive contribution to the most recent agenda for economic recovery.

In addition to identifying historical variations in the state's regulatory project, cultural differences must also be taken into account. The manner in which core states interpret and shape informal work will differ from the attitude of peripheral states. Unlike the United States or European countries, peripheral areas may be the object of international agency recommendations that the state foster informal work in order to relieve unemployment, or even take administrative action "where necessary . . . to limit the expansion of the formal sector."[21] What examples like these imply is that while the role of the state is important in structuring informal work, it is not this role that accounts for its existence. Rather, state activity is itself subject to historical and cultural variation with respect to informal work. This key point was overlooked by early commentators, who defined informal work in terms of a "sector" of unenumerated or unregulated economic activity practice primarily by the urban poor.

Early Perspectives on Informal Work

Scholars first noted informal work in the early years of the 1970s. In places as diverse as Third World countries and the United States,[22] in both capitalist and socialist economies,[23] and at levels of social organization as intimate as the home and as impersonal as the international system,[24] informal work seemed to make a sudden and ubiquitous appearance. Some suggested that its contributions to income and gross national product were substantial enough to constitute a distinct economy parallel to, or articulated with, the economy made up of regularly produced goods and services. Thus the literature of economists, anthropologists, and sociologists makes numerous references to the "underground" or "subterranean economy," as well as to the "informal sector."[25]

This sectoral division was defined in terms of the political prerogatives of the state to enumerate or regulate economic activities, and was believed to appear in response to conditions associated with the global economic crisis of the times. But insofar as this crisis was manifested differently in different parts of the world, research agendas inevitably reflected the sociopolitical priorities of the region in which the research was embedded.[26] This in turn made it difficult to synthesize empirical findings coherently, or to transfer them cross-culturally. Yet each contained elements that are helpful in understanding informal work.

Informal Work as the Unenumerated Residual

From 1973, when the first two articles discussing the informal sector were published, the most common standard by which it has been distinguished from its counterpart, the formal sector, is based on the political prerogative of the state to enumerate economic activities. A central feature of these perspectives is that aggregate measures of the gross national product, labor and capital productivity, and the unemployment rate have relied exclusively on statistical data collected by state agencies. Some activities remain unenumerated, introducing, in effect, an error term of unknown proportions into the aggregates on which social and economic policies are subsequently based.

The central public policy issue defined here is not so much the *absolute size* of the informal sector, but rather the degree of its stability relative to the formal sector—that is, *the size of the error term*. The key determinant of this error term is the rate at which informally produced goods and services are substituted for formally produced ones.[27] Because social and economic policies are assumed to be only as good as the information that underlies them, the effectiveness of public policy declines as this error term grows larger.

This tendency to define the informal sector as "economic activities that normally fall outside the purview of economic analysis"[28] or as enterprises that "escape enumeration"[29] resulted in a concept that defined by creating a residual category. For diverse reasons, many income-producing activities remain uncounted. Consequently, the residual said to make up the informal sector included activities as diverse as drug dealing, moonlighting, bartering, and self-employment.

The problem was that although all these activities produce income, they had little in common that would warrant placing them in the same category. Nevertheless, one was as likely to be used to illustrate what was meant by the informal sector as another, and the premature suggestions for policy were as diverse as the activities this residual definition was capable of containing. On one hand, some said, we may want to design "a culture of unemployment" where the moonlighters and barterers might cooperate with government agencies in exchange for the privilege of supporting themselves without adequate employment.[30] On the other hand, "since the power to tax is the power to destroy," we might want to legalize the drug trade and other vices, and retrain those currently employed in law enforcement as tax enforcement agents. In this way, the informal sector would "retreat as quickly as it has advanced,"[31] and this troublesome residual would disappear altogether!

Defining the informal sector as an artifact produced by imperfections in state data collection procedures did not tell us anything about the distinctive nature of the activities within it. Why are some economic activities more easily enumerated than others? Hart pointed out that enterprises run with some measure of bureaucracy, and in which work is more thoroughly rationalized, are more easily surveyed than those in which this is not the case. He also noted that these characteristics form the basis of the distinction between wage earning and self-employment, where the former involves recruiting labor on a "permanent and regular basis for fixed rewards," in contrast to the dynamics of the latter.[32]

It can certainly be argued that firms employing wage workers take on a higher visibility than the self-employed person operating on a smaller scale, and that in order to document wage payments and workers' performance, they indeed keep records that must be opened on the demand of government authorities. But at the same time, many of the self-employed maintain records, comply with their tax obligations, participate voluntarily in social security programs, and so are regularly enumerated as self-employed.[33] Equating self-employment with the informal sector can be a helpful strategy, not because self-employment remains unenumerated, but because of what Hart pointed out as features of self-employment that differ from wage earning: the latter is characterized by fixed rewards paid on a (more or less) permanent and regular basis. The former is not.

Instead, the working relationships of the self-employed depend more on their ability to promote and sell their services by the job or project, and are often relationships established by virtue of being the lowest bidder. This means that income derived from self-employment at the same kind of work may vary from project to project. In contrast, wage earners may work on different projects over the span of their employment with a firm although the hourly rate of pay remains the same.

The self-employed were featured at the heart of numerous discussions of the informal sector,[34] for in fact, they work within an employment relationship in which the dynamics and the outcomes differ radically from those peculiar to the employer-employee relationship. They have less security, fewer benefits, but greater independence from direct supervision and managerial control. By focusing on how employment relationships differed along these dimensions, these earlier contributions to the literature provided a key to understanding informal work. It is not the same as true self-employment, because informal workers are subject to a kind of control not imposed on the self-employed. And yet the manner in which both are remunerated causes income to fluctuate in a manner different from that of the wage worker.

Informal Work as the Unregulated Residual

The role of the state goes beyond just measuring the gross national product and collecting revenue commensurate with its size. The state is also involved in regulating the relations between capital and labor and the conditions under which work is performed. This important fact was noted by Portes and Walton when they defined the informal sector not simply as the residual of unenumerated activities, but as activities characterized by the "absence of routine state regulation.[35] Safa also stressed the unregulated nature of many small-scale, labor-intensive manufacturing and service industries as a key criterion in assigning them to the informal sector.[36] Others touched on a similar theme in referring to the informal sector as "unprotected."[37]

This distinction between enumeration and regulation amounted to a great deal more than substituting one term for another. Among the regulatory concerns of the state are the enforcement of the minimum wage and working hours, collection of social security benefits, and the establishment of health and safety codes governing the conditions under which labor can be employed. The initial fixation on the informal sector as unenumerated, and therefore as an untaxed part of the economy, defined an arena of social action in which participants' motives were tainted from the outset with somewhat criminal intentions. Since the state is also the enforcer of labor legislation, where regulations can be more easily circumvented there are potential costs as well as potential benefits to those income earners.

But there remained two problems with basing the distinction between the formal and informal sectors on the regulatory activities of the state. First, it defined by creating another residual category—this time, the category of everything left over when the state has exhausted its regulatory powers. This is a reference point that fluctuates historically, cross-culturally, and according to budgetary and political pressures to regulate or ignore in the first place. Equating the informal sector with the residual category of what escapes routine state regulation means that today the informal sector includes one thing, but tomorrow it may be made up of something else as regulations change.

Second, in some countries at least, the accretion of regulations that stem from the political process may result in an apparatus so complex that in the strictest sense, there remain few truly unregulated activities. In the United States, for example, that most personal of transactions, bartering, must be listed as taxable income. The fact that many scoff at Internal Revenue Service injunctions to "list the fair market value of all goods and services traded"[38] does not mean that this regulation will disappear, nor that means of enforcement are not being sought.

Other activities typically associated with the informal sector are likewise subject to some form of regulation. Payment for work in cash is not, per se, illegal, however more difficult it is to detect. In the United States, as elsewhere, subcontracting in the construction industry was often featured as an example of unregulated work, insofar as cash payment may be used to conceal wages below union scale, unpaid overtime, and other benefits. Nevertheless, special agents are routinely dispatched to firms in this industry by local industrial relations departments seeking to enforce regulations governing the proper methods of cash payment accounting.[39] Industrial homework in the knitted skiwear industry is not unregulated, however popular the example it provided of informal sector work. Rather, the workers who produce these garments are at the center of a debate involving questions as to which of several regulations should be invoked.[40]

The regulatory activities of the state, then, did not by themselves carve out a distinctive sector. Instead, they pointed to the existence of a range of working relationships—between employers and their employees, between the self-employed and their clients, *and* between informal workers and those for whom they ultimately labor. When the state does intervene, it is generally in order to determine which of the first two of these relationships is in effect, for each of them entails a distinct set of legal rights and obligations.

In an alternative model of employment relations, informal work confounds elements of wage work *and* self-employment. Therefore, it is not so much a question of its being *unregulated* as it is a matter of two contradictory sets of regulations applying to it simultaneously! How is this conundrum manifested in practice?

In the employer-employee relationship, the employer is responsible for ensuring that regardless of fluctuations in product demand, changes in the costs of production, or any of the other contingencies faced by private producers of goods and services, employees receive at least the average social wage for their work.[41] This includes not only a legally defined hourly rate of pay, but limits on the number of hours they can be required to work without additional compensation or periods of rest and contributions to whatever programs of social security have been historically and culturally established. In return, the employer has a legally recognized right to control the design, quality, and pace of the work employees perform.

These aspects of the working relationship differ in the case of self-employment. It is not the client who is legally responsible for ensuring that the self-employed person's labor yields the minimum social wage. Instead, the self-employed themselves are responsible for ensuring that as a result of contracting to perform the work, the price—either stipulated in advance or arrived at after the fact—is sufficient to equal the minimum social wage when costs are deducted and the remainder averaged over the hours it took to complete the work. They can achieve this by working at a faster pace or for longer hours than they might legally be required to do as employees, or they can allow their average wage to fall below the legal minimum. In neither case are they in violation of any law. On the other hand, they are recognized as free to control the conditions of their own labor, and have the means to do so—that is, they own their own equipment and find work in a relatively open market.

To the extent that informal workers do not participate in the *legal* relationship of employee and employer, they too find themselves responsible for ensuring that their work yields what is considered a just return. But in a number of ways, the *social* relationship between informal workers and their "clients" is more similar to the one characterizing wage work than it is to self-employment. Informal workers do not control the conditions of their own labor, and hence, remain subject to those for whom they work.

The collapse of the legal and social elements of two distinct employment relationships, wage work and self-employment, creates the third category—informal work. It is characterized by material outcomes that can include less than the minimum wage, failure to pay taxes and social benefit contributions, or more extensive working hours at a more intensive pace than it is possible to impose on wage workers. And yet, despite the fact that in the social relations of their work informal workers are not truly self-employed, the legal regulations governing employers' use of labor do not apply to them. (For an example of what can happen when regulations governing both wage work and self-employment are applied at the same time, see pages 42–43.) For all legal intents and purposes, they are as free as the self-employed to suffer the risks they confront.

Although a sectoral division of the labor force based on the regulatory activities of the state did not immediately result in a clarification of why homework, subcontracting, barter, and cash payment should be considered under a single rubric, this approach to informal work still proved helpful. It elucidated the variety of employment relationships that exist alongside wage work, and the differences in their dynamics and outcomes. By grouping them within a single category, it became possible to examine similarities in the social relationships into which participants' work brings them. Finally, it was far less pejorative in its connotations than such concepts as the "underground economy." Remember that the income on which the inhabitants of the so-called underground may pay no taxes is income earned by laboring for someone else—for firms and enterprises that contract for labor they need pay no benefits. The concept of informal work developed here emerges out of the problems posed by this earlier perspective.

Informal Work as an Outgrowth of Late Capitalism

The origins of the informal sector were discussed not only in terms of the political prerogatives of the state to intervene in the economy, but in terms of tendencies in the contemporary world economy to create categories of labor that are more highly exploited and less easily protected. Economic interpretations like these were based on characteristics of the informal workers chosen for study, such as their income, occupation, enterprise structure, and human capital assets. These were discussed with respect to the role such labor plays in the regional and world economy, where the informal sector was said to serve unique economic functions.

As we have seen, these economic interpretations provide only partial answers to questions regarding the origins and maintenance
of the informal sector.

However, insofar as they were based on innovative studies of
the actual practice of informal work, they vividly illustrated the
degree to which work conducted inside the familiar setting of office and factory could account for only a portion of the goods and
services produced in society. Looking beyond the familiar relations of employers and their workers, they showed arising from
the streets, from homes, from facilities as simple as a handcart,
productive activities that previously went unnoticed. Interest in
the informal sector located these activities in a broad economic
context where their contributions to a single system of production
and circulation was highlighted. What role did the informal sector
play in the development of urban and national economies? Given
variations in the position of these formations in the global setting,
how should the informal sector be viewed from one region to the
next? Answers to questions like these were based on often poign-
ant studies of workers assigned to the informal sector on the basis
of characteristics noted above.

Informal Work and Participants' Characteristics

Those who conceptualized the informal sector as an economically
dynamic scene within the larger productive system began to unravel the complex working relations contained within what had
appeared as self-employment. Detailed field research into the
working lives of scavengers who set out each morning to sort
through yesterday's refuse[42] and of families who operate commercial enterprises out of the cramped quarters of a front room[43] contributed rich support to the idea that such activities were closely
articulated with the structure of the local economy. The fact that
particular occupations could result in income which at times *ex-
ceeded* the prevailing minimum wage led some to suggest (with
an appropriate degree of caution) that "the 'reserve army of the
underemployed and unemployed' may not be the economic disas-
ter it is often thought to be."[44] That is, the informal sector might
represent a potential source of autonomous economic growth in
underdeveloped countries where investment in the formal sector
was insufficient or inappropriate to the task of increasing the level
of employment.

Other studies based on similar occupations suggested that the informal sector was but the latest and most insidious mechanism for exploiting labor. These argued that this sector had no capacity for generating economic growth on its own, since studies of "typical" informal sector occupations revealed them to be dependent on formal sector firms. Indeed, when large corporations in Columbia's paper industry were shown to rely on "self-employed" rag pickers to provide 60 percent of their waste paper, or 16 percent of national raw material requirements, and yet did not count any of them among their regular labor force, there was reason to believe this was true.[45]

Unique occupations such as street trading or rag picking do indeed spring up in the substantial niches created by large and more familiar firms. But the use of occupation as a basis for defining a separate sector was unsatisfactory for two reasons. First, it remained unclear which occupations belonged on the informal sector list and which did not. If their amenability to enumeration was the criterion, then the fact that many street traders cannot operate without purchasing permits from local authorities would seem to disqualify them from the consideration they received. The incomes and activities of physicians and private consultants are often difficult to scrutinize with precision. Did these occupations warrant inclusion? And if so, what did they have in common with their less affluent counterparts? Occupational studies of the informal sector tended more to be studies of occupations whose participants were poor. They suggested that informal work and poverty went hand in hand without disproving the possibility that informal work might include activities that were highly profitable, at least in the short run.

A second problem with identifying the informal sector in terms of particular occupations was that frequently the occupations selected had their counterparts in the formal sector. For example, Tokman's study of competition between formal and informal sector retailing examined a trade that belonged in each category.[46] The same was true for building construction, small appliance repair, or food preparation, activities other investigators highlighted as belonging in the informal sector.[47] This did not help answer the better questions: What circumstances accounted for the practice of a particular occupation within one working relationship (outwork, independent contracting, for example) versus another (i.e., employee)? How did we determine when to assign a particular activity to one sector and when to another? This was not always clear.

Size of enterprise was also suggested as a convenient measure of the "informality" of its activities. Thus, Souza and Tokman included

> . . . all those engaged in domestic service, casual laborers, the self-employed, and employers, white-collar, blue collar and family workers in enterprises with a total staff of not more than four persons.[48]

But because this tended to "overestimate the size of the informal sector" (and moreover, might cause us to mistake our dentist, his receptionist and two hygienists as an instance of what we are realy talking about) they subsequently revised their definition to include only those whose income was low. Again, the informal sector was equated with urban poverty, closing the door on understanding its role in the economy as anything more than a means of absorbing and exploiting the surplus labor force.

The occupational approach, like the new attention paid the self-employed, was valuable in that it provided examples of the complex relationships between apparently simple, loosely structured activities and a more elaborate system of production and circulation. The establishment of these relationships was discovered to occur through the workings of social networks existing between members of particular occupations and the firms that ultimately benefited from their labor. Between the exploited rag picker and the paper company were found waste paper buyers and warehouses equipped to channel the product of random individual effort into a socially useful form. Between the corporation investing in the construction of an office building and the independent contractor who came in with relatives and friends to prepare the building site there could be hosts of intermediaries—agents, contractors, subcontractors—that organized his "independence" into a collective effort.

Insofar as it is necessary, then, to view informal work as resulting from complex sets of social relations that can be contrasted in the ways suggested above, it is necessary to look beyond the examples provided by the poor, by those whose activities stand out because they are shocking in what they require of people trying to make a living. The findings of these studies pointed out that behind the tidy framework of the office and factory world, there were other structures that shaped people's work as well. The fact that they became visible when we looked at the poor did not mean we should look no further. Rather, it suggested we might look at all kinds of work in the manner in which we had begun looking at these.

Another approach in discussing the informal sector was to explain its appearance in terms of its participants' personal characteristics. Where people failed to find employment within the regular workplace, a setting with a stratified labor market, the informal sector was seen as "merely the bottom layer in the hierarchy of activities."[49] It was then assumed that if people worked informally, the reason must lie in some difference in their human capital assets. Poor as they were, they could not invest in a "real" enterprise, and had to rely on others to provide equipment, inventory, and credit, making them increasingly dependent in the bargain.[50] They were less educated than their formal sector counterparts, unskilled, or if not that, then in possession of skills acquired outside the school system.[51] They were older, they were younger.

Those *selected* from among the urban poor in Third World cities for study of 'the" informal sector—for this is where these studies are based—may indeed have been all those things. The implication that they were there because the informal sector was the choice for those who had no choice may have been true for some. But the social relations that define informal work need not be restricted to those whose human capital assets leave them unqualified for regular employment. (In fact, those who have education, skill, and high-paying white-collar occupations may participate as well.)

The inclusion of certain occupational groups such as builders and auto mechanics also called into question the idea that informal work was the exclusive preserve of marginal, unskilled workers, even where the Third World was concerned. Such activities were at the heart, not the margins, of an urban economy in which auto repair still requires a knowledge of the internal combustion engine and buildings are expected to remain standing! To make a living at garbage picking required some skill, and Birkbeck noted that there were "many people on the garbage dump who profess no desire to leave" when the alternative was a lower echelon job in a formal sector enterprise where the work could be long, arduous, and badly paid.[52]

If these studies offered limited promise for understanding informal work as something more general than an income strategy for hard times in poor countries, it was because similar studies had not been conducted in places where people seem to have it easier. The concept of the informal sector was tightly intertwined with theories of underdevelopment, with concerns about unemployment, and with the projected future direction of economic growth in the Third World. In the United States, by nobody's standards suffering from underdevelopment, the concept was adapted to suit discussions of sagging public revenues and growing deficits. Here, unemployment (a problem from which the United States has suffered) was thought to be better handled by measures designed to reduce inflation and stimulate investment that would presumably create jobs. The informal sector was more likely to go by the name "underground economy," and to provoke the image of a bloated source of free money for those whose irresponsibility fueled the inflationary fires. It is not surprising that these studies produced a wealth of information on particular aspects of the informal sector in the Third World, and a new category of deviance in the core.[53]

Nevertheless, each of these approaches to the "informal sector" provided valuable insights into the manner in which informal work constituted a unique employment relationship that had gone unnoticed. First, the spotlight cast on the self-employed as a part of what was conceptualized as a separate sector of the economy illuminated a wide variety of working arrangements within the self-employment rubric—homework, subcontracting, cash payment, and the like. In contrasting the reward structures of self-employment and wage work, these early studies laid the groundwork for a model of employment relations in which informal work is established as a unique category.

Second, the empirical studies generated by the informal sector concept shed considerable light on the subtle ties existing between casually organized, apparently independent activities, and highly visible enterprises thought to rely strictly on the wage labor of their employees. These connections remain as a central concern of this investigation of informal work in a core region of the global economy.

Finally, the very difficulty encountered in the attempt to assign workers to a "formal" or "informal sector," based on their occupation, income, or human capital assets, suggested that informal work represented a generalized phenomenon. If it did not fit neatly into a static sectoral model, perhaps it was necessary to identify the dynamic conditions and processes that led workers from a variety of occupational and socioeconomic statuses to labor informally, rather than as employees. This investigation has shown that the explanation is in part located in the demand of firms for a flexible labor supply. But at the same time, this demand cannot be satisfied unless social structures thought of as private and noneconomic in nature—the home, the family, the friendly sentiment—are also activated and transformed into productive inputs.

The Intimate Inputs of Informal Work Today

Even the briefest glance at the past reveals wage work emerging as a source of subsistence *in addition* to other activities workers routinely conducted. Furthermore, if the laborers to which Adam Smith referred could rely on nonwage work with family and neighbors during the "cheap years" when manufacturing employment declined, it was because these networks remained intact and viable throughout periods when wage work was plentiful. But worker's reliance on a wage gradually became more exclusive, and perhaps it is not surprising that the accepted definition of work came to be more exclusive as well—coterminous, in fact, with employment at a job physically removed from home and family, friends and neighbors.

Naturally, the fact that wage work came to represent an increasingly important source of subsistence did not mean that the household, the family, and the lively structure of friendship and neighborliness were obliterated from the social map. Yet, their contributions to survival came to be ignored by social theorists. Home life was now conceived as a private domain where women carried out the tasks of reproduction and consumption; work was assigned to a more public realm of society in which wage earners labored behind the walls of profit-making enterprises.

Recent perspectives on informal work and the household unit call these assumptions into question. If production and reproduction have indeed become so unalterably divided within the social practices of society, the dynamic flow of labor and resources observed between informal workers and firms becomes impossible to explain, for it is a flow that depends heavily on their continued interaction. Thus, a principal consideration the concept of informal work raises for general social theory is that within it, the components of the production/reproduction dichotomy must be reintegrated under the more useful rubric of what are called "household survival strategies" (see Chapter 5). Pahl defines such strategies in terms of "the different kinds of work undertaken by members of a household and the use of other sources of labor on which they can draw."[54] Household workers need not be co-resident, and Mingione distinguishes between resources internal to the unit (material goods and the disposable labor of its members) and external resources such as contributions from public subsidies, friends, community, and extended family solidarity.[55]

Theoretically, a household can satisfy the subsistence needs of its members through complete reliance on its own resources. Kin and neighbors can contribute their labor to gardening, raising animals, building their own housing, and bartering surpluses with others, for example. On the other hand, a household can provision itself completely through the purchase of goods and services out of the wage and salary earnings of its members. Food, clothing, shelter, child care—even in the extreme case, the services of servants—all can be bought as commodities on the market.

Few households today fall neatly into either category. More commonly survival strategies combine aspects of each. The typical strategy practiced, however, can vary historically, culturally, and at the level of the individual household over time. Mingione therefore refers to "cycles of social reproduction" in which preindustrial patterns characterized by a high degree of self-provisioning may change into the familiar patterns of industrial society, with their greater dependence on the wage labor of household members.[56] He is careful to point out as well, however, that this shift has been far from simple and linear.

Differences in the pace of urbanization and industrial development also interact with the household unit in different ways from region to region of the global economy at any given time. Wage labor in some settings does not contribute the same share to survival as it does in others. It may also be the case that inflation, unemployment, and other manifestations of economic crisis are reflected in an "informalizaton" of household survival strategies where previously wage earnings satisfied the greatest part of subsistence needs. This will mean that even in core countries like the United States, there can be an increase in households' reliance on "extra formal market contributions to survival."[57]

In addition to historical and cultural variations in survival strategies, the patterns of work in which households engage may fluctuate over the lifetime of individual units. Pahl demonstrates empirically for the Isle of Sheppey how the "domestic cycle" of marriage, the birth of children, and retirement structure the way in which the unit's members allocate their labor to wage work, domestic work, and informal work.[58]

Vinay's research in Italy reveals this same dynamic operating in what she calls the "family life cycle" of the households she studied. In the first stage of this cycle, the young family, still without children, is mainly involved in wage work. The second stage begins upon the first child's arrival. Housework increases at this time, but so does the need for income. Vinay discovers the wife/mother withdrawing from full-time wage work to involve herself in informal work out of the home. This enables her to carry out the domestic work that typically falls to the woman in the gender division of labor, *and* to contribute cash earnings to household income as well. The arrival of other children intensifies this dynamic, as older children join with her in domestic tasks and informal work. The husband/father may now add moonlighting at a second job to his main wage activity. Finally, upon the couple's retirement, they rely on contributions from the combined wage and informal work of their adult offspring.[59]

These more recent perspectives on informal work focus on the household, moving beyond dualistic models in which work and home, production and reproduction are separated into physically and socially distant categories. Previous studies of informal work show such models to be historically and culturally imprecise, for a distinctive feature of informal work is that its very practice is founded upon "intimate inputs." These inputs include family labor, the assistance of friends and acquaintances, and the diversion of consumption goods into income-producing activities, all of which are channeled into the production of goods and services for firms that sell them as commodities on a market. How, and under what conditions are these intricate connections established and maintained? And what effects do they have on household members?

A number of relationships between household and firm have been suggested in studies of peripheral and semi-peripheral regions. Informal work is shown there to cheapen the cost of labor force reproduction in three ways. Workers can provide child care for themselves, and it therefore need not be included in a wage. The expenses of participating in regular employment are reduced insofar as travel expenses, special clothing, and the like can be avoided. Finally, benefits such as health insurance or retirement funds are not typically collected by informal workers.

The costs of production are also lowered. The household's contributions of space, cheap labor, and utilities represent savings in the firm's production budget. And where firms find a supply of informal labor that can be as readily let go as it can be put to work, their regular work force of employees is kept to a minimum. This means they can adjust rapidly to changing needs for labor without going through hiring and layoff procedures. Administrative costs are reduced, and firms are enabled to maintain an image of stability during periods of fluctuation in the market.

Some argue that as firms restructure their operations to adapt themselves to the economic contractions of the last fifteen years, informal work has increased in all regions of the global economy.[60] However, they propose that the potential for informal work to expand dramatically is also conditioned by the strength of family ties, and by the degree to which households can substitute direct subsistence production for the purchase of goods with cash. Their implication is that in core regions like the United States, where urban and suburban residential patterns make this difficult, and where even the nuclear family is unstable, households will find it difficult to incorporate informal work into their survival strategies.

There are two reasons why this notion bears further exploration. First, it tends to limit the "intimate inputs" of informal work to those arising directly out of the biological family or the immediate residential community. These may indeed provide the primary bases of informal work in some regions. In fact, they can still play a role in the conduct of formal enterprise as well.[61]

But the "family" is a social, not a natural construction, and as Rapp *et al.* point out, its "boundaries are always decomposing and recomposing in continuous interaction with larger domains."[62] The more cogent question, they suggest, is under what economic and social circumstances are nuclear and nonnuclear kin relationships strong, and when are community, neighborhood, and peer ties more important? The latter play an important role in facilitating informal work where the extended or nuclear family is unavailable to the household.

Second, it may be true that in some urban areas land is too expensive or its uses too regulated to enable households to rely on direct subsistence production as a significant strategy in their overall survival. But for the very reason that reliance on cash income is great, households are confronted with the need to maximize cash resources through whatever means available. Possible strategies in these regions are for some household members to maintain regular wage or salary employment while others work informally, or for individual members to combine or to alternate wage and informal work.

~

Appendix B
Research Methods

How do we investigate an activity like informal work, which by definition is located at the intersection between the sociable world of family and friends, and the commercial world of the firm? If informal workers are not listed in the yellow pages of the telephone directory, how might we learn about their relationship to the enterprises that do appear there? First, we will find census data useful, for in order to understand the economy in which their labor is embedded, we must draw a statistical picture of its industrial composition. Thus, I frequently cite in this study figures collected by the United States Bureau of the Census, as well as by public and private research institutions.

Second, the San Francisco Bay Area in which this research was conducted is home to one of the major centers of high-technology industry—Silicon Valley in the South Bay. This means that the region serves as an everyday example in popular publications of what the spread of the "sunrise" sector might mean for the rest of us. The business pages of local newspapers offer daily coverage of the newest start-up companies, rumored acquisitions, or the latest bankruptcies, and Sunday supplements often feature articles on the "high-tech life style." Where appropriate, I draw on sources like these for background material, and for the occasional statistic not collected by official agencies but of sufficient practical interest to be compiled by local business associations.

But these secondary sources bring us no closer to the day-to-day experiences I wanted to tap in the lives of informal workers and the firms for which they ultimately labor. What I needed was primary data on informal work, and when I first began this research,

I despaired of ever completing it. There was clearly no listing from which to draw a random sample of individuals—that is, of workers who fall outside the category of the employee, who have close ties to one or a few firms, and whose work depends heavily on personal and household resources. But as I lamented this seemingly insurmountable difficulty with personal acquaintances of my own, I made a surprising discovery. Field contacts, and even data, were readily available!

For two years, I had been acquainted with someone involved in the home manufacture of electronic components for a producer of scientific instrumentation. He had never thought to mention this, since he didn't think it particularly noteworthy. But when I assured him of my interest, he agreed to an interview and provided introductions to others who became part of the group of individuals on which this study is based. Another acquaintance ran a word processing operation out of his spare bedroom, and he also consented to an interview. To the best of my knowledge, only two people in my immediate circle are directly involved in informal work. Yet, through them and their friends I was referred to eleven additional respondents, and these in turn led me to twenty-two more.

Throughout 1983, I conducted interviews until I had collected information from thirty-five informal workers, all but two of whom worked exclusively out of their homes. I introduced myself to them in a telephone call, and after indicating who had referred me, I explained my interest in learning about how people make a living in ways other than having a job as someone else's employee. Being a stranger to all but two of the people upon whom I called, I invited prospective respondents to contact the Sociology Department for confirmation that I was indeed affiliated with the University of California. None of them did so. Only two out of thirty-seven people refused to be interviewed; both said they were too busy at the time with their work. The rest seemed more than happy to interrupt their schedules and meet me with no more introduction than the name of a friend and my word that I was with a respected institution, the University of California.

Two interviews took place in coffee shops. Another was conducted during a high-speed auto journey over Silicon Valley expressways, while my respondent drove to pick up several blueprints from a client. The rest of the interviews took place in people's homes. There, I was hospitably offered refreshments and invaluable insights into the practical intricacies of informal work.

Previous research on informal work suggests that it is not confined to particular occupations or industries, and through the contacts my initial exploration yielded, I could have investigated a range of activities diverse enough to cover the entire occupational structure of the region—construction, gardening, and trades, for example. But I decided instead to limit my investigation to those two components of local industry that account for the region's reputation as a model of the modern, "information society" economy: electronics manufacture and business services (see Chapter 2 for a description of the importance of these two sectors to the "industrial-information economy").

In the manufacturing category, I interviewed eight "cottage assemblers," individuals who make electronic components in their homes. There are two subgroups of respondents in the business service category. Nine individuals provide clerical services, such as typing, typesetting, and word processing; eighteen are professional-technical workers who do computer programming, engineering, technical writing, and similar tasks. I found that even with this limit placed on my interest in informal work, I had entered a social network that my interviewing could not exhaust. Everyone knew someone else who, with the right introductions, would be happy to talk with me about their work. In order for this project ever to achieve written form, it was necessary for me to leave the field before tapping all possibilities for an interview.

The interview itself was structured to raise several issues through a variety of questions (see "Individual Interview Schedule," below). After obtaining information about standard demographic variables (age, marital status, household living and working arrangement, education, and experience), I explored the nature of informal work from the perspective of those who perform it. How, I asked, did they themselves interpret their employment status? What were their typical products or services? Who were their typical clients? How did they get started, and how do they persevere? Here, I looked for connections I anticipated might exist between firms and informal workers, and for possible distinctions between work that is put out of the firm and work that remains in-house. In other words, if informal work provides a way to cheapen the cost of labor, what factors prevent all work from being subcontracted?

Other issues covered in the interview included the structure of the enterprise. Who else did it involve? How were needs for capital and equipment met? How likely was it that such activities might expand into a regular enterprise with employees and a more impersonal public status? The answers to questions like these are important in determining how dependent on others informal workers might be, and whether they might not more properly be considered as budding entrepreneurs.

Naturally, an important concern surrounding informal work has to do with the comparability of the material rewards it generates to those associated with regular wage or salary employment in the same field. I addressed this question in two ways. Preferring not to use the personal interview as an occasion for insisting on exact household income figures, I inquired about the basis of remuneration. Was it by the hour, the piece, the project, or some other arrangement? I also determined the average number of hours worked and, where piece rates prevailed, the number of pieces that could be completed in a given time. In this way, we have a basis for estimating average income for each respondent.

Second, I asked respondents to complete and return a questionnaire in which I asked for exact household income, its sources, as well as other pertinent information (see "Follow-up Questionnaire," below). Each respondent was provided with a stamped, self-addressed envelope. Fifteen people returned the questionnaire, although several who did chose to avoid some part of the income question. On the other hand, some people volunteered additional information on sensitive issues such as compliance with tax and zoning regulations. All respondents revealed whether they are covered by other benefits such as health insurance or retirement plans. This information, coupled with their subjective comparisons of informal work to the regular workplace, allows us to contrast the costs and rewards associated with their current situation versus regular employment at a similar occupation.

Not long after I began these interviews, it became clear that these individuals who do not appear on the payroll of any local firm depend for their living on the regular enterprise that surrounds them. It seemed essential to explore from their clients' point of view the factors that structure the demand for their services. Therefore, in addition to my thirty-five interviews with informal workers, I conducted interviews within twelve locally-based firms. Five of these are firms named as actual clients of individuals that I interviewed; the remainder are similar to the kinds of enterprise mentioned as "typical clients."

Again, I described my interest in working arrangements outside the normal employment relationship and requested an interview with someone involved in the decision either to bring employees into the workplace or to subcontract the work. In the case of large firms, this might be the personnel manager or a purchasing agent. I was more likely with small companies to be referred to the president or vice-president.

Only one firm of the original thirteen I contacted denied me entry. This company had recently undergone investigation by the California Department of Industrial Relations for violation of the codes regulating the use of industrial homeworkers, and they were vehement in their refusal to discuss their subcontracting practices with me. The others agreed to my visit.

But in contrast to the refreshing hospitality of the individual respondents—according to writers on the "underground economy," people with something to hide—these prospective interviewees were considerably more circumspect in setting up an appointment. Most of them requested that I confirm my identity in an advance letter on university stationery. One accepted my invitation that he inquire about my credentials with someone in the Sociology Department. Refusing my offer to provide him the telephone number, he acquired it himself, and on reaching the department secretary, elicited from her my physical description!

Later, respondents within some of the firms explained their caution in terms of concern that I might be engaged in industrial espionage, or in "headhunting," a lucrative trade in which personnel brokers attempt to seduce employees from one firm into going to work for a competitor. But once convinced that my interests were harmlessly academic, these respondents also granted me an interview. They spoke frankly, sometimes cynically, about the considerations and arrangements that led them to use informal workers rather than regular employees. As we will see, these firms constitute the essential term in the equation describing the function of informal work in the economy.

Interviews lasted from an hour to an hour and a half. Three individual respondents preferred not to be tape recorded, and with them, I took handwritten notes. The remaining individuals, and all representatives of the companies I visited, agreed to my recording our conversations.

I personally transcribed all the taped interviews verbatim, and followed the method suggested in *Analyzing Social Settings* for disaggregating the mass of text this produced.[1] This means that a chronologically intact set of transcripts was maintained for the purpose of reviewing field data from beginning to end. Another set was broken down into the conceptual categories embodied in the inteview schedule (typical clients, structure of informal enterprise, system of remuneration, etc.). Responses to these issues were compiled separately according to gender and occupational category (professional-technical, clerical, and manufacturing). The resulting body of materials was then distilled a second time into more finely grained subcategories intended to allow increasingly specific topics of analysis to arise out of the data themselves, and to capture variations in response to the interview themes.

This is clearly not a random sample of informal workers, nor of local firms that use such labor. Nevertheless, I am persuaded that the "snowball" technique has generated data through which we can reliably begin to understand the key dimensions of informal work with respect to the kinds of activities discussed here. Respondents in each category spontaneously raise similar issues, and allude to similar dynamics that consistently set their work apart from self-employment on one hand, and from wage work on the other. Moreover, the information derived from individual respondents is subsequently corroborated by representatives inside the firms. The findings of this study should therefore serve as useful guides in elaborating future investigation through large-scale survey research based on random samples of households and firms.

Individual Interview Schedule

Age	Years of Experience
Occupation	Employment Status
Education	

How did you get started in this kind of work? What would I need to do if I wanted to get involved?

Describe a typical working day.

Describe some of your typical clients. Are they firms? Individuals? What do they do?

How do you go about getting work?

What special kinds of equipment do you need? How do you acquire and finance it? If you wanted to expand, how would you go about it?

Are there any particular new technologies that will have an impact, positive or negative, on your ability to make a living in this way?

How do you go about setting a price, or a value, on your work for the client? Is it by the hour, the piece, the project, or what?

How does this compare to working in a company in terms of hours, benefits, sociability, professional training, and the like?

Under what circumstances would you decide to look for a job?

How much would someone with your training and experience make in a company? How does your income compare to that? How much of your income is derived from your working on your own like this?

Do you belong to any professional societies or clubs?

Does working at home have any particular effects, positive or negative, on your home and social life?

Are there any particular government regulations, federal, state, or local, that have any positive or negative effects on your ability to work as you do?

Some people say that in the future, more people will be working out of their homes, or will have their own businesses, rather than jobs in which they work as someone else's employee. What do you think about that?

Are there any points we haven't covered that you think are important in understanding your work?

Can you suggest someone else with whom I might talk?

Follow-up Questionnaire

Please answer the following questions without signing your name, and return in the stamped, self-addressed envelope. Thank you for your help with this research.

Demographic Information

1. Age

2. Sex (check one): ___/___
   male/female

3. Marital status: married ____
   single ____

4. Number of children at home: ____

5. Highest grade completed:
   (Check one) ____ high school
   ____ some college
   ____ B.A. degree
   ____ B.S. degree
   ____ master's degree
   ____ Ph.D. degree

Occupational Information

6. Check which of the following occupations best describes what you do to make a living.
   ____ typist
   ____ word processor
   ____ assembler
   ____ engineer
   ____ other (Describe:) _____

   ____ computer programmer
   ____ technical writer
   ____ software author
   ____ computer consultant

7. In what city do you work? _____

8. Are you required to: _____ register as a fictitious business?
   _____ obtain a city business license?
   _____ get a home-based business permit?
   _____ get an independent contractor's license?

9. How long have you worked in your current situation?   _____ Years
   _____ Months

10. How many partners, if any, do you have   _____
    How many full-time employees, if any, do you have?   _____
    How many part-time employees, if any, do you have?   _____
    How many helpers and assistants, if any, do you have?   _____

Relations With Clients

11. When you agree to work for a client, do you obtain from them a written contract, or do you work by verbal agreement?
    _____ verbal agreement
    _____ written agreement

12. What things do you negotiate in advance of performing the work?
    _____
    _____

13. How do you charge for your work? (Check as many as apply, and list your rates.)

	RATE			RATE
_____ by the hour	_____		_____ royalties on sales	_____
_____ by the page	_____		_____ advances against	
_____ by the piece	_____		royalties	_____
_____ by the project	_____		_____ other (Explain)	_____
			_____	

14. Has anyone shown an interest in investing in, or buying, your business?   _____ yes
    _____ no

    IF YES, please describe the offer briefly, and mention your response to it: _____
    _____
    _____
    _____

Material Returns and Benefits

15. What was your total gross income from your business in 1982—that is, how much did you earn *after* paying expenses, but *before* paying taxes?
    $ _____

16. What was your total net income from your business in 1982—that is, how much did you earn after paying both expenses and taxes?
    $ _____

17. Do you have either a spouse or a living partner who has regular paid employment at a job?   _____ yes
                                                                        _____ no

    > IF YES, how much did their net wages and salaries contribute to the total household income in 1982?
    > $_____

18. Do you have either a spouse or a living partner who works independently, as you do?   _____ yes
                                                                        _____ no

    > IF YES, how much did his or her fees, royalties, or earnings contribute to the total household income in 1982?
    > $ _____

19. Did you have any regular paid employment in addition to your independent work?   _____ yes
                                                                        _____ no

    > IF YES, how much additional income did this employment contribute to the total household income in 1982?
    > $ _____

20. Do you carry health insurance?   _____ yes
                                            _____ no

    > IF YES, are you covered under a:
    > _____ policy provided by a spouse's job?
    > _____ privately purchased policy?
    > _____ other (Explain) _____

21. Do you make regular contributions to: _____ social security?
                                                  _____ retirement plan?

Operating Equipment

22. Please check the pieces of equipment you currently use in your work, and list the value of each:

	VALUE		VALUE
_____ typewriter	$_____	_____ software	$_____
_____ word processor	_____	_____ modem	_____
_____ printer	_____	_____ other	_____
_____ computer(s)	_____		

23. From what sources have you obtained your equipment, and how much does each source account for, of the total investment? (Check all that apply)

	AMOUNT
____ bank loan	$_____
____ loan from family	_____
____ loan from friend	_____
____ personal savings	_____
____ venture capital fund	_____
____ loan of actual equipment	_____ (value)
____ equipment leasing	_____ (lease payment)

~

Notes

CHAPTER 1. **What Is Informal Work?**

1. John Naisbitt, "Executive briefing: Naisbitt sites [sic] trends to year 2000," *Government Technology* 1(Fall 1987):26.
2. Dan Shafer, *Silicon Visions: The Future of Microcomputer Technology* (New York: Prentice Hall Press, 1986), p. 76.
3. *Ibid,* p. 86.
4. Eugene H. Becker, "Self-employed workers: An update to 1983," *Monthly Labor Review* 107(1984):14.
5. R. E. Pahl, "Does jobless mean workless? Unemployment and informal work" (unpublished manuscript, June 1987), pp. 14–15.
6. "11% still jobless in California," *San Francisco Chronicle,* (5 February 1983):12. A closer look at the Bay Area does show intraregional variation in unemployment, as well as other measures of socioeconomic well-being. In 1980, the national unemployment rate was 7.1 percent (U.S. Bureau of the Census *Census of Manufactures* [Washington, D.C.: Government Printing Office, 1982a] p. 375), a figure higher than the 5.4 percent rate for the San Francisco–Oakland SMSA. But when we break these figures down, we find that central-city residents of San Francisco were unemployed at a rate of 6.5 percent; in Oakland, 7.3 percent—*higher* than the national average. The pattern holds as well for the San Jose SMSA (U.S. Bureau of the Census *Census of Service Industries*, Geographic Area Statistics, U.S. Summary [Washington, D.C.: Government Printing Office, 1982b], p. 428). Per capita income is also subject to variation within the region: In the San Francisco–Oakland SMSA, per capita income averaged $9,650 in 1979. But residents of the city of Oakland averaged $1,916 less than this figure. In the San Jose SMSA, non-central

city residents averaged $2,226 more in per capita income than those living within the central city (*ibid,* 429).

7. These figures are derived from Table 173, pp. 1684–1685 of the U.S. Census for 1970, and Table 120, pp. 244–246 of the U.S. Census for 1980 (U.S. Bureau of the Census, 1970 *Census of Population,* Characteristics of the Population, Vol. 1, Part 6 [Washington, D.C.: Government Printing Office, 1970 and 1980]). It is interesting to note in addition that between 1979 and 1980 alone, U.S. self-employment grew by 3 percent, while total employment increased by only 0.3 percent (Barry Molefsky, "America's underground economy," in *The Underground Economy in the United States and Abroad,* ed. Vito Tanzi [Lexington: Lexington Books, 1982], p. 59). And between 1983 and 1984, the Labor Department indicates that 410,000 additional people were counted in the former category. ("Labor letter," *Wall Street Journal,* 12 February 1985:1). Regional census figures are not yet available. But if national statistics are any indication, we might expect the Bay Area trend to have continued.

8. Alejandro Portes and Saskia Sassen-Koob, "Making it underground: Comparative material on the informal sector in Western market economies," *American Journal of Sociology* 93(1987):35.

9. Maria Patricia Fernandez-Kelly and Anna Garcia, "The making of an underground economy: Hispanic women, home work and the advanced capitalist state," *Urban Anthropology* 14(1985):75.

10. Alejandro Portes, Silvia Blitzer, and John Curtis, "The urban informal sector in Uruguay: Its internal structure, characteristics and effects," *World Development* 14(1986):730.

11. Figures derived from United States Bureau of the Census, *Current Population Reports,* Series P-60:1969–1986.

12. Alejandro Portes and John Walton, *Labor, Class and the International System* (New York: Academic Press, 1981), p. 103.

13. Carl Simon and Ann Witte, *Beating the System: The Underground Economy* (Boston: Auburn House Publishing Company, 1982), p. 12.

14. Portes and Walton, *Labor, Class and the International System,* p. 103.

15. C. Birkbeck, "Self-employed proletarians in an informal factory: The case of Cali's garbage dump," *World Development* 6(1978):1173.

CHAPTER 2. **The Industrial-Information Economy**

1. Alan Bernstein, Bob DeGrasse, Rachael Grossman, Chris Paine, and Lenny Siegel, *Silicon Valley: Paradise or Paradox?* (Mountain View: Pacific Studies Center, 1977) p. 4; Lenny Siegel and Herb Borock,

Background Report on Silicon Valley, prepared for the U.S. Commission on Civil Rights (Mountain View: Pacific Studies Center, 1982), pp. 13–14.

2. AnnaLee Saxenian, *Silicon Chips and Spatial Structure: The industrial Basis of Urbanization in Santa Clara County, California.* Working Paper 345 (Berkeley: Institute of Urban and Regional Development, 1981), p. 58.

3. Bernstein et al., *Silicon Valley: Paradise or Paradox?,* p. 111.

4. *Ibid.,* p. 7

5. San Francisco Chamber of Commerce, *San Francisco: the Financial, Commercial and Industrial Metropolis of the West Coast* (San Francisco: H. S. Crocker Company, 1915), p. 15.

6. *Ibid.,* p. 41.

7. It is perhaps more apt to say this growth took place *because* the city was destroyed. Naturally, the process of reconstruction stimulated employment in the building trades. But the 1906 fire, as well as five major conflagrations before it, provided an incentive as well to the growth of the local insurance industry. Where wealth was more easily destroyed than created, the inhabitants realized "it was about time that they should be protected by insurance . . . a necessary bulwark to the credit system." By 1868, there were twenty-two insurance companies in San Francisco, many of them headquartered there (*ibid.,* p. 49).

8. *Ibid.,* p. 53.

9. Unless otherwise noted, figures for 1977 and 1982 cited in this section are derived from Tables 1 through 4a in U.S. Bureau of the Census, *Census of Service Industries* (Washington, D.C.: Government Printing Office, 1977b and 1982b). Figures for 1983 are derived from Table 1B and Table 2 in (U.S. Bureau of the Census *County Business Patterns—1984* [Washington, D.C.: Government Printing Office, 1984]).

10. SRI International, *High Technology and the California Workforce in the 1980s. A Report on California's Technological Future: Emerging Economic Opportunities in the 1980s.* Prepared in cooperation with the California Employment Development Department for the Department of Economic and Business Development (1982), p. 43.

11. Howard Aldrich, Catherine Zimmer, and Trevor Jones, "Small business still speaks with the same voice: A replication of 'the voice of small business and the politics of survival,'" *Sociological Review* 31(1986):353.

12. Unless otherwise noted, all figures cited in this section are derived from Tables 1a through 6 of the 1977 and 1982 *Census of Manufactures* (U.S. Bureau of the Census, 1977a and 1982a). Figures for

1983 are derived from Table 1B and Table 2, *County Business Patterns—1984* (U.S. Bureau of the Census, 1984).

13. It is interesting to note that despite the slow growth rate in manufacturing employment, manufacturing output as a percentage of gross national product has remained fairly stable over the last thirty years. It amounted to 24.5 percent in 1950, 23.3 percent in 1960, 24.1 percent in 1970, and 23.8 percent in 1980 and 1984. Some use these figures to argue that aside from some "troubled industries," the United States is *not* deindustrializing ("Is U.S. industry dying? A rosy minority view," *Wall Street Journal,* 31 December 1984:1).

14. For the state as a whole, manufacturing occupied 23 percent of the work force, and 27 percent worked in the service sector.

15. Bank of America, *Regional Perspectives: Santa Clara County—1983 Outlook* (Economics Policy Research: Regional Marketing and Corporate Communications Department, 1983), p. 2.

16. *Ibid.*

17. "Silicon Valley to grow," *Global Electronics Information Newsletter,* 35(September, 1983):3.

18. Colin Norman, *Microelectronics at Work: Productivity and Jobs in the World Economy,* No. 39(Washington, D.C.: Worldwatch Institute, 1980), p. 40.

19. An example of the value embodied in such products is provided by a respondent in a Sunnyvale firm that produces scientific instruments: Fifteen dollars worth of components assembled in four hours by a worker paid $6 an hour yields a product that sells for $390. Naturally, this does not include overhead costs—one of the primary incentives I will argue firms experience for putting out work to cottage assemblers.

20. A. J. Scott, "Industrial organization and the logic of intrametropolitan location: I. Theoretical considerations," *Economic Geography* 59(1983):236.

21. Siegel and Borock, *Background Report on Silicon Valley,* p. 72.

22. AnnaLee Saxenian, *Silicon Chips and Spatial Structure,* p. 140.

CHAPTER 3. **The Structure of Informal Enterprise, the Uses of Informal Labor**

1. United States Bureau of the Census, *Census of Population and Housing,* Summary Characteristics for Governmental Units and SMSAs, California (Washington, D.C.: Government Printing Office, 1980a), pp. 6–20.

2. I conducted these as "blind" interviews, not mentioning to the firm representative that I had talked with one of their informal workers.

I did, however, tell all respondents in the companies that I had been interviewing people in the local area who worked informally, and that my questions in general were informed by those conversations.

3. United States Bureau of the Census, *County Business Patterns—1984* (Washington, D.C.: Government Printing Office, 1984).

4. F. John L. Young, *The Contracting Out of Work: Canadian and U.S.A. Industrial Relations Experience,* Research Series Number 1 (Ontario: Industrial Relations Center, 1964).

5. United States Congress, *Miscellaneous Tax Bills II. Hearing Before the Subcommittee on Taxation and Debt Management Generally of the Committee on Finance* (Washington, D.C.: Government Printing Office, September 17, 1979c), p. 48.

6. Angela Dale, "Social class and the self-employed," *Sociology* 20(1986):432.

7. Maria Patricia Fernandez-Kelly and Anna Garcia, "The making of an underground economy: Hispanic women, home work and the advanced capitalist state," *Urban Anthropology* 14(1985):73–75.

8. David H. Rothman, "The computer cottage hysteria," *Washington Post* (7 July 1985): B1.

9. "IRS ruling raises cloud over contract work status," *Computerworld* 22(1988):105.

10. *Ibid.*

11. "Text of message from the President on the state of the union," *New York Times* (26 January 1984):12.

12. Between 1977 and 1982, receipts for equipment rental and leasing services increased nationally by over 120 percent (U.S. Bureau of the Census, *Census of Manufactures* [Washington, D.C.: Government Printing Office, 1977a], p. 11).

13. Dan Clawson, *Bureaucracy and the Labor Process: The Transformation of U.S. Industry 1860–1920* (New York: Monthly Review Press, 1980).

14. Lenny Siegel and Herb Borock, *Background Report on Silicon Valley,* Prepared for the U.S. Commission on Civil Rights (Mountain View: Pacific Studies Center, 1982), pp. 38–39.

15. *Ibid.,* p. 40.

16. Lourdes Beneria and Martha Roldan, *The Crossroads of Class and Gender: Industrial Homework, Subcontracting, and Household Dynamics in Mexico City* (Chicago: The University of Chicago Press, 1987), p. 38.

17. Peter Hall, Ann R. Markusen, Richard Osborn, and Barbara Wachsman, "The American computer software industry: Economic development prospects," in *Silicon Landscapes,* Peter Hall and Ann Markusen, eds. (Boston: Allen & Unwin, 1985), pp. 31–52.

18. Randy Hodson, "Working in 'high-tech': Research issues and opportunities for the industrial sociologist," *Sociological Quarterly,* 26 (1985): 354.

CHAPTER 4. **Individual Motives and Structural Requirements**

1. Vito Tanzi, *The Underground Economy in the United States and Abroad,* (Lexington: Lexington Books, 1982), p. 90.

2. Keith Hart, "Informal income opportunities and urban employment in Ghana," *Journal of Modern African Studies* 11(1973):61–89.

3. J. I. Gershuny and R. E. Pahl, "Work outside employment: Some preliminary speculations," *New Universities Quarterly* 34(1979): 120–135.

4. Alejandro Portes and John Walton, *Labor, Class and the International System* (New York: Academic Press, 1981); C. Birkbeck, "Garbage, industry, and the 'vultures' of Cali, Colombia," in *Casual Work and Poverty in Third World Cities,* ed. R. Bromley and C. Gerry (New York: John Wiley, 1979).

5. "The Silicon Valley style," *Newsweek* (8 June 1981):80.

6. "Managing by mystique at Tandem Computers," *Fortune* (June 28, 1982): 84–91.

7. "Software to go," *Forbes* (20 June 1983):94.

8. Peter Hall, Ann R. Markusen, Richard Osborn, and Barbara Wachsman, "The American computer software industry: Economic development prospects," in *Silicon Landscapes,* ed. Peter Hall and Ann Markusen (Boston: Allen & Unwin, 1985), p. 54.

9. A 1982 American Electronic Association survey shows that employee turnover in the Bay Area averaged 24 percent. Although the rate for salaried employees is lower (16.6 percent), this means that each year firms must replace one of every four employees ("Turnover," *Global Electronics Information Newsletter,* May 1983:3). Siegel and Borock explain that what accounts for this mobility among top level employees is their leaving to start companies on their own, and salary competition between local firms (Lenny Siegel and Herb Borock, *Background Report on Silicon Valley,* prepared for the U.S. Commission on Civil Rights [Mountain View: Pacific Studies Center, 1982], p. 41). There is evidence that turnover rates are decreasing, however.

10. Richard Osborn, Barbara Wachsman, Anne Markusen, and Peter Hall, *The California Software Industry: Problems and Prospects. A Report to the California Commission on Industrial Innovation* (Berkeley: Institute of Urban and Regional Development, 1982), p. 72.

11. Client specifications, of course, can be an important qualifier to the degree of freedom experienced by the worker. Repetitive work, such as assembly or computer coding, can be quite dull, and there may be little leeway for introducing more interesting variations on it. Some report turning down such jobs—when times are good. But if work is slow, they must accept jobs in which, by the nature of the task, opportunities for creativity are minimal.

12. There is always a certain amount of risk to the firm in putting work out where these conditions are not met. For example, according to the *Wall Street Journal,* many businesses have recently turned to independent computer consultants for help in the specialized field of selecting and installing office automation systems. It is a field confusing even to the experts, and "includes many incompetent practitioners ready to take unsuspecting clients for a useless ride." The "ride" may include inappropriate hardware, pirated software, and expensive regrets over having placed "confidence in somebody's business card that says 'computer consultant.'" ("Hiring a computer consultant can help, but the field is full of incompetents," *Wall Street Journal,* 25 February 1985, p. 31).

13. Karl Marx, *Capital: A Critique of Political Economy.* (Volume I), ed. Frederick Engles, revised and amplified according to the Fourth German Edition by Ernest Untermann (New York: Modern Library, 1906), p. 60.

14. Michael Burawoy, "Between the labor process and the state: The changing face of factory regimes under advanced capitalism," *American Sociological Review* 48(1983):589.

15. "Strategic systems plans gone awry," *Computerworld* 22(1988):105.

16. David Talbot, "Fast times for high-tech: Meet the moguls who are reprogramming our future," *Mother Jones* (December 1983):26.

17. "Warner debt soars after Atari losses," *Los Angeles Times* (9 November 1983):1 IV.

18. "A new effort to revive Osborne," *San Francisco Chronicle* (14 December 1983):31.

19. "Soothsayers look at 1983 in Silicon Valley," *San Francisco Chronicle* (2 January 1983):D1.

20. Bureau of National Affairs, "Flexible staffing: Exclusive results of survey on U.S. firms' use of non-regular employees," Special Supplement to *Employee Relations Weekly* 4(8 September 1986):6.

21. Nancy Sullivan, comments made at the California Employment Development Department Seminar on California's Changing Labor Market, 17 February 1988.

22. U.S. Bureau of the Census, *Statistical Abstract of the United States 1982–83,* 103rd Edition (Washington, D.C.: Government Printing Office, 1982c), p. 406.

23. U.S. Bureau of the Census, *Census of Manufactures* (Washington, D.C.: Government Printing Office, 1982a).

24. Several of these admit that were it not for the insurance available through their spouse's regular employment, they would find it necessary to seek regular work themselves. In this respect, some firms may be providing an indirect subsidy to other firms by underwriting health benefits for their informal workers!

25. This issue seemed to make several respondents thoughtful, or slightly anxious, during the interview, and they stated that until I mentioned it, they had not given the matter much thought. I later heard from two people I had interviewed when they wrote and called with follow-up information, and they claimed they were still thinking about our conversation. These contacts leave me with the impression that my questions caused some respondents to evaluate their activities with respect to a more long-term perspective. Though as of last report, none have left the field, the field is not quite as I found it, either.

26. Margrethe H. Olson and Sophia B. Primps, "Working at home with computers: Work and nonwork issues," *Journal of Social Issues* 40(1984):103.

27. Jill Rubery and Frank Wilkinson, "Outwork and segmented labour markets," in *The Dynamics of Labour Market Segmentation,* ed. Frank Wilkinson (London: The Academic Press, 1981), p. 117.

CHAPTER 5. **Bringing Work Home**

1. "Running a firm from home gives women more flexibility," *Wall Street Journal* (31 December 1984):11.

2. United States Congress, *Amending the Fair Labor Standards Act to Include Industrial Homework,* Hearing Before the Subcommittee on Labor of the Committe on Labor and Human Resources, February 9(Washington, D.C.: Government Printing Office, 1984), p. 79. In 1942, it was estimated that 20 percent of the work force labored at home. Although the combined figures for today's full-time and part-time home-based work force total only 13 percent of the whole, estimates of its growth trend indicate it will once again stand at the 1942 level by the end of this decade (*ibid.,* p. 35).

3. Francis Horvath, "Work at home: New findings from the Current Population Survey," *Monthly Labor Review* 109(1986):35.

4. "Telecommuters could top 7.2 million this year, a report says," Labor Letter, *Wall Street Journal* (5 February 1985):1.

5. United States Congress, *Amending the Fair Labor Standards Act to Include Industrial Homework,* p. 118.

6. "A job with a view," *Forbes* (12 September 1983):144. Jack M. Nilles is quoted in this article.

7. United States Congress, *A Bill,* H.R. 2531, First Session, Ninety-eighth Congress (Washington, D.C.: Government Printing Office, 1983), p. 1–2.

8. Bettina Berch, "The resurrection of outwork," *Monthly Review* 37(1985):41.

9. United States Congress, *Amending the Fair Labor Standards Act to Include Industrial Homework,* p. 6.

10. *Ibid.,* p. 77.

11. Eileen Boris, "Regulating industrial homework: The triumph of 'sacred motherhood,'" *The Journal of American History* 71(1985):762.

12. "Home computers are nurturing working mothers," *San Jose Mercury News* (13 March 1983):2D.

13. Harriet B. Presser and Wendy Baldwin, "Child care as a constraint on employment: Prevalence, correlates, and bearing on the work and fertility nexus," *American Journal of Sociology* 85(1980):1203.

14. Jessie Bernard, "The good-provider role: Its rise and fall," in *Work and Family: Changing Roles of Men and Women,* ed. Patricia Voydanoff (Palo Alto: Mayfield Publishing Company, 1984), p. 54. Between 1957 and 1976, the proportion of men and women who found marriage and parenthood burdensome and restrictive increased from 42 percent and 47 percent respectively, to 57 percent collectively. While it seems that no one is really happy with the arrangement, men's disaffection with family life has different implications insofar as family breakup generally results in women assuming sole responsibility for child rearing. The proportion of working men with positive attitudes toward marriage dropped from 68 percent in 1957 to 39 percent in 1976 (*ibid.,* p. 54).

15. Stuart Ewen, *Captains of Consciousness: Advertising and the Social Roots of the Consumer Culture* (New York: McGraw-Hill, 1976), p. 191.

16. Barbara Ehrenreich and Deirdre English, *For Her Own Good:150 Years of the Experts' Advice to Women* (New York: Anchor Books, 1978), p. 283.

17. Paul Blumberg, *Inequality in an Age of Decline* (New York: Oxford University Press, 1980), p. 201.

18. It is also a home that is shrinking. Between 1978 and 1982, the median size of a new home in the United States decreased from 1655 square feet to 1520 square feet. This is a change equivalent to losing a 13-by-10-foot room ("Space-savvy furniture," *San Francisco Chronicle,* 7 March 1984:36). Cottage industry may be growing, but the cottage most certainly is not.

19. C. Wright Mills, *White Collar* (New York: Oxford University Press, 1951), p. 238.

20. Blumberg, *Inequality in an Age of Decline,* pp. 233–235.

21. Emile Durkheim, *The Division of Labor in Society* (Toronto: The Macmillan Company, 1893), p. 58.

22. *Ibid.,* p. 60.

23. Neil J. Smelser, "Processes of social change," in *Sociology: An Introduction,* 2nd Edition, ed. Neil J. Smelser (New York: John Wiley and Sons, 1973), p. 752.

24. Talcott Parsons, *The Evolution of Societies* (Englewood Cliffs: Prentice-Hall, 1977), pp. 166–167.

25. *Ibid.,* p. 195.

26. Bernard, "The good-provider role: Its rise and fall," p. 46.

27. Harry Braverman, *Labor and Monopoly Capital: The Degradation of Work in the Twentieth Century* (New York: Monthly Review Press, 1974), p. 277.

28. Kenneth Keniston, *All Our Children: The American Family Under Pressure* (New York: Harcourt Brace Jovanovich, 1977), p. 14. But according to Burawoy, the productive function of the family was not so immediately reduced, even under the paternalistic factory regime in nineteenth century Lancashire. Worker dependence on one employer, and the employment of more than one family member in the same mill resulted in the family becoming "a potent instrument of incorporation and deference in many mill communities. Rather than a linear differentiation . . . , the family was now *reconstituted* within the context of paternalism" (Michael Burawoy, "Marx and the satanic mills: Early factory politics," *American Journal of Sociology* 90[1984]:262).

29. Marlene Dixon, *Women in Class Struggle* (San Francisco: Synthesis Publications, 1978), p. 49.

30. Braverman, *Labor and Monopoly Capital,* p. 276.

31. Renate Bridenthal, "The dialectics of production and reproduction in history," *Radical America* 10(1976):4; Women's Work Study Group, "Loom, broom and womb: Producers, maintainers and reproducers," *Radical America* 19(1976):37; Dixon, *Women in Class Struggle,* p. 9.

32. Women's Work Study Group, "Loom, broom and womb," p. 37.

33. Braverman, *Labor and Monopoly Capital,* p. 281.

34. *Ibid.,* pp. 279–281.

35. *Ibid.*

36. Ivan Szelenyi, "Structural changes of and alternatives to capitalist development," *International Journal of Urban and Regional Research* 5(1981):2.

37. Wolfgang Glatzer and Regina Berger, "Household composition, social networks and household production," in *The Economics of the Shadow Economy: Proceedings of the International Conference on the Economics of the Shadow Economy,* eds. Wulf Gaertner and Alois Wenig (Berlin: Springer-Verlag, 1985), p. 332.

38. Despite popular accounts to the contrary, there has been little change in the domestic division of labor. In 1975, women continued to bear the same proportion of the home workload as they did in 1965—over two-thirds. And among full-time workers in 1975, wives register more total work time than husbands (64 hours per week versus 61 hours per week) due to their cooking, cleaning, and laundering responsibilities (Arland Thornton and Deborah Freedman, "The Changing American Family," *Population Bulletin* 38 [1983] :27).

39. Dixon, *Women in Class Struggle,* p. 52.

40. Women's Work Study Group, "Loom, broom and womb," p. 37.

41. Presser and Baldwin, "Child care as a constraint on employment," p. 1209.

42. Arland Thornton and Deborah Freedman, "The changing American family," p. 27.

43. Michael Burawoy, "Between the labor process and the state: The changing face of factory regimes under advanced capitalism," *American Sociological Review* 48(1983):596.

44. In 1975, President Gerald Ford urged housewives to help fight inflation by comparison shopping at many stores for the lowest-cost item, spending more time preparing low-cost homecooked meals, and going through the house turning off lights in empty rooms (Women's Work Study Group, "Loom, broom and womb: Producers, maintainers and reproducers" *Radical America* 19[1976]:45). Sociological theory aside, there is still no place like home for dealing with the problems of the day.

45. In Santa Clara County, for example, 83 percent of the technicians are male, whereas 80 percent of clerical workers and 68 percent of the operatives are female. These characteristics are typical of the labor force found in other high-tech regions such as Boston and Dallas (Lenny Siegel and Herb Borock, *Background Report on Silicon Valley,* prepared for the U.S. Commission on Civil Rights [Mountain View: Pacific Studies Center, 1982], pp. 44–45).

46. Lourdes Beneria and Martha Roldan, *The Crossroads of Class and Gender: Industrial Homework, Subcontracting, and Household Dynamics in Mexico City* (Chicago: The University of Chicago Press, 1987), p. 48.

47. "G.I. Pain," *Global Electronics Information Newsletter* 23(July 1982):4.

48. Maria Patricia Fernandez-Kelly, "Gender and industry on Mexico's new frontier," in *The Technological Woman: Interfacing with Tomorrow,* Jan Zimmerman, ed. (New York: Praeger Publishers, 1983), p. 25.

49. "Women in electronics find Silicon Valley best and worst," *New York Times* (2 March 1984):1. For instance, Sandra Kurtzig, founder and president of Ask Computer Systems, no longer speaks to women's groups. Feeling little sympathy for women's complaints about gender discrimination in the industry, she says, "I feel I am just a business person who happens to be a woman. If you do a good job in managing a company, you'll be respected. If anything, it is an advantage to be a woman—it sets you apart. . . . [Women's groups] don't want to hear what I say. All they do is feed on each other's can't-do-it-syndrome" (*ibid,* p. 11). Why there are so few women managing companies is apparently not an issue for her.

50. Robert Goffee and Richard Scase, "Business ownership and women's subordination," *Sociological Review* 31(1983):633.

51. It is important to note that the elderly and disabled, i.e., the nonproductive population, are also featured frequently as beneficiaries of policies promoting homework.

52. United States Congress, *Amending the Fair Labor Standards Act to Include Industrial Homework,* p. 7.

53. Frank Schiff, "Flexiplace: An idea whose time has come," *IEEE Transactions on Engineering Management* 30(1983):27.

54. Jack M. Nilles, F. Roy Carlson, Paul Gray, and Gerhard J. Hanneman, *The Telecommunications-Transportation Tradeoff* (New York: John Wiley and Sons, 1976), pp. 75–76. We are reminded here of one respondent's prospective employer and his worries over what would happen "when little Johnny gets the chicken pox." In addition to the fact that women are expected to answer for how they intend to look after their children while they work, it seems that the troublesome child so often in need of their tender mercies is a male—little "Johnny." Either female children are perceived as being less needy of their mothers' attentions, or male employers are expressing some oedipal anxiety over the abandonment represented by working mothers!

55. Sheila Allen, "Production and reproduction: The lives of women homeworkers," *Sociological Review* 31(1983):660.

56. Kathleen E. Christensen, "Women and home-based work," *Social Policy* 15(1985):57.

57. Michael Burawoy, "The functions and reproduction of migrant labor: Comparative material from South Africa and the United States," *American Journal of Sociology* 81(1976):1051.

58. Southern California Association of Governments, *Implementation Plan: Telecommuting Pilot Project for the Southern California Asso-*

ciation of Governments Central City Association, Telecommuting Subcommittee, January 1986, p. 3.

59. California Department of Industrial Relations, *Annual Report* (1977), p. 6; California Department of Industrial Relations, *Annual Report* (1978), p. 11. California Department of Industrial Relations, *Annual Report* (1980), p. 22.

60. "Black market in Silicon Valley," *San Jose Mercury News* (31 August 1980):1.

61. "What color is your umbrella?" *Parents Monthly* 6(1988):1–3.

62. Bernard, "The good-provider role: Its rise and fall," p. 46.

63. "Worksteaders clean up," *Newsweek* (9 January 1984):87.

64. Linda Lee Small, "How to get up in the morning and other tricks to working from home," *Ms. Magazine* August (1981):35.

65. "Running a firm from home gives women more flexibility," *Wall Street Journal* (31 December 1984):11.

66. "Women in electronics find Silicon Valley best and worst," *New York Times* (2 March 1984):1.

67. Rosa Luxemburg, *The Accumulation of Capital* (New Haven: Yale University Press, 1913), p. 365.

68. *Ibid.,* p. 361.

69. *Ibid.,* p. 366.

70. Margaret Benston, "The political economy of women's liberation," in *Woman in a Man-Made World: A Socioeconomic Handbook* (Second Edition), eds. Nona Glazer and Helen Youngelson Waehrer (Chicago: Rand-McNally College Publishing Company, 1977), p. 220. These are precisely the forms of production that Luxemburg demonstrates lie at a point of tension between capital's need to transform them through exploitation and to preserve them so that they might be exploited. (See Chapter XXVII, "The Struggle Against Natural Economy" and Chapter XXIX, "The Struggle Against Peasant Economy" in Luxemburg, *The Accumulation of Capital*).

71. Juliet Mitchell, "Women: The longest revolution," in *Woman in a Man-Made World: A Socioeconomic Handbook* (Second Edition), eds. Nona Glazer and Helen Youngelson Waehrer (Chicago: Rand-McNally College Publishing Company, 1977), p. 175.

72. Mingione, "Informalization and Restructuring: The Problem of Social Reproduction of the Labor Force," paper delivered at the Tenth World Congress of Sociology, Tepoztlán, Mexico (August 1982).

CHAPTER 6. Concluding Thoughts on Informal Work

1. Richard Edwards, *Contested Terrain: The Transformation of the Workplace in the Twentieth Century* (New York: Basic Books, 1979), p. 158.

2. Bureau of National Affairs, "Flexible staffing: Exclusive results of survey on U.S. firms' use of non-regular employees," *Special Supplement to Employee Relations Weekly* 4(8 September 1986):5.

3. Patricia Mokhtarian, "Telecommuting on the move in city of Los Angeles," *Telecommunity* 3(1987):2.

4. Kathryn Yates, "An agent of change," *Government Technology* 1(Fall 1987):13.

5. Raffaele De Grazia, *Clandestine Employment: The Situation in the Industrialized Market Economy Countries* (Geneva: International Labour Organization, 1984), p. 13.

6. Patricia L. Mokhtarian and Richard Spicer, "Telecommuting gathers speed as traffic slows down," *Government Technology* 1(Fall 1987):14.

7. Alejandro Portes and Saskia Sassen-Koob, "Making it underground: Comparative material on the informal sector in Western market economies," *American Journal of Sociology* 93(1987):53.

8. C. Birkbeck, "Self-employed proletarians in an informal factory: The case of Cali's garbage dump," *World Development* 6(1978):1179.

9. David Beers, "9 to 5 in Barbados," *In These Times* 8(1984):23

APPENDIX A.

1. Cited in Eileen Boris, "Regulating industrial homework: The triumph of 'sacred motherhood,'" *Journal of American History* 71(1985):757.

2. Adam Smith, *The Wealth of Nations* (London: J. M. Dent and Sons, Ltd., 1776), p. 76.

3. E. P. Thompson, *The Making of the English Working Class* (New York: Vintage Press, 1963), p. 261.

4. T. S. Ashton, "The domestic system in the early Lancashire tool trade," *Economic History Supplement to the Economic Journal* 1(1926):136.

5. *Ibid.*

6. "Current topics," *Economic Journal* 2(1892):757.

7. Thomas Wright, *Some Habits and Customs of the Working Class* (London: Tinsley Brothers, 1867), p. 85.

8. Stuart Henry, *The Hidden Economy* (London: Martin Robertson, 1978).

9. Martin Bennett, personal communication, Davis, California, 17 March 1984.

10. Helen Dendy, "The industrial residuum," *Economic Journal* 3(1893):601.

11. *Ibid.*, p. 609.

12. *Ibid.,* p. 616.

13. C. Osborn, "The hand-working and domestic industries in Germany," *Economic Journal* 12(1903); 134.

14. G. M. Oakeshott, "Artificial flower-making: An account of the trade and a plea for municipal training," *Economic Journal* 13(1903):125.

15. Emily Hobhouse, "Dust-women," *Economic Journal* 19(1900):411.

16. *Ibid.*

17. Dan Clawson, *Bureaucracy and the Labor Process: The Transformation of U.S. Industry 1860–1920* (New York: Monthly Review Press, 1980), p. 119.

18. *Ibid.,* p. 106.

19. *Ibid.,* p. 123.

20. Luther Whiteman and Samuel Lewis, *Glory Roads: The Psychological State of California* (New York: Crowell, 1936), p. 166.

21. Paolo Souza and Victor Tokman, "The informal urban sector in Latin America," *International Labour Review* 114(1976):365.

22. For a thorough discussion of the informal sector in peripheral countries, see "Unequal exchange and the urban informal sector," pp. 67–106 in Alejandro Portes and John Walton, *Labor, Class and the International System* (New York: Academic Press, 1981). Perspectives such as those found in Carl Simon and Ann Witte, *Beating the System: The Underground Economy* (Boston: Auburn House Publishing Company, 1982); Vito Tanzi, *The Underground Economy in the United States and Abroad* (Lexington: Lexington Books, 1982); and Dan Bawly, *The Subterranean Economy* (New york: McGraw-Hill, 1982) demonstrate how differently the issue is framed in core regions.

23. For example, see Gregory Grossman, "The 'Second Economy' of the USSR," in *The Soviet Economy: Continuity and Change,* ed. Morris Bernstein (Boulder: Westview Press, 1981).

24. The approaches of J. I. Gershuny and R. E. Pahl ["Work outside employment: Some preliminary speculations," *New Universities Quarterly* 34(1979):120–135] in the United Kingdom; Patricia Ferman and Louis Ferman ["The structural underpinnings of the irregular economy," *Poverty and Human Resources Abstracts* 8(1973):3–17], and Louis Ferman, Louise Berndt, and Elaine Selo [*Analysis of the Irregular Economy: Cash Flow in the Informal Sector* (University of Michigan–Wayne State University: Institute of Labor and Industrial Relations, 1978)] in the United States are primarily concerned with the production and trade of consumer goods and services at the neighborhood level. This is in contrast to the more global analyses of the Third World informal sector made by Portes and Walton, *Labor, Class and the International System.*

25. This approach is best exemplified by the work of economists at-

tempting to estimate its size in terms of dollars (see Edgar L. Feige, "How big is the irregular economy?" *Challenge* Nov./Dec. 1979:5–13; Peter Gutmann, "Statistical illusions, mistaken policies," *Challenge* Nov./Dec. 1979:14–17); unreported income and taxes (see Berdj Kenadjian, "The direct approach to measuring the underground economy in the United States," and Peter Reuter, "The irregular economy and the quality of macroeconomic statistics," both in *The Underground Economy in the United States and Abroad,* ed. Vito Tanzi [Lexington: Lexington Books, 1982]); or the number of "jobs" implied by estimates of the income generated (see Peter Gutmann, "The subterranean economy," *Financial Analysts Journal* Nov./Dec. 1977:26). For example, Feige claims that the underground economy has recently grown at a rate four times faster than the regular economy, and amounted to 26.6 percent of the total economy in 1978(Feige, "How big is the irregular economy").

26. For example, our understanding of informal work in core countries like the United States and Great Britain was largely shaped by concern over the effect economic recession was having on patterns of consumption, and on the state's ability to generate revenue. The former led to studies of the manner in which neighbors, friends, and households coped with inflation and unemployment through the substitution of informally produced goods and services for commercially produced ones (Ferman *et al., Analysis of the Irregular Economy;* J. I. Gershuny, *After Industrial Society? The Emerging Self-Service Economy* [Atlantic Highlands: Humanities Press, 1978]; Gershuny and Pahl, "Work outside employment"; R. E. Pahl, "Employment, work and the domestic division of labor," *International Journal of Urban and Regional Research* 4 [1980]:1–19).

The notion of an "underground economy" arose out of United States economists' attempts to define social policies that would correct sagging public revenues (see note 25). It is a pejorative term with sinister connotations of dishonest citizens lurking about a shadowy region where they hope to turn an easy buck and avoid, scot-free, their social obligations. This concept has worked its way into the popular press and presidential speeches. According to President Reagan, for example, it is "immoral to make those who are paying taxes pay more to compensate for those who aren't paying their share." Consequently, one of his proposals for improving the state of the union is to bring the underground economy "into the sunlight of honest tax compliance" ("Text of message of the President on the state of the union," *New York Times,* 26 January 1984:12).

Studies conducted in Third World countries were based on different preoccupations from those that characterized research in core states. Informal work was conceptualized in those regions as a strategy through which local economies coped with high rates of rural-to-urban migration (P. Bairock, *Unemployment in Developing Countries: The Nature of the Problem and Proposals for Its Solution* [Geneva: International Labour Organization, 1973], p. 85); a potential mechanism for the peaceful absorption of the unemployed (Keith Hart, "Informal income opportunities and urban employment in Ghana," *Journal of Modern African Studies* 11 [1973]:89); or as a structural feature of peripheral accumulation through which indirect subsidies could be transferred to core-nation capital invested in the Third World (Portes and Walton, *Labor, Class and the International System*, p. 106). The term "informal sector" was intended to emphasize the fact that informal work did not make up a separate economy of its own, but rather, could be thought of as a unique sector articulated with regular systems of production in a single economy. This insight is central to the analysis of informal work we consider here, though a sectoral approach is not used.

27. Stephen Smith, *Britain's Shadow Economy* (Oxford: Clarendon Press, 1986), p. 3.

28. J. D. Uzzell, "Mixed strategies and the informal sector: Three faces of reserve labor," *Human Organization* 39(1980):40.

29. Keith Hart, "Informal income opportunities and urban employment in Ghana," p. 68.

30. J. I. Gershuny and R. E. Pahl, "Work outside employment: Some preliminary speculations," p. 121. Actually, the United States Internal Revenue Service is already attempting to lay claim to barter "income" by requiring that citizens list "the fair market value of all goods and services traded" when submitting their income statements (Commissioner of Internal Revenue, *Federal Income Tax Form and Instructions, Package 1040A* [Washington, D.C.: Department of the Treasury, 1980], p. 3). Of special interest are clubs that organize individual barter activities into impersonally traded "banks" of goods and services (U.S. Congress, *Underground Economy, Hearings, Commerce, Consumer and Monetary Affairs Subcommittee of the Committee on Government Operations*, September 5 and 6 [Washington, D.C.: Government Printing Office 1979a). Contrast this with the attitude of the 1930s federal government that actively involved itself in subsidizing a "reciprocal economy" among the unemployed (Luther Whiteman and Samuel Lewis, *Glory Roads: The Psychological State of California* [New York: Crowell, 1936], pp. 158–174).

31. Edgar L. Feige, "How big is the irregular economy?" p. 13.

32. Hart, "Informal income opportunities and urban employment in Ghana," p. 68.

33. It is true that the self-employed have much lower compliance rates than wage and salary workers whose income tax and social security contributions are regularly withheld by employers. For example, re-

sults of the Taxpayer Compliance Measurement Program conducted by the Internal Revenue Service suggest a 97 percent compliance rate among wage and salary workers, and only a 60 to 64 percent compliance rate among the self-employed (U.S. Congress, *Underground Economy, Hearings*). Furthermore, 62 percent of the workers who list themselves as independent contractors pay no social security tax (U.S. Congress, *Descriptions of Proposals Relating to Independent Contractors Scheduled for a Hearing Before the Subcommittee on Select Revenue Measures of the Committee on Ways and Means* [Washington, D.C.: Government Printing Office, 1979b], p. 30). It is interesting to note, however, that compliance within these groups *increases* with income, a fact difficult to reconcile with popular explanations alleging that the "underground economy" grows as marginal tax rates increase. A more likely hypothesis is that the poor cannot afford to sacrifice their already low incomes to the state, and yet are not eligible for the legal tax shelters enjoyed by the more affluent.

34. C. Birkbeck, "Self-employed proletarians in an informal factory: The case of Cali's garbage dump," *World Devleopment* 6(1978):1173–1185; R. Bromley, "Organization, regulation and exploitation in the so-called 'urban informal sector': The street traders of Cali, Colombia," *World Development* 6(1978):1161–1171; Keith Hart, "Informal income opportunities and urban employment in Ghana"; Dipak Mazumdar, "The urban informal sector," *World Development* 4(1976):655–679; S. V. Sethuraman, "The urban informal sector: Concept, measurement and policy," *International Labour Review* 114(1976):69–81; Souza and Tokman, "The informal urban sector in Latin America," pp. 355–365.

35. Portes and Walton, *Labor, Class and the International System*, p. 62.

36. Helen Safa, "Urbanization, the informal economy and state policy in Latin America," *Urban Anthropology* 15(1986):137.

37. Mazumdar, "The urban informal sector," p. 655; Alejandro Portes, Silvia Blitzer, and John Curtis, "The urban informal sector in Uruguay: Its internal structure, characteristcs, and effects," *World Development* 14(1986):729.

38. Commissioner of Internal Revenue, *Federal Income Tax Form and Instructions, Package 1040A*, p. 3.

39. Personal communication. Nance Milberger, Assistant Manager, California State Department of Industrial Relations, San Francisco, California; 3 April 1982.

40. "Federal 'help' for these workers could cost them their incomes," *Wall Street Journal* (30 June 1980):15; "The flap over the cottage industry ban," *Christian Science Monitor* (12 December 1983):27. In

1980, the United States Department of Labor under the Carter administration brought suit against a company that relied on industrial homeworkers to produce its line of knitted ski hats, claiming that the knitters were employees subject to the Fair Labor Standards Act of 1938. A year later, Secretary of Labor Ray Donovan of the Reagan administration revoked regulations governing this particular industry, thereby making his department the object of another lawsuit initiated by the International Ladies Garment Workers Union. Other voices added to this clamor now include the National Association of Cottage Industries. This organization is dedicated on behalf of its 42,000 members to advocating laws that will be helpful to such home-based workers. According to its director, Coralee Kern Smith, what is needed is a "non-union union" of such workers ("The flap over the cottage industry ban," p. 27).

41. Employers are required to meet only a legal minimum wage in order to comply with the law. However, differences in wage scales for various occupations normally result in the average wage for many of them being higher than what is required by law. Thus, although employers are not *prohibited* from paying skilled workers the minimum wage, they are more likely to offer something closer to the average package of wages and benefits for any given occupation or profession. This I refer to throughout the present work as the "average social wage."

42. Birkbeck, "Self-employed proletarians in an informal factory"; C. Birkbeck, "Garbage, industry, and the 'vultures' of Cali, Colombia," in *Casual Work and Poverty in Third World Cities*, eds. R. Bromley and C. Gerry (New York: John Wiley, 1979).

43. Hart, "Informal income opportunities and urban employment in Ghana," p. 79.

44. *Ibid.*, p. 88.

45. Birkbeck, "Garbage, industry, and the 'vultures' of Cali, Colombia," p. 171.

46. Victor Tokman, "Competition between the informal and formal sectors in retailing: The case of Santiago," *World Development* 6(1978):1187–1198.

47. Cathy A. Rakowski, "The planning process and the division of labour in a new industrial city: The case of Ciudad Guayana, Venezuela," in *Capital and Labour in the Urbanized World*, ed. John Walton (London: Sage, 1985), p. 198.

48. Souza and Tokman, "The informal urban sector in Latin America," p. 356.

49. *Ibid.*,

50. Bromley, "Organization, regulation and exploitation in the so-called 'urban informal sector,'" p. 1165.

51. Rob Davies, "Informal sector or subordinate mode of production? A model," in *Casual Work and Poverty in Third World Cities* eds. R. Bromley and C. Gerry (New York: John Wiley, 1979), p. 91; Sethuraman, "The urban informal sector: Concept, measurement, and policy," p. 71; Tokman, "Competition between the informal and formal sectors in retailing: The case of Santiago," p. 1195.

52. Birkbeck, "Self-employed proletarians in an informal factory," p. 1179.

53. In the five years following its 1973 appearance in the social scientific literature, over one hundred articles on the informal sector were published (Bromley, "Organization, regulation and exploitation in the so-called 'urban informal sector,'" p. 1033), and there was so little agreement between them as to its origins and composition, some scholars favored scrapping the whole idea of an informal sector. Insofar as formal-informal sector distinctions were reminiscent of previously unseated dichotomies such as "traditional" versus "modern" economies, interest in the informal sector was criticized as being one more "simplistically dualistic differentiation" based on the assumption that "a reformed capitalism is capable of spreading 'development' to the contemporary underdeveloped world" (C. Gerry, "Petty production and capitalist production in Dakar: The crisis of the self-employed," *World Development* 6 [1978]:1147). Gerry concluded that a concept based on such an assumption warranted "no further discussion" (*ibid.*), and that questions about "what *is* the informal sector" could be productive "only of tautology" (*ibid.,* p. 1151). Those who continued discussing the informal sector anyway were put aside as "neo-dualists" (R. Bromley and C. Gerry, "Who are the casual poor?" in *Casual Work and Poverty in Third World Cities,* eds. R. Bromley and C. Gerry [New York: John Wiley, 1979], p. 4), whose "insipid term informal" simply meant "not formal," a term wanting replacement with a more precise and meaningful description (Bromley, *op. cit.,* p. 1162).

54. R. E. Pahl, *Divisions of Labour* (Oxford: Basil Blackwell, 1984) p. 30.

55. Enzo Mingione, "Informalization and households' survival strategies in industrialized countries," in *The Capitalist City: Global Restructuring and Community Politics,* eds. Michael F. Smith and Joe R. Feagin (New York: Basil Blackwell, 1987).

56. Enzo Mingione, "Informalization and Restructuring: The Problem of Social Reproduction of the Labor Force," paper delivered at the Tenth World Congress of Sociology, Mexico, August 1982, p. 6.

57. Mingione, "Informalization and households' survival strategies in industrialized countries," p. 9.

58. Pahl, *Divisions of Labour,* p. 231.

59. Paola Vinay, "Family life cycle and the informal economy in central Italy," *International Journal of Urban and Regional Research* 9(1985):92.

60. Enzo Mingione, "Informalization, restructuring and the survival strategies of the working class," *International Journal of Urban and Regional Research* 7(1983):311; Ivan Szelenyi, "Structural changes of and alternatives to capitalist development," *International Journal of Urban and Regional Research* 5(1981):9.

61. Larissa Lominitz and Marisol Perez-Lizaur, "Social relations and capital accumulation: The case of the Mexican bourgeoisie," in *Capital and Labour in the Urbanized World,* ed. John Walton, (London: Sage Publications, 1985), p. 232.

62. Reyna Rapp, Ellen Ross, and Renate Bridenthal, "Examining family history," *Feminist Studies* 5(1979):175.

APPENDIX **B.**

1. John Lofland, *Analyzing Social Settings* (Belmont: Wadsworth Publishing Company, Inc., 1971), pp. 117–133.

~

References

"A job with a view." 1983. *Forbes,* September 12:143–150.

"A new effort to revive Osborne." 1983. *San Francisco Chronicle,* December 14:31.

ALDRICH, HOWARD, CATHERINE ZIMMER, AND TREVOR JONES. 1986. "Small business still speaks with the same voice: a replication of 'the voice of small business and the politics of survival.'" *Sociological Review* 34(2):335–356.

ALLEN, SHEILA. 1983. "Production and reproduction: The lives of women homeworkers." *Sociological Review* 31(4):649–665.

ASHTON, T. S. 1926. "The domestic system in the early Lancashire tool trade." *Economic History Supplement to the Economic Journal* 1(1):131–140.

BAIROCK, P. 1973. *Unemployment in Developing Countries: The Nature of the Problem and Proposals for Its Solution.* Geneva: International Labour Organization.

BANK OF AMERICA. 1983. *Regional Perspectives: Santa Clara County— 1983 Outlook.* Economics Policy Research: Regional Marketing and Corporate Communications Department.

BAWLY, DAN. 1982. *The Subterranean Economy.* New York: McGraw-Hill.

BECKER, EUGENE H. 1984. "Self-employed workers: An update to 1983. *Monthly Labor Review* 107(7): 14–18.

BEERS, DAVID. 1984. "9 to 5 in Barbados." *In These Times* 8(18):23–24.

BENERIA, LOURDES, AND MARTHA ROLDAN. 1987. *The Crossroads of Class and Gender: Industrial Homework, Subcontracting, and Household Dynamics in Mexico City.* Chicago: The University of Chicago Press.

BENSTON, MARGARET. 1977. "The political economy of women's liberation." In Nona Glazer and Helen Youngelson Waehrer (Eds.), *Woman in a Man-Made World: A Socioeconomic Handbook,* Second Edition. Chicago: Rand-McNally College Publishing Company.

BERCH, BETTINA. 1985. "The resurrection of outwork." *Monthly Review* 37(6):37–46.

BERNARD, JESSIE. 1984. "The good-provider role: Its rise and fall." In Patricia Voydanoff (Ed.), *Work and Family: Changing Roles of Men and Women.* Palo Alto: Mayfield Publishing Company.

BERNSTEIN, ALAN, BOB DEGRASSE, RACHAEL GROSSMAN, CHRIS PAINE, AND LENNY SIEGEL. 1977. *Silicon Valley: Paradise or Paradox?* Mountain View: Pacific Studies Center.

BIRKBECK, C. 1978. "Self-employed proletarians in an informal factory: The case of Cali's garbage dump." *World Development* 6(9/10):1173–1185.

———. 1979. "Garbage, industry, and the 'vultures' of Cali, Columbia." In R. Bromley and C. Gerry (Eds.), *Casual Work and Poverty in Third World Cities.* New York: John Wiley.

"Black market in Silicon Valley." 1980. *San Jose Mercury News,* August 31:1.

BLUMBERG, PAUL. 1980. *Inequality in an Age of Decline.* New York: Oxford University Press.

BORIS, EILEEN. 1985. "Regulating industrial homework: The triumph of 'sacred motherhood.'" *The Journal of American History* 71(4):745–763.

BRAVERMAN, HARRY. 1974. *Labor and Monopoly Capital: The Degradation of Work in the Twentieth Century.* New York: Monthly Review Press.

BRIDENTHAL, RENATE. 1976. "The dialectics of production and reproduction in history." *Radical America* 10(2):3–11.

BROMLEY, R. 1978. "Organization, regulation and exploitation in the so-called 'urban informal sector': The street traders of Cali, Colombia." *World Development* 6(9/10):1161–1171.

BROMLEY, R., AND C. GERRY. 1979. "Who are the casual poor?" In R. Bromley and C. Gerry (Eds.), *Casual Work and Poverty in Third World Cities.* New York: John Wiley.

BURAWOY, MICHAEL. 1976. "The functions and reproduction of migrant labor: Comparative material from South Africa and the United States." *American Journal of Sociology* 81(5):1050–1087.

———. 1983. "Between the labor process and the state: The changing face of factory regimes under advanced capitalism." *American Sociological Review* 48(5):587–605.

———. 1984. "Marx and the satanic mills: Early factory politics." *American Journal of Sociology* 90(2):247–282.

BUREAU OF NATIONAL AFFAIRS. 1986. "Flexible staffing: Exclusive results of survey on U.S. firms' use of non-regular employees." *Special Supplement to Employee Relations Weekly* 4(September 8):1–8.

CALIFORNIA DEPARTMENT OF INDUSTRIAL RELATIONS. 1977. *Annual Report.*

——. 1978. *Annual Report.*

——. 1980. *Annual Report.*

CHRISTENSEN, KATHLEEN E. 1985. "Women and home-based work." *Social Policy* 15(Winter):54–57.

CLAWSON, DAN. 1980. *Bureaucracy and the Labor Process: The Transformation of U.S. Industry 1860–1920.* New York: Monthly Review Press.

COMMISSIONER OF INTERNAL REVENUE. 1980. *Federal Income Tax Form and Instructions, Package 1040A* Washington, D.C.: Department of the Treasury.

"Current Topics." 1892. *Economic Journal* 2(8):775–757.

DALE, ANGELA. 1986. "Social class and the self-employed." *Sociology* 20(3):430–434.

DAVIES, ROB. 1979. "Informal sector or subordinate mode of production? A model." In R. Bromley and C. Gerry (Eds.), *Casual Work and Poverty in Third World Cities.* New York: John Wiley.

DE GRAZIA, RAFFAELE. 1984. *Clandestine Employment: The Situation in the Industrialized Market Economy Countries.* Geneva: International Labour Organization.

DENDY, HELEN. 1893. "The industrial residuum." *Economic Journal* 3(9):600–616.

DIXON, MARLENE. 1978. *Women in Class Struggle.* San Francisco: Synthesis Publications.

DURKHEIM, EMILE. 1893. *The Division of Labor in Society.* Toronto: The Macmillan Company.

EDWARDS, RICHARD. 1979. *Contested Terrain: The Transformation of the Workplace in the Twentieth Century.* New York: Basic Books, Inc.

EHRENREICH, BARBARA, AND DEIRDRE ENGLISH. 1978. *For Her Own Good: 150 Years of the Experts' Advice to Women.* New York: Anchor Books.

"11% still jobless in California." 1983. *San Francisco Chronicle,* February 5:12.

EWEN, STUART. 1976. *Captains of Consciousness: Advertising and the Social Roots of the Consumer Culture.* New York: McGraw-Hill.

"Federal 'help' for these workers could cost them their incomes." 1980. *Wall Street Journal,* June 30:15.

FEIGE, EDGAR L. 1979. "How big is the irregular economy?" *Challenge* Nov/Dec:5–13.

FERMAN, LOUIS, LOUISE BERNDT, AND ELAINE SELO. 1978. *Analysis of the Irregular Economy: Cash Flow in the Informal Sector.* University of Michigan–Wayne State University: Institute of Labor and Industrial Relations.

FERMAN, PATRICIA, AND LOUIS FERMAN. 1973. "The structural underpinnings of the irregular economy." *Poverty and Human Resources Abstracts* 8(1):3–17.

FERNANDEZ-KELLY, MARIA PATRICIA. 1983. Gender and industry on Mexico's new frontier. In Jan Zimmerman (Ed.), *The Technological Woman: Interfacing with Tomorrow.* New York: Praeger Publishers.

FERNANDEZ-KELLY, MARIA PATRICIA, AND ANNA GARCIA. 1985. "The making of an underground economy: Hispanic women, home work and the advanced capitalist state." *Urban Anthropology* 14(1–3):59–90.

GERRY, C. 1978. "Petty production and capitalist production in Dakar: The crisis of the self-employed." *World Development* 6(9/10):1147–1160.

GERSHUNY, J. I. 1978. *After Industrial Society? The Emerging Self-Service Economy.* Atlantic Highlands: Humanities Press.

GERSHUNY, J. I. AND R. E. PAHL. 1979. "Work outside employment: Some preliminary speculations." *New Universities Quarterly* 34:120–135.

"G.I. pain." *Global Electronics Information Newsletter,* issue number 23. July.

GLATZER, WOLFGANG, AND REGINA BERGER. 1985. "Household composition, social networks and household production." In Wulf Gaertner and Alois Wenig (Eds.), *The Economics of the Shadow Economy: Proceedings of the International Conference on the Economics of the Shadow Economy.* Berlin: Springer-Verlag.

GOFFEE, ROBERT, AND RICHARD SCASE. 1983. "Business ownership and women's subordination: A preliminary study of female proprietors." *Sociological Review* 31(4):625–648.

GROSSMAN, GREGORY. 1981. "The 'second economy' of the USSR." In Morris Bornstein (Ed.), *The Soviet Economy: Continuity and Change.* Boulder: Westview Press.

GUTMANN, PETER. 1977. "The subterranean economy." *Financial Analysts Journal* Nov/Dec:26.

———. 1979. "Statistical illusions, mistaken policies." *Challenge* Nov/Dec:14–17.

HALL, PETER, ANN R. MARKUSEN, RICHARD OSBORN, AND BARBARA WACHSMAN. 1985. "The American computer software industry: Economic development prospects." In Peter Hall and Ann Markusen [Eds.], *Silicon Landscapes.* Boston: Allen & Unwin.

HART, KEITH. 1973. "Informal income opportunities and urban employment in Ghana." *Journal of Modern African Studies* 11(1):61–89.

HENRY, STUART. 1978. *The Hidden Economy.* London: Martin Robertson.

"Hiring a computer consultant can help, but the field is full of incompetents." 1985. *Wall Street Journal,* February 25:31.

HOBHOUSE, EMILY. 1900. "Dust-women." *Economic Journal* 19(39):411–420.

HODSON, RANDY. 1985. "Working in 'high-tech': Research issues and opportunities for the industrial sociologist." *Sociological Quarterly* 26(3):351–364.

HORVATH, FRANCIS W. 1986. "Work at home: New findings from the Current Population Survey." *Monthly Labor Review* 109(11):31–35.

"IRS ruling raises cloud over contract work status." 1988. *Computer world* 22(12):105.

"Is U.S. industry dying? A rosy minority view." 1984. *Wall Street Journal,* December 31:1.

KENADJIAN, BERDJ. 1982. "The direct approach to measuring the underground economy in the United States." In Vito Tanzi (Ed.), *The Underground Economy in the United States and Abroad.* Lexington: Lexington Books.

KENISTON, KENNETH. 1977. *All Our Children: The American Family Under Pressure.* New York: Harcourt Brace Jovanovich.

LOFLAND, JOHN. 1971. *Analyzing Social Settings.* Belmont: Wadsworth Publishing Company, Inc.

LOMNITZ, LARISSA, AND MARISOL PEREZ-LIZAUR. 1985. "Social relations and capital accumulation: The case of the Mexican bourgeoisie." In John Walton (Ed.), *Capital and Labour in the Urbanized World.* London: Sage Publications.

ROSA LUXEMBURG. 1913. *The Accumulation of Capital.* New Haven: Yale University Press.

"Managing by mystique at Tandem Computers." 1982. *Fortune,* June 28:84–91.

MARX, KARL. 1873. *Capital: A Critique of Political Economy* (Volume I). Edited by Frederick Engels; revised and amplified according to the Fourth German Edition by Ernest Untermann (1906). New York: Modern Library.

MAZUMDAR, DIPAK. 1976. "The urban informal sector." *World Development* 4(8):655–679.

MILLS, C. WRIGHT. 1951. *White Collar.* New York: Oxford University Press.

MINGIONE, ENZO. 1982. Informalization and Restructuring: The Problem of Social Reproduction of the Labor Force. Paper delivered at the Tenth World Congress of Sociology, Tepoztlán, Mexico. August.

——. 1983. "Informalization, restructuring and the survival strategies of the working class." *International Journal of Urban and Regional Research* 7(3):311–339.

——. 1987. "Informalization and households' survival strategies in industrialized countries." In Michael F. Smith and Joe R. Feagin (Eds.), *The Capitalist City: Global Restructuring and Communty Politics.* New York: Basil Blackwell.

MITCHELL, JULIET. 1977. "Women: The longest revolution." In Nona Glazer and Helen Youngelson Waehrer (Eds.), *Woman in a Man-Made World: A Socioeconomic Handbook,* Second Edition. Chicago: Rand-McNally College Publishing Company.

MOKHTARIAN, PATRICIA. 1987. "Telecommuting on the move in city of Los Angeles." *Telecommunity* 3(5):1–2.

MOKHTARIAN, PATRICIA L., AND RICHARD SPICER. 1987. "Telecommuting gathers speed as traffic slows down." *Government Technology* No. 1(Fall):13–14.

MOLEFSKY, BARRY. 1982. "America's underground economy." In Vito Tanzi (Ed.), *The Undergrond Economy in the United States and Abroad.* Lexington: Lexington Books.

NAISBITT, JOHN. 1987. "Executive briefing: Naisbitt sites [sic] trends to year 2000." *Government Technology* No. 1(Fall):26–28.

NILLES, JACK M., F. ROY CARLSON, PAUL GRAY, AND GERHARD J. HANNE-MAN. 1976. *The Telecommunications-Transportation Tradeoff.* New York: John Wiley and Sons.

NORMAN, COLIN. 1980. *Microelectroncis at Work: Productivity and Jobs in the World Economy,* No. 39. Washington, D.C.: Worldwatch Institute.

OAKESHOTT, G. M. 1903. "Artificial flower-making: An account of the trade and a plea for municipal training." *Economic Journal* 13(44):123–131.

OLSON, MARGRETHE H., AND SOPHIA B. PRIMPS. 1984. "Working at home with computers: Work and nonwork issues." *Journal of Social Issues* 40(3):97–112.

OSBORN, C. 1903. "The hand-working and domestic industries in Germany." *Economic Journal* 13(49):133–136.

OSBORN, RICHARD, BARBARA WACHSMAN, ANNE MARKUSEN, AND PETER HALL. 1982. *The California Software Industry: Problems and Prospects.* A Report to the California Commission on Industrial Innovation by the Institute of Urban and Regional Development; University of California, Berkeley. August.

PAHL, R. E. 1980. "Employment, work and the domestic division of labor." *International Journal of Urban and Regional Research* 4(1):1–19.

——. 1984. *Divisions of Labour.* Oxford: Basil Blackwell, Limited.

———. 1987. "Does jobless mean workless? Unemployment and informal work." Unpublished manuscript. June.

PHILLIPS, J. D. 1962. *The Self-Employed in the United States.* Urbana: University of Illinois Press.

PORTES, ALEJANDRO. 1982. "The Informal Sector: Definition, Controversy and Relations to National Development." Paper prepared for the Third Seminar of the Working Group on Latin American Urbanization, Tepoztlan, Mexico. August 22–24.

PORTES, ALEJANDRO, SILVIA BLITZER, AND JOHN CURTIS. 1986. "The urban informal sector in Uruguay: Its internal structure, characteristics, and effects." *World Development* 14(6):727–741.

PORTES, ALEJANDRO, AND SASKIA SASSEN-KOOB. 1987. "Making it underground: Comparative material on the informal sector in Western market economies." *American Journal of Sociology* 93(1):30–61.

PORTES, ALEJANDRO, AND JOHN WALTON. 1981. *Labor, Class and the International System.* New York: Academic Press.

PRESSER, HARRIET B., AND WENDY BALDWIN. 1980. "Child care as a constraint on employment: Prevalence, correlates, and bearing on the work and fertility nexus." *American Journal of Sociology* 85(5):1202–1213.

RAKOWSKI, CATHY A. 1985. "The planning process and the division of labour in a new industrial city: The case of Ciudad Guayana, Venezuela. In John Walton (Ed.), *Capital and Labour in the Urbanized World.* London: Sage Publications.

RAPP, RAYNA, ELLEN ROSS, AND RENATE BRIDENTHAL. 1979. "Examining family history." *Feminist Studies* 5(1):174–200.

REUTER, PETER. 1982. "The irregular economy and the quality of macroeconomic statistics." In Vito Tanzi (Ed.), *The Underground Economy in the United States and Abroad.* Lexington: Lexington Books.

ROTHMAN, DAVID H. 1985. "The computer cottage hysteria." *Washington Post,* July 7:162–164.

RUBERY, JILL, AND FRANK WILKINSON. 1981. "Outwork and segmented labour markets." In Frank Wilkinson, Ed., *The Dynamics of Labour Market Segmentation.* London: The Academic Press.

"Running a firm from home gives women more flexibility." 1984. *Wall Street Journal,* December 31:11.

SAFA, HELEN. 1986. "Urbanization, the informal economy and state policy in Latin America." *Urban Anthropology* 15(1–2):135–163.

SAN FRANCISCO CHAMBER OF COMMERCE. 1915. *San Francisco: The Financial, Commercial and Industrial Metropolis of the West Coast.* San Francisco: H. S. Crocker Company.

1983 "Beyond silicon: Shooting for the moon in Los Altos Hills." *San Francisco Examiner,* April 10:1(Scene/Arts).

1983 "Home computers are nurturing working mothers." March 14:2D.

SAXENIAN, ANNALEE. 1981. *Silicon Chips and Spatial Structure: The Industrial Basis of Urbanization in Santa Clara County, California.* Working Paper 345. Institute of Urban and Regional Development, University of California, Berkley.

SCHIFF, FRANK. 1983. "Flexiplace: An idea whose time has come." *IEEE Transactions on Engineering Management* 30(1):26–30.

SCOTT, A. J. 1983. "Industrial organization and the logic of intra-metropolitan location: I. Theoretical considerations." *Economy Geography* 59(3):233–250.

SCOTT, ALISON MACEWEN. 1979. "Who are the self-employed?" In R. Bromley and C. Gerry (Eds.), *Casual Work and Poverty in Third World Cities.* New York: John Wiley.

SETHURAMAN, S. V. 1976. "The urban informal sector: Concept, measurement and policy." *International Labour Review* 114(1):69–81.

SHAFER, DAN. 1986. *Silicon Visions: The Future of Microcomputer Technology.* New York: Prentice Hall Press.

SIEGEL, LENNY, AND HERB BOROCK. 1982. *Background Report on Silicon Valley.* Prepared for the U. S. Commission on Civil Rights. Mountain View: Pacific Studies Center.

"Silicon Valley to grow." 1983. *Global Electronics Information Newsletter,* Issue Number 35. September.

SIMON, CARL, AND ANN WITTE. 1982. *Beating the System: The Underground Economy.* Boston: Auburn House Publishing Company.

SMALL, LINDA LEE. 1981. "How to get up in the morning and other tricks to working from home." *Ms. Magazine* 19(2):35–36.

SMELSER, NEIL J. 1973. "Processes of social change." In Neil J. Smelser (Ed.), *Sociology: An Introduction,* 2nd edition. New York: John Wiley and Sons.

SMITH, ADAM. 1776. *The Wealth of Nations* (Volume I). London: J. M. Dent and Sons, Ltd.

SMITH, STEPHEN. 1986. *Britain's Shadow Economy.* Oxford: Clarendon Press.

"Software to go." *Forbes,* June 20:93–102.

"Soothsayers look at 1983 in Silicon Valley." 1983. *San Francisco Chronicle,* January 2:D1.

SOUTHERN CALIFORNIA ASSOCIATION OF GOVERNMENTS. 1986. *Implementation Plan: Telecommuting Pilot Project for the Southern California Association of Governments.* Central City Association. Telecommunications Task Force. Telecommuting Subcommittee. January.

SOUZA, PAOLO, AND VICTOR TOKMAN. 1976. "The informal urban sector in Latin America." *International Labour Review* 114(3):355–365.

"Space-savvy furniture." 1984. *San Francisco Chronicle*, March 7:36.

SRI INTERNATIONAL. 1982. *High Technology and the California Workforce in the 1980s. A Report on California's Technological Future: Emerging Economic Opportunities in the 1980s.* Prepared in cooperation with the California Employment Development Department for the Department of Economic and Business Development.

"Strategic systems plans gone awry." 1988. *Computerworld* 22(11):1.

SULLIVAN, NANCY. 1988. Comments made at the California Employment Development Department Seminar on California's Changing Labor Market. February 17.

SZELENYI, IVAN. 1981. "Structural changes of and alternatives to capitalist development." *International Journal of Urban and Regional Research* 5(1):1–4.

TALBOT, DAVID. 1983. "Fast times for high-tech: Meet the moguls who are reprogramming our future." *Mother Jones*, December:23–59.

TANZI, VITO. 1982. *The Underground Economy in the United States and Abroad.* Lexington: Lexington Books.

"The flap over the cottage industry ban." 1983. *Christian Science Monitor*, December 12:27.

"Text of message from the President on the state of the union." 1984. *New York Times*, January 26:12.

"Telecommuters could top 7.2 million this year, a report says." 1985. Labor letter. *Wall Street Journal*, Febuary 5:1.

"The Silicon Valley style." *Newsweek*. June 8:80–81.

THOMPSON, E. P. 1963. *The Making of the English Working Class.* New York: Vintage Press.

THORNTON, ARLAND, AND DEBORAH FREEDMAN. 1983. "The changing American family." *Population Bulletin* 38(4):1–44.

TOKMAN, VICTOR. 1978. "Competition between the informal and formal sectors in retailing: The case of Santiago." *World Development* 6(9/10):1187–1198.

"Turnover." 1983. *Global Electronics Information Newsletter.* Issue Number 32. May.

UNITED STATES BUREAU OF THE CENSUS. 1969–1986. *Current Population Reports.* Consumer Income. Series P-60. Washington, D.C.: Government Printing Office.

———. 1970. *Census of Population.* Characteristics of the Population (Volume 1, Part 6). Washington, D.C.: Government Printing Office.

———. 1977a. *Census of Manufactures.* Washington, D.C.: Government Printing Office.

———. 1977b. *Census of Service Industries.* Washington, D.C.: Government Printing Office.

——. 1980a. *Census of Population and Housing.* Summary Characteristics for Governmental Units and SMSAs. California. Washington, D.C.: Government Printing Office.

——. 1980b. *Census of Population.* Characteristics of the Population (Volume 1, Part 6). Washington, D.C.: Government Printing Office.

——. 1982a. *Census of Manufactures.* Washington, D.C.: Government Printing Office.

——. 1982b. *Census of Service Industries.* Geographic Area Statistics. U.S. Summary. Washington, D.C.: Government Printing Office.

——. 1982c. *Statistical Abstract of the United States* 1982–83. 103d Edition. Washington, D.C.: Government Printing Office.

——. 1984. *County Business Patterns—1984.* Washington, D.C.: Government Printing Office.

UNITED STATES CONGRESS. 1979a. *Underground Economy. Hearings. Commerce, Consumer and Monetary Affairs Subcommittee of the Committee on Government Operations,* September 5 and 6. Washington, D.C.: Government Printing Office.

——. 1979b. *Descriptions of Proposals Relating to Independent Contractors Scheduled for a Hearing Before the Subcommittee on Select Revenue Measures of the Committee on Ways and Means.* Washington, D.C.: Government Printing Office.

——. 1979c. *Miscellaneous Tax Bills II. Hearing Before the Subcommittee on Taxation and Debt Management Generally of the Committee on Finance.* September 17. Washington, D.C.: Government Printing Office.

——. 1983. *A Bill.* H.R. 2531. First Session, Ninety-eighth Congress. Washington, D.C.: Government Printing Office.

——. 1984. *Amending the Fair Labor Standards Act to Include Industrial Homework.* Hearing Before the Subcommittee on Labor of the Committee on Labor and Human Resources, Febuary 9. Washington, D.C.: Government Printing Office.

Uzzell, J. D. 1980. "Mixed strategies and the informal sector: Three faces of reserve labor." *Human Organization* 39:40

Vinay, Paola. 1985. "Family life cycle and the informal economy in central Italy." *International Journal of Urban and Regional Research* 9(1):83–97.

"Warner debt soars after Atari losses." 1983. *Los Angeles Times,* November 9:1IV.

"Wanted: Electronics illustrators." 1988. *Bay Area Computer Currents.* 5(16):49.

"What color is your umbrella?" 1988. *Parents' Monthly* 6(5):1–3.

WHITEMAN, LUTHER, AND SAMUEL LEWIS. 1936. *Glory Roads: The Psychological State of California.* New York: Crowell.

"We promise: Each handknit Aran crew is a bit different!" 1987. *Lands' End Catalog*. November:56.

1985. "Labor letter: A special news report on people and their jobs in offices, fields and factories." February 12:1.

"Women in electronics find Silicon Valley best and worst." *New York Times,* March 2:1.

WOMEN'S WORK STUDY GROUP. 1976. "Loom, broom and womb: Producers, maintainers and reproducers." *Radical America* 19(2);29–45.

"Worksteaders 'clean up.'" 1984. *Newsweek,* January 9:86–87.

WRIGHT, THOMAS. 1867. *Some Habits and Customs of the Working Class.* London: Tinsley Brothers.

YATES, KATHRYN. 1987. "An agent of change." *Government Technology* No. 1(Fall):13.

YOUNG, F. JOHN L. 1964. *The Contracting Out of Work: Canadian and U.S.A. Industrial Relations Experience.* Research Series Number 1. Ontario: Industrial Relations Center.

Index